INVESTIGATING
CSI

Other Titles in the Smart Pop Series

INVESTIGATING
CSI

An Unauthorized Look
Inside the Crime Labs of
Las Vegas, Miami, and New York

POLICE LINE DO NOT CROSS   POLICE LINE DO NOT

POLICE LINE DO NOT

EDITED BY

DONN CORTEZ

WITH LEAH WILSON

BENBELLA BOOKS, INC.
Dallas, Texas

BenBella Books, Inc.
6440 N. Central Expressway, Suite 617
Dallas, TX 75206
www.benbellabooks.com
Send feedback to feedback@benbellabooks.com

Printed in the United States of America
10 9 8 7 6 5 4 3 2 1

Library of Congress Cataloging-in-Publication Data

Investigating CSI : inside the crime labs of Las Vegas, Miami, and New York / edited by Donn Cortez With Leah Wilson.
    p. cm.
    ISBN 1-932100-93-8
    1. CSI: crime scene investigation (Television program) 2. CSI: Miami (Television program) 3. CSI: NY (Television program) I. Cortez, Donn. II. Wilson, Leah.

    PN1992.77.C75I58 2006
    791.45'75—dc22

                                                    2006022475

Proofreading by Jessica Keet and Stacia Seaman
Cover design by Todd Michael Bushman
Text design and composition by John Reinhardt Book Design
Printed by Bang Printing

Distributed by Independent Publishers Group
To order call (800) 888-4741
www.ipgbook.com

For media inquiries and special sales contact Yara Abuata at yara@benbellabooks.com

Contents

CONTENTS

CSI: Carefully Scripted Introduction

I'M REMINDED OF THE EPISODE of *CSI* where Grissom is supposed to give a speech introducing Ecklie, his immediate superior who's just won an award. Not only does Grissom despise Ecklie—who cares more about political maneuvering than science—but Grissom hates giving speeches. Minutes before the speech is due, he's still doodling notes on a napkin. When his beeper goes off, summoning him to a crime scene, he quickly hands the napkin to Catherine and tells her to give the speech instead.

All that's written on the napkin is Ecklie's name.

Umm....

Fortunately, there are two major differences between me and Grissom. First, I don't despise what I'm about to introduce—on the contrary, I'm a huge fan of the franchise and in fact have written several *CSI: Miami* novels. Second, I actually have something to say.

You see, I investigated a murder the other day.

I found the body in my front yard at around 11 A.M, and IDed the vic immediately as a long-time resident of my house. Careful observation of the body gave me an approximate TOD of two to three hours earlier; the victim was known to stay inside during the night. I had cut the lawn the previous evening, and the body lay on top of the clippings.

The head and neck were mutilated, suggesting an animal attack. However, an eye was missing, and crows are common in the neighborhood—plus, the body itself wasn't ripped apart as a predator would do. I surmised that the head and neck had been subjected to anthrophagy—predation by animals after the fact.

In case you hadn't figured it out yet, the DB was that of a pigeon, one of a pair that lives in my attic. But who killed him (or her)?

My first suspect was a hawk—one had previously killed a pigeon in our back yard. However, the hawk had disemboweled its vic, and also hung the body over the top of a fence (not uncommon for birds of prey, possibly to keep other animals from eating their kill). This DB was lying on the ground.

There was a spatter on a nearby leaf, but no blood trail, and the mown grass was undisturbed; therefore, the body hadn't been dragged. I found it beneath a small tree and beside a fence—most likely, it had been perched on the fence when it was killed. The blood droplet beneath seemed to support that.

I gloved up, then examined the body carefully. I found a fair bit of blood on its back, indicating an exit wound, and a small round hole in its breast. There were short, fibrous objects jutting from the hole, which I carefully pulled out. Feathers. Something had punched into the chest, pushing the feathers inside the wound, but whatever it was hadn't been traveling fast enough to destroy the feathers themselves. I surmised it was probably a small projectile, traveling at a relatively low velocity—most likely a pellet from an air pistol. I searched the area, but didn't locate the pellet.

Possible suspects included several of my neighbors. Pigeons crap all over everything, and their cooing can be extremely loud—especially when perched on your eaves. (Actually, for a while I was the prime suspect.) However, after studying the angle of the wound and where the body was found, I determined the most likely point of origin was across the street. There's a duplex there, rented out to several low-income families, and a favorite hangout for a group of guys who favor backward baseball caps, loud rap music, and sports cars they shouldn't be able to afford. The evidence, however, was only circumstantial, and I kept the place under surveillance for additional proof.

The next day, I saw an eight-year-old over there running around with an air pistol. I nodded to myself in satisfaction, slipped on my sunglasses, and put on *The Who's Greatest Hits*.

I admit it. I am a CSI geek.

Nor am I alone. As several of the essays in this collection will cite, the CSI franchise is one of the most successful on television. The original currently holds the number one slot in America, and *CSI: Miami* is number one worldwide.

CSI is more than just a trio of hit shows, however. It's a way of life.

Certain shows do more than just entertain us—they change the way we look at things. CSI is such a set of shows. What they do—what they show us, every week—is that science is more than some abstract concept only specialists can understand. It shows us how things work, how things are interconnected, and how everything we do and touch leaves a history and affects the future. It's raised the public consciousness to such a degree that juries now *expect* DNA results instead of being mystified by them. And, through a combination of charismatic actors, special effects, and sharp writing, it's made science *cool*.

Warren Ellis, a writer for whom I have a lot of admiration, once compared CSI to *Blade Runner*. He has a point: the flashy computer graphics, the emphasis on technology to solve crimes, the neon-lit *noir*ish feel of it all. *Blade Runner* is one of those movies William Gibson cites as an influence on his own writing, and he's hardly the only cyberpunk writer to pick up on it. Gibson once said that he wanted to romanticize computers the way Bruce Springsteen romanticized cars, and it could be argued that CSI has done the same thing for the Gas-Chromatograph Mass Spectrometer—or, as we CSI geeks like to say, the GC mass-spec.

I have my own theory why the CSI shows are so popular, which breaks down into three parts. The first is demographics. See, I believe the CSI shows are aimed not at male geeks, but at female mystery fans—of which, as book sales in that genre will attest, there are many. Women on the whole read more fiction than men, and mysteries written by women and featuring female protagonists tend to do well. As the Baby

Boom generation ages, more and more women in their fifties are filling their leisure time with Patricia Cornwell or Kathy Reichs.

And with Catherine Willows, Sara Sidle, Calleigh Duquesne, and Stella Bonasera.

Unlike the typical female lead on television, none of these women are in their twenties. While they are attractive, they're also smart, tough, and experienced. The beefcake factor, on the other hand, is definitely high; George Eads, Gary Dourdan, Adam Rodriguez, and Jonathon Togo are all young, buff, and handsome. The leads in the series—Gil Grissom, Horatio Caine, and Mac Taylor—all have a decidedly paternal bent, more dignified elder statesmen than young mavericks. To me, this says that while the cool gadgets and special effects may draw a certain amount of male technophile attention, the real audience of these shows is intelligent, experienced women—many of whom used to sing along to The Who's "My Generation."

Second, I think the planet is growing a brain.

I mean that in a very literal way. Human beings evolved emotions before thought, so it makes sense that we'd develop a global network based on feelings before one built on intellect. That's what television is—more than anything it's a planetary system for conveying emotion. Even news programs are driven more by fear, outrage, and sheer entertainment value than factual content, and advertising appeals even more directly to our emotional natures.

But the Internet has changed all that. A global, interactive repository of information and experience, one you can draw on at any time, the World Wide Web has radically changed not just information but people's attitudes toward information. It used to be that if you were given a piece of data, you could either disbelieve it, trust that it was true, or verify it by going to the library and doing some research. This approach was time-consuming and limited in scope, and as a result many people believed what they were told simply because it was easier.

Not anymore. These days, looking stuff up on the Web has become a reflex. Need to know the rules to a game, how to make an exotic dish, how to repair an appliance, how to buy stocks or raise llamas or launch a rocket? All available within seconds. Hear a song you like? You can have a list of everything that artist has ever done in less than the time it takes to listen to one of her tunes. Want to know more about a breaking news story? More and more, people are hitting the Net before they tune in to CNN.

Information isn't the sole province of experts anymore. It's everywhere. And shows like CSI, with all their high-tech jargon, are far more accessible as a result.

See, learning is insidious. The more you know, the more you want to know. And it makes perfect sense that a franchise that has at its very heart the quest for information would wind up becoming the top show on TV. If the Internet is in the process of becoming the world's brain, then CSI is a crash-course in sensory input. A CSI doesn't just look at the world through his eyes; he evaluates it on every level from the atomic to the temporal, from the psychological to the biological, from the chemical to the genetic. There's no such thing as a single, discrete object; there are only collections of events that interact with each other on a myriad of levels, leaving a history of their behavior behind.

Or maybe people just enjoy seeing someone get killed by a stuffed swordfish from the swordfish's point of view.

Which brings us to point number three: the black humor. Which is not a reference to old reruns of *The Cosby Show*, or the latest Chris Rock HBO Special. It's more along the lines of the terrible puns Grissom delivers with a straight face during the opening teaser—you know, like when he found the body of a Civil War re-enactor who'd used a corset to squeeze his belly into a column roughly the size of a stovepipe? "What a waist. . . ."

The humor, always understated and very dry, hasn't been injected for any artificial reason; it's one of the ways real CSIs handle the stress of a job that requires dealing with death and the ramifications of violence every day. Though I would love to sit in on a pitch where they decided to be a little more blatant about it. . . .

WRITER: Okay, then Catherine turns the body over and finds the spine ripped out.
PRODUCER: Yeah, that's good.
WRITER: But as she flips the corpse over . . . there's a loud farting noise! Grissom's put a whoopee cushion on the other side!
PRODUCER: You're fired.

Okay, maybe not.

Death is a fact of life. It's the period at the end of the sentence, the punch line to the joke, the sudden stop at the bottom. When it's your job to confront it, day after day, you better have some kind of coping mechanism in place or you'll go crazy.

I should know.

We all deal with death—and by extension, with grief—in different ways. There's a *Saturday Night Live* sketch that plays with this idea; I can't remember which cast was involved, or even when it was on exactly, though it had to have been prior to the mid-eighties. Someone—let's pretend it was Tom Hanks—has to break the news to a couple that somebody close to them has died. They react badly, screaming and wailing. Overwhelmed by their pain, Hanks changes his story—it was a bad joke, just a gag, so-and-so isn't really dead. The couple is so relieved they aren't even angry. But now Hanks is overcome by guilt; knowing he can't keep up the charade forever, he admits that, actually, so-and-so *is* dead. More wailing and crying...and Hanks tells them that no, really, he was kidding again.

This repeats several times. It is as heart-wrenching to watch as it is hilarious, and apparently it made a big impression on a friend of mine—let's call him Curtis.

I've always been a big fan of Robert A. Heinlein. Curtis knew this. On the day Heinlein died, Curtis heard about it before I did. And—not having any particular connection to Heinlein himself—he pulled the same stunt on me. He's dead; he's not dead; I'm kidding; no, I'm not. I thought it was in poor taste, but Curtis used to be a prison guard, and his notion of bad taste was considerably different from mine.

Years pass. Curtis and I fall out of touch. One day, I run into him on the street. He tells me he's looking for a place to rent, and I mention that my place will be empty soon. It's a lovely little apartment, the main floor of a house with two bedrooms and a nice backyard, and the rent is reasonable. My wife and I have been there for several years. If it's so nice, he wants to know, then why am I moving?

Because my wife has AIDS, I tell him. She doesn't have long to live, and I'm not going to stay there by myself once she's gone.

I know what you're thinking—but I wasn't setting him up. My wife, Evelyn, died in 1995, within a few weeks of that conversation. Or maybe it was months; that time is kind of blurred and unreal in my memory. No, the truth is a little more disturbing.

Grief makes you...strange. Not yourself. When you know—and I mean know, with utter certainty—that someone close to you is about to die, you do much of your grieving beforehand. In the days and hours before Ev's death, I was doing a lot of that, and so were my friends. And humor was definitely a part of that process—we found ourselves making jokes, saying things that afterward seemed horribly out-of-place. The humor was black and absurd and utterly necessary.

And then came the morning she died.

I was all alone with her, which was a minor miracle; since she'd developed dementia she had to be monitored twenty-four hours a day, and there was always at least one other support person or day-care nurse present. Somehow, she timed it between shifts—it was just me and her.

This next part, I've never told anyone.

The first person I called after she died was Curtis. For some reason, I had fixated on the idea that he had to be notified immediately, so he could work out the whole rent thing. I wasn't really rational. When he answered the phone, I told him my wife had just died.

I let him get halfway through his condolences before I told him I was joking.

And then I told him I wasn't.

I don't remember if I did it more than once. Looking back now, I see the actions of someone who was completely irrational; who had just said goodbye to his wife, held her as she died, and whose first reaction was—somehow—to try to make a joke.

Curtis didn't rent the place. As a matter of fact, he never talked to me again. I can't say I really blame him; if I'd gotten that insane phone call, I'd put as much distance between the caller and myself, too. Craziness is scary.

But I wasn't really crazy. I was just trying to deal with a huge overload of pain—and one of the best painkillers that exists is a sense of humor. Cops know it, doctors know it...and crime scene investigators know it.

The essays collected here fall roughly into three groups: the ones that deal with the CSI shows as entertainment, the ones that deal with it as

science, and the ones that examine its influence on the general public—
including the so-called "CSI Effect." In the first group, we have Adam
Roberts, who takes a less than serious look at some possible future CSI
spin-offs; Matthew Woodring Stover, who—despite the kind of cyni-
cal snarkiness one usually has to watch *House* to experience—has some
valuable insights to share; while both Bruce Bethke and Nick Mamatas
explore the reasons for the series' overwhelming popularity. There's also
Katherine Ramsland, a forensic authority with a book detailing the science behind the CSI shows, but her essay isn't about technology; it deals
with the symbolic importance of each show's male lead, and what that
person represents. Janine Hiddlestone examines how each show has a
very distinctive color scheme, and what moods and themes those color
schemes convey.

Writers who've taken a more analytical look at the technical and scientific aspects of the shows include Elizabeth Engstrom, who delves
into Grissom's fascination with entomology; Christine Kruse-Feldstein,
a genuine Miami-Dade CSI who contrasts the glamour of the Miami
show with brutal reality; Doranna Durgin, who provides an entertaining
look at the wily fingerprint; and Timothy Palmbach, who compares the
investigative and courtroom techniques of yesterday with today's.

Studying the impact of the show on the world at large are Kristine
Kathryn Rusch, who looks at whether watching CSI produces smarter
criminals; Rick Workman, one of the CSIs working the Vegas graveyard
shift that producer Anthony Zuiker studied when designing the show;
and Sharon Plotkin, a real-life CSI who compares her own experiences
as a female crime scene investigator with those of her fictional counterparts.

Whether offering personal experience, carefully reasoned analysis, or
truly offbeat opinions, all of these writers have something interesting to
say. So sit back, put on some Who, and enjoy.

Donn Cortez
Vancouver, BC
June 23, 2006

Detective Kruse-Feldstein is the real thing, a CSI who works in Miami. Her world, as you will soon see, is far removed from the sex and glitter of the television show; computer-generated gore can't compare to the gut-churning reality a law-enforcement officer faces every day.

DET. CHRISTINE KRUSE-FELDSTEIN

The Reality of *CSI: Miami*

O N TELEVISION, CRIME SCENE INVESTIGATORS operate in a glamorous world of beautiful mansions and wealthy people. Everyone has that plastic surgery sculptured body, and is a model or some high-powered person. The crime scene investigator on television is always pristine, with his or her hair in place—he or she never sweats, is never dirty, and always wears the latest fashions, from low-rider pants and form-fitting belly-exposing shirts to high heel open-toe shoes.

In reality, crime scene investigators have little contact with the rich and the famous. We never interview or interrogate suspects; the lead detective does that—and he or she would never show the suspect the evidence in a sealed bag. Most of our profession is going into dirty, cluttered houses to deal with the nasty conditions in which people live. We deal with the decomposing bodies. (Decomposition happens very quickly in South Florida's heat.) We deal with the victims who lie about their involvement in crimes. (I cannot count how many times I have heard victims say, "I was just walking down the street and got shot for no reason." I normally tell them that people do not shoot at you for no reason, especially not several times with an AK-47. Usually that means they intend to kill you, or at least send a very strong message.) We deal with the raw and unpleasant aspects of life on the streets. We deal with a side of life that most people cannot even imagine. Let me give you a glimpse of the work of a real crime scene investigator.

First, let me talk about living conditions. Most of the houses you, as a crime scene investigator, go into are not recently cleaned by a maid, or even cleaned once a week by a working mom. The houses are cluttered, dirty, and a lot of times infested by insects and rodents.

A typical alcoholic's house, for instance, is cluttered with hundreds of empty bottles of the cheapest liquor and beer on the market; most never buy the industrial size bottles that you get at your local warehouse retailer, but the small and the mini-size bottles. Often, in the houses you enter, there are layers and layers of dirt, dust, and junk. A lot of the time you have to maneuver around piles of accumulated crap inside the house. Sometimes you have to walk sideways down hallways to get around the corners, especially if you are wearing your duty belt with your gun on your side. Most of the houses we go in, your boots stick to the carpet or linoleum flooring. As you walk inside there are so many roaches that you have to immediately return outside to get the duct tape. Yes, the duct tape: we duct tape our pant legs to our boots. Why? Because if you stand still for more than thirty seconds the roaches will crawl up the inside of your pant leg. You also have to watch out for rats and other rodents. I've worked plenty of scenes where I could hear the rats scurrying inside the house.

Another thing you have to watch out for is "the bucket." A lot of times, individuals use a bucket to go to the bathroom in instead of using the toilet. Now, if you are dealing with an alcoholic who died of natural causes in bed, you just need to be careful of it. But if the victim has been part of a violent act, or as moving around in a drunken stupor, you may find the bucket tipped over, and urine, feces, and maggots all over the floor...which you have to walk on.

A lot of alcoholics die naked; I cannot count how many times I've gone into a house with a decomposed body and found them completely naked or without pants. When that happens, you look on the floor and in the bathroom. If you find soiled pants with fecal matter, or fecal matter in the toilet or on the floor, it's a good indication of a heart attack. I have found that heart attack victims lose their bowels and are often in the middle of cleaning themselves or the house when they have "the big one."

With decomposing bodies there is the fluid as well. As the body breaks down it releases gases and fluids. As the blisters in the skin fill up, the fluid eventually gets too heavy for the skin to hold, and the blisters break and spatter onto the floor. I have learned the hard way how to best move these blister-covered bodies. A term we have used in the field is called "blessing the body." This consists of getting a wire hanger or other throwaway sharp object and puncturing the lower part of the blisters. The fluid then gently rolls down instead of going everywhere the way it does when you move the victim and the blisters forcefully pop.

Then there is the issue of odor. It's not very pleasant at all. The smell seems to linger on everything: your hair, your clothes, your shoes. Of course you spray yourself down with antiviral disinfectant, but the smell is still there. Just like the macho man who puts on too much cologne and can't smell it, you stop being able to smell yourself either. Sometimes, after working a decomped body, you get hungry. Not realizing that you stink, you sit down at a restaurant, only to have the people sitting behind you ask to move. Or you hear people say, "What's that smell?"

One other thing about decomposing bodies is the maggots. Even inside houses, the flies will find a way inside and maggots will be crawling on the body. You look for normal entomological activity: maggots should first be found on the head area and some of the genitalia, at warm, moist openings where they can access the inside of the body. If you see a maggot mass in the stomach, it might indicate an area of trauma because the midsection has no natural openings. A lot of times we see maggot masses on the legs of older people. When that happens, I look for diabetic medication in the house—something to explain why a maggot mass is forming. Diabetics sometimes have open sores on their legs or slow-healing wounds.

Once in a while you get a change of pace. It is definitely different when you go inside the house of a schizophrenic person and find it totally covered with aluminum foil. The walls, ceilings, windows, doors—

everything covered. Most schizophrenics I've talked to do it to reflect the thoughts beamed into their heads by the Russians, space aliens, or the government—the usual perpetrators. When I used to work as a road officer, I would carry aluminum pie plates that you can get at the grocery store. Whenever a schizophrenic person came up to me and complained of beams radiating into their head, I would give him a pie plate and tell him to wear it on his head, explaining that it would reflect any beams. He would then go down the street with the pie plate on his head, thinking that it worked.

Home invasion robberies involve a different set of conditions. It will be 100-plus degrees outside, but you walk into the victim's residence only to find that it's even hotter inside. Every surface is covered with dirt or greasy substances from the kitchen. As you process the scene, your uniform sticks to your body and the sweat just drips off you. You try not to drip on the area that you are processing, because the littlest bit of any liquid turns the fingerprinting powder into a smeared mess. Typically, there are hardly any latent prints of value in situations like that. But you still end up coming out of the house with powder all over you and your uniform. It also never fails: you always have an itch on your face when you are dealing with powder. Every time you blow your nose black fingerprint powder comes out in the tissue.

Also, you would not believe how many people can live in one house. I am not talking about mom, dad, and kids. I am talking about mom, dad, five children, grandma, grandpa, mom's sisters, their children, and the list goes on and on. I have got to admit large families get very creative in the house as far as furniture, decorating, and sleeping arrangements. A colleague and I have been to houses where the family uses a toilet as a flower pot...inside the house.

I have also had victims start speaking about catching the "perps" and gotten the famous "But they do not do it that way on CSI!" lecture. I have to try to explain that what you see on television is not necessarily how things are done in real investigations.

Take my uniform, for example. No, it does not consist of jeans, a nice shirt, and heels. My uniform consists of SRT boots, which are a lot like army boots; BDU-type pants, which are the pants with the cargo pockets on the sides; a polo shirt; and my duty belt with my firearm. My hair is usually pulled up and secured, for several reasons. First, I do not want to put traces of my hair into the crime scene. More importantly from a comfort standpoint, I don't need my hair falling into my face when my gloved hands are bloody.

I sometimes wear protective gear, such as Tyvek® suits. Tyvek suits are made to protect you, so they are hot and do not breathe at all. If you are in a house that has no air conditioning, and it is summer, you can easily dehydrate and end up needing hydration from fire rescue paramedics. It is great if you want to lose a couple of pounds for an important night, but it's also dangerous.

I have also learned over the years that even with the suits, you want to wear gloves—layers of gloves. You wear the first pair of gloves underneath the Tyvek® suit, and then add another pair over the suit's, secured with duct tape. Then add a few more pairs. As you work the scene your hands get bloody, and if you have to take a photo, or collect another piece of evidence, you do not want to transfer trace or mix serological evidence—so you are continuously putting new gloves on. It's much easier to just cut a pair off and move immediately on to the next task.

I work a lot of suicides. Being seasoned in crime scene, and having seen so many, I do not feel sorry for the victim—with the exception of the terminally ill dealing with a lot of pain. Suicide is the victim's choice; it's a voluntary act. Maybe this is just a coping mechanism for me, but I know several professionals in the field who feel the same way. It's the family that I feel for.

I have also found that most leave one-page suicide notes. There are the occasions where you have multiple envelopes addressed to different people and one for the police. The one-liner suicide notes, though, tend to be the most bizarre. I had one once that said, "Life is like a box, you must think outside of it." That was it; no other reason why this guy hanged himself in the closet. Other strange ones have included notes that were just highlighted lyrics to songs. I guess they contained a life lesson that the person was trying to communicate.

Some suicide victims make elaborate plans for their death. I had a case where a woman checked herself into a hotel room and failed at taking an overdose of prescription medication. So she took the shower curtain off, laid it on the bed, and then shot herself in the chest.

Most suicide victims use firearms, but you also get the hangings, the overdoses, and sometimes the carbon monoxide poisonings.

With firearms, sometimes you deal with uniform officers who feel it is necessary to unload the weapon "for officer safety." The person is dead; it's not likely that they are going to shoot you. Regardless, it's important, especially when the firearm is a revolver, to document the positions of the casing and cartridges, and how the cylinder rotates in the firearm. You check all of that.

With a hanging you check how the ligature is tied around the neck and if it is consistent with the way the person is hanging and the use of the person's dominant hand, right or left. Most times the victim has been cut down by either fire rescue or a family member.

You also have to watch for the occasional autoerotic case. When a family member finds the victim in an embarrassing position, with "visual aids" around, he or she sometimes hides the aids. That may be the difference between a life insurance company ruling the death a suicide or ruling it an accidental; most policies do not pay out for suicides.

A word on sex: I have found that the more money you make, the kinkier your sex life is. You would not believe how many houses I go into, investigating some kind of death or other crime, and find drawers filled with strap-ons, dildos, vibrators, bondage equipment, and of course, photos and videos—and most of these homes belong to heterosexual couples.

Sometimes, you're in a house, looking for suicide notes, prescription medications, or anything else that will help explain why a person died, and come across photos of the recently deceased with his or her partner in a sex act. The other person in the photos is in the other room. You have to pull yourself together, and be able to speak professionally to that person.

You occasionally have to go into jails or prisons to investigate a death or other crime. It never fails—you end up having to try to document the crime scene while you can see several inmates having "self-relations." The first time I witnessed this, the homicide detective whispered in my ear, "You know they are staring at you while they are touching themselves." Considering the eye candy kind of guy that he is, I had to respond, "No, they are staring at you."

I usually just want to go up to the indiscreet inmate and say something like, "Hey, it looks like a penis, only smaller!"

One last thing about the sex stuff: I've had cases where the lead detective has wanted me to go into a house of prostitution to find a condom and other serological evidence. It's like finding a needle in a haystack, there are so many condoms from so many johns; I can spend days just collecting and packaging used condoms. I have to say, "Can you narrow it down a little bit for me?"

Most non-suicide shootings are related to drugs or gang activity. It sometimes gets old, working a shooting where the victim tells you that he will "take care of the matter" himself. The stray bullet that hits an innocent bystander or a child is the exception.

When dealing with shooting scenes, you frequently use wooden dowel rods instead of lasers to show the bullet's trajectory. These show up better in photos and are disposable. If you get blood on the dowel rod, or it breaks, it's pennies to replace. A lot of times you are on the ground outside, on your hands and knees looking for a casing or projectile (bullet). I wear tile setter knee pads—they help your knees when you are on the ground for some time. Otherwise, pebbles and other road debris grind against your knees. In the summer this can be especially grueling, because it is hot on the asphalt. I am not seventeen anymore; my knees and back hurt after a while.

In addition to shootings that happen outside, you also have inside shooting scenes. It really is fun destroying walls and furnishings inside houses that belong to drug dealers in order to search for money, drugs, projectiles, or other items of evidentiary value. The same goes for disassembling vehicles that have been used in crimes.

Fortunately, the county doesn't reimburse drug dealers for police acts of vandalism, so our paychecks would be safe... *if* some renegade ever did something like that.

You also deal with the homeless and prostitutes. I can tell you this: a homeless person's feet smell worse than any decomposed body I have ever encountered. So does a prostitute's underwear. It's one of those smells that is like "Pandora's box": once it's been opened, there's no closing it. I had one prostitute at the jail put her hands on the table and spread her legs in the typical pat down position. All the jailers, the other working inmates, and the prisoners in the process of being booked all backed up four feet. And she still had her jeans on. You have to wonder what man would actually pay for that. (Most men want oral sex from prostitutes, but there are the few who do want intercourse.)

The worst kinds of cases, though, are elderly homicide victims, children, and (thank God I've never had to work one) police officers who have been killed in the line of duty.

After completing a crime scene, you take all the evidence back to headquarters to send to the forensic laboratory. At this point, you've spent all day on a crime scene, plus, lots of times, overtime. Sometimes I am there as long as eighteen hours on the scene, alone. After rejuvenating yourself with a cup of coffee from an all-night coffee and donut shop, you have to separate the mountain of evidence into different piles: what evidence is going to which section of the lab. Some items of evidence may end up going to several different sections. For instance, one shirt may go to the Trace, Biology, and Firearms sections, while another shirt may just go to Biology. Once everything is separated you have to write and/or type out a property receipt for each item that gives a description of that item—not "one T-shirt," but "one white Hanes T-shirt, size XXL, with suspected bloodstains and gunshot powder patterns." This takes hours in itself.

On your down time you write reports. This is as important as actually working the crime scene. You have to articulate through your writing what you did on the scene, and attorneys try to catch you on how you phrase things. It doesn't matter how good I am at my job; if I cannot write a good report, the rest of my skills are worthless.

The other important thing you do is go to court and testify. If you cannot relate to the jury, the case could be lost. I had one attorney try to confuse a jury once by saying that the cartridge (bullet) could not have come from the Beretta 9mm firearm because the head stamp on the cartridge was from S&W. I had to explain to the jury: You wear a specific size in clothing—say, a woman's 8 or 12. But you can go out and buy a pair of jeans from different companies, like Guess, Levi's, or DKNY. Your size is like the firearm. The pair of jeans you buy is like the bullet—it can be many different brand names, and still fit on your body. The jury completely understood.

On a lighter note, every profession has its own related humor, and crime scene is no exception. Since the *CSI: Miami* team drives Hummer H2s, I constantly get asked, "Where is your Hummer?" "Bite me," is my usual response. There's also a lot of on-scene stress relief humor from all the violence and death that we encounter. But one of the most fun are the practical jokes in the office. I have two co-workers who are consistently playing jokes on each other. It's endless: opening lockers to find the whole thing filled with shredded paper, phone books, or other surprises. You never know what those two are going to do next. It's really almost a cross between Barney Fife and *Reno 911*.

Sometimes you have to chuckle about some of the observers who ride along with us from time to time. One particular observer, who was studying forensic science, came with me to the scene of a double homicide. She was shocked to find out that when you move a victim with gunshot wounds, blood pools out. I think she may need to rethink what she wants to do for a living.

I have had other observers show up wearing shorts, T-shirts, and open-toed shoes. Now, I understand that civilians may not completely comprehend what goes on at a crime scene. But there is something to say for a good first impression. If you are even remotely considering getting into this profession, show up dressed appropriately, and do not say things like, "Oh, my God, I am having a Court TV moment" or "a real *CSI* moment." That is not going to make a good impression.

Being a crime scene investigator is a great job, but you have to know what you're getting into. On the personal end, crime scene can be trying on your home life. You work homicides or domestic-related incidents on most major holidays, as well as working late most nights, and it can get old. Just because the clock says it's time to go home, you can't—not if you are at the scene of a crime. Often, you work late, and then have to go in early for court the following day. There have been times that I've taken catnaps at traffic lights. Good thing I keep my doors locked.

Some cases really do touch our hearts more than others. I will never forget the old lady sleeping in her bed with a gunshot wound to the head. Or the pizza delivery guy, working three jobs trying to make ends meet for his family, who didn't understand English and was shot and killed by robbers on Christmas Eve. Or the SIDS cases, where the mom and dad tried to do everything right. Or the child drowned in the pool, or with her head stuck in the window of a vehicle. Or the child-related homicides that have taught me the most dangerous place for a child is with mom's new boyfriend. It's those kinds of cases, where I can help grieving families find closure—where I can help put the guilty away and exonerate the innocent—that makes this profession worth every sleepless night and every missed holiday.

Crime Scene **Detective Christine Kruse-Feldstein** has been with the Miami-Dade Police Department for over ten years. She also has experience in law enforcement in Kentucky and has been a part of a volunteer fire department working as an emergency medical technician. Overall she has been involved in law enforcement or fire rescue for sixteen years. One of Christine's favorite sayings is, "I do not respond unless you are raped, robbed, shot, stabbed, or dead."

The so-called "CSI Effect"—the influence the shows have had on the public and their expectations when it comes to forensics—has been the subject of much speculation. Rick Workman has a unique perspective on this: a real-life CSI working the graveyard shift in Vegas, he was one of the people Anthony Zuiker studied when creating the show in the first place.

RICK WORKMAN

The CSI Effect

CSI—The Beginning

My first exposure to the concept of the *CSI* television series was as a senior crime scene investigator (CSI) for the Las Vegas Metropolitan Police Department (LVMPD), where I was assigned to the graveyard shift.

I was in a shift briefing in late 1999 when a supervisor told us that Anthony Zuiker was going to ride with us to crime scenes for six weeks, doing research for a show about CSIs and forensics.

We'd had camera crews and reporters travel with us in the past, but they were normally from the local TV news or newspapers. Occasionally a regional or national television crew would show up to film the aftermath of a major crime scene, like Tupac Shakur's murder in Las Vegas in 1996, or when a camouflage-clad Zane Floyd, armed with a shotgun, hunted people in a Las Vegas supermarket, killing four employees and wounding a fifth in 1999. But the news crews were interested in body counts, victims, and suspect information, not forensic processes.

Until Zuiker, no one had paid much attention to the virtually unknown world of forensics. But we wondered out loud if anyone would watch a television show where its stars spend hours brushing powder onto a piece of evidence to develop a fingerprint, or adding drops of phenolphthalein onto red-stained cotton swabs to determine if the red substance is blood. How do you capture the emotions on the face of a fingerprint examiner as he waits fifteen minutes or more, even hours, while a computer silently performs its work, sorting through millions of fingerprints in its electronic records? How do you keep the attention of the audience while showing a piece of high-tech equipment running through its time-consuming cycles of replicating and analyzing genetic material?

Zuiker began riding with the younger CSIs on each shift. Although the older CSIs usually had the most experience and technical knowledge, he wouldn't ride in a vehicle with anyone over thirty years old. He believed at the time that the show's target audience was going to be young adults, under thirty, and wanted to spend more time getting to know the younger CSIs.

Zuiker went from crime scene to crime scene, trying to learn the CSI business from the inside out. Our shift usually gathered for lunch each night, where he began telling us about some of his ideas for the *CSI* pilot and first season. In return, we bombarded him with details of the most interesting crime scenes we had worked. He was creating characters and stories as we spoke with him, and we were amazed at his ability to take an idea and turn it into so many different possibilities so quickly. Several of his characters were to be loosely based on some of our CSIs. Some of our unusual habits, quirks, and sayings would later be repeated on the screen as well.

Zuiker had an impressive drive and desire to turn his dream into a reality, and his attitude made us want to dig deeper into ideas for shows.

Earlier TV Crime Dramas Treated the Forensic Process as an Automatic Process—or Magic

There have been many popular "police" shows on television, but before *CSI*, none that showed the inner workings of a real forensic lab—none that showed the time-consuming and painstaking steps required of the scientific work behind the scenes.

Successful shows like *Law and Order*, which first aired in 1990, and

NYPD Blue, which began in 1993, have familiarized us with the routines of police work: locating witnesses, interrogating suspects, arresting the "guilty," and winning or losing the case in trial. But the fast pace of those shows gave very little attention, and even less respect, to the crime scene investigators, forensic scientists, and others who worked in the crime labs.

In the seventh season *NYPD Blue* episode "These Shoots Are Made for Joaquin," fingerprint examiner Preston Ross was dressed in a suit with a bow-tie. His stereotypical style of clothing and his mannerisms immediately painted a negative picture of him (and with him, his fellow lab workers). Ross was proud of his ability to recover a fingerprint from a revolver involved in a murder and explained to Detective Sipowicz how he had determined the order in which the print was left on the revolver. But his explanation was quickly dismissed, and he was portrayed as an overzealous lab rat to be seen, but not heard.

Traditional police shows on television have mentioned "fingerprints," "ballistics," and "forensics" for years, but almost as if that piece of the criminal justice and law enforcement world had some sort of magic to it. A detective leaves a crime scene and grabs some lunch. As soon as he returns to his desk he gets a call. He is told that "ballistics matched the bullet to the gun found in the suspect's apartment" or "forensics found only one fingerprint in the apartment and it didn't match the suspect." The process itself remained unknown.

In some shows, the typical procedure is for the crime scene investigators to begin taking photographs as detectives arrive. Within minutes, the scene has been processed for fingerprints and trace evidence, detectives are tossing the place (searching in and under everything), the body is being removed, and everyone is leaving the crime scene. The detectives order tests from the crime lab, and lab results miraculously appear by report or phone call in a matter of minutes or hours. Just like magic.

Why Cops, Prosecutors, and Real CSIs Hate the World's Most Popular TV Show

With all the success Zuiker's three CSI shows have had—the original version is now in its sixth season, its television audience ranges between fourteen and twenty-nine million viewers per episode (per Nielsen's Top 10 TV Ratings), and it's widely syndicated, and is broadcast in over thirty countries—it may be surprising to learn that not everyone is happy with the new phenomenon. From its inception, a huge black cloud has been cast upon the series.

That cloud obviously doesn't cast a shadow among the millions in the viewing audience, but rather, within the halls of justice and in law enforcement agencies across the country. Many prosecutors, detectives, and police officers speak in very unkind terms about the shows. They talk openly about the (perceived) negative impact on the viewing public and on our jury system. It is also a common occurrence to hear forensic chemists, DNA analysts, and other forensic scientists and managers talking in negative terms about the CSI shows.

Most surprising to me is the fact that many of the CSIs, whose profession is so widely publicized and hailed by the show, have turned against it. Many CSIs will not publicly admit, at least not in front of police officers, forensic scientists, or other CSIs, that they watch or like the show. So many CSIs I know deny watching it that I am not sure how many actually do. During a recent trip to a crime scene investigation unit in Arizona, I saw a CSI poster with a red circle and red slash drawn through it, showing someone's obvious dislike of the show.

So what is all the uproar about?

The CSI Effect and the One-Hour Investigation

The "CSI Effect" has been discussed and written about in many major television, newspaper, and Internet news reports. The term itself can be described in three parts:

- The belief by prosecutors, detectives, and police officers that the show "incorrectly" leads the public to believe that there can be no crime solved, and no one convicted, unless there are substantial, even overwhelming amounts of physical evidence to prove the facts—that eyewitness testimony and good-old-fashioned detective work is not enough.
- The fear that the viewing audience will believe that all of the techniques and equipment used in the shows are representative of a "real" crime laboratory.
- Concern about the way "one-hour investigations" misrepresent what happens in real life.

The CSI Effect: No Evidence, No Case

The first part of the CSI Effect is the belief by prosecutors, detectives, and police officers that the show leads the public to somehow believe, incorrectly, that there can be no crime solved, and no one convicted, unless there is substantial physical evidence to prove the facts.

Many prosecutors believe that jurors now place an unrealistic burden on the prosecution to provide physical evidence as proof of the facts of a crime, primarily due to their reliance on and belief of what they have seen during episodes of CSI. There have been reports of court trials where the jury expected to see results of the analysis of physical evidence because of their newfound knowledge of forensics courtesy of CSI. When none or not as much physical evidence as they might have expected was presented, the jurors made "incorrect" decisions based on false assumptions about the weight the potential evidence would have carried had it been analyzed and presented in court. Some jurors have questioned why a particular evidence-processing technique might have been used but was not attempted or presented in court.

Prosecutors have complained of jurors acquitting "guilty" defendants because *CSI* misled them into believing something they should not have, or disregarding testimony that they should have considered more carefully.

I have seen the disappointment and dismay on the faces of detectives and prosecutors when they are told that there is very little useful forensic evidence in a particular murder case or other major crime. This has always been a tough situation to deal with, but the CSI Effect seems to add more significance, at least in the minds of prosecutors, detectives, and police officers.

The popularity of CSI may have helped to shift the burden of proof slightly further to the police and prosecutors, which has been the crux of our criminal justice system. In *Commentaries on the Laws of England* (1765–1769), Sir William Blackstone wrote ". . . for the law holds, that it is better that ten guilty persons escape, than one innocent suffer."

Where do we draw the line? No matter the number, one is too many.

Thanks to the evolution of DNA technology and programs like the Innocence Project, many convicted persons, even some with death sentences, have been exonerated of crimes for which they were originally convicted. Since the inception of the Innocence Project, more than 170 people in the United States have been exonerated, including 14 who were at one time sentenced to death (Innocence Project home page).

Our courtrooms across the country are frequently filled with jurors armed with more, albeit not necessarily complete, information and "education" regarding certain processes used in a criminal case.

What can be so wrong with that?

Since the late 1800s, we have known that microscopic evidence—hair, fibers, fingerprint evidence, biological fluids, etc.—is important in establishing the connections between suspects, evidence, and crime scenes. In 1892, Dr. Edmond Locard, director of the Lyon Laboratory of Police Techniques and vice president of the International Academy of Criminology, wrote in the *Manual of Police Techniques*: "It is impossible for the lawbreaker to act—above all with the intensity that a criminal act presupposes—without leaving traces of having been on the scene."

What CSI does for the public is remind them of the possibility that potential evidence can exist at most, if not all, crime scenes. What the shows do not always do is explain how difficult or time-consuming the process to locate, document, collect, and process it is. The sad reality is that, in most cases, spending days or weeks searching for evidence at a crime scene is not a realistic option. There is no law enforcement agency in the country—or in the world, for that matter—that has the equipment, personnel, uninhibited access to the crime scene, and time necessary to process each crime scene until every last piece of microscopic evidence has been recovered and analyzed. That is not a realistic expectation, and also not necessary in most cases.

I've been asked by local and federal prosecutors to have guns fingerprinted in order to prove that a particular suspect had that gun in his possession. Some request it even though the arresting officer found the gun in the suspect's waistband during the pat-down search. The problem is, if a CSI or latent print examiner (LPE) processes the gun and does not recover a fingerprint that can be identified as the suspect's, he or she will be hauled into court to explain why not. Prosecutors must be prepared and able to explain not only the process, but the potential for positive or negative results.

Police officers must continue to hone their writing skills and carefully describe, in minute detail, the events of each case and the information and events that led to their actions and conclusions. When all is said and done, the integrity of the police officer or detective, and of the CSI handling the evidence, is more important than the presence of physical evidence itself. In fact, without careful documentation of the chain of custody of evidence[1] and careful handling, preparation, preservation, and security of the evidence, as testified to by real people, the evidence is worthless in court anyway.

Prosecutors must be able to skillfully explain to jurors that *CSI* is *just* a television show, broadcast for entertainment purposes. They must use their jurist skills to explain that there are many different ways of proving a real case and that the testimony of law enforcement professionals, witnesses, and experts is often the most appropriate, and must be given due consideration.

I have been on the witness stand giving "negative print testimony." In negative print testimony, an expert witness explains how fingerprints may or may not be deposited at a scene, and the chance of actually recovering an identifiable print that may belong to a particular subject. This is the type of testimony that may be required in the instance mentioned earlier, regarding the processing of a gun removed from a suspect's waistband. When this testimony is presented well by the prosecution and the expert witness, any potential CSI Effect should be greatly diminished or eliminated. Negative print testimony, and similar testimony related to other types of forensic evidence, has been used for many years—well before the CSI series started.

When a prosecutor asks for a firearm to be processed for prints, and none are recovered, the next logical question a CSI fan may ask is, why didn't they process the gun for DNA? That would be a very good question. Why not?

Before we answer the question of why not, let's talk about why.

Without turning this into a science lesson, here's a brief explanation about DNA provided by the President's DNA Initiative, *Advancing Justice through DNA Technology*:

DNA (the abbreviation for deoxyribonucleic acid, which is the genetic material present in the cells of all living organisms) is the fun-

---

[1] Chain of custody is basically the documentation and proof at each step as the evidence changes hands from collection through processing stages, storage in the evidence vault, and removal for court.

damental building block for an individual's entire genetic makeup. A person's DNA is the same in every cell (with a nucleus). The DNA in a person's blood is the same as the DNA in their skin cells, semen, and saliva. DNA is contained in blood, semen, skin cells, tissue, organs, muscle, brain cells, bone, teeth, hair, saliva, mucus, perspiration, fingernails, urine, etc.

You may imagine after reading this that DNA can be contained in nearly any residue you might leave behind on things that you touch.

The grips of many handguns are manufactured with a rough surface to help the shooter maintain a better grip on the gun when shooting. However, this rough surface makes it extremely difficult to recover identifiable fingerprints. That's where the partnership (DNA and fingerprints) comes in. The same surfaces that make recovering fingerprints difficult also tend to scrape, abrade, or rub off skin cells that may contain DNA. The reverse is also true: smooth surfaces are less likely to collect DNA but are often great sources of fingerprints. In other words, the smooth surfaces of a firearm, such as the barrel or other smooth metal parts, may be an excellent source for fingerprints, and the rough surfaces may be a better source of DNA. Both should always be considered when evidence is processed.

However, there are several reasons why they often aren't. I'll list a few here, although there are many more.

One reason is because many people in law enforcement agencies, particularly detectives and police officers charged with conducting interviews and arresting the bad guys, still rely on "good-old-fashioned" police techniques. Even processing for fingerprints often takes a back seat to other investigative techniques (as it should whenever that method is practical, effective, and more efficient).

Also, many law enforcement supervisors and managers still appear to have a difficult time realizing or accepting the true investigative value of DNA. I have been told on more than one occasion that "I will get DNA analysts and DNA equipment when we have all the cops we need." The fact is that, through DNA (and the century-old fingerprint processing routine), more victims are identified (which is often the most important step in beginning a successful homicide investigation), more suspects are identified and apprehended, fewer (relative) numbers of crimes are committed, more lives are saved, and crime is actually reduced, effectively adding more seasoned police officers to the street without the additional salary expenses.

Another reason DNA is not analyzed as often as it should be is because of a lack of sufficient laboratory analysis capability nationwide. Nearly every public forensic DNA laboratory in the U.S. is overwhelmed with backlogs of DNA samples that have not yet been analyzed.

In March 2003, the U.S. Department of Justice released a Special Report, "Report to the Attorney General on Delays in Forensic DNA Analysis" which summarized:

> Forensic DNA evidence has tremendous potential to solve some of our nation's most serious crimes. It has solved rape and homicide cases that could not have been solved with traditional law enforcement techniques. DNA has also exonerated persons charged with or convicted of crimes they did not commit. However, DNA currently is not used to its full potential in the criminal justice system.

The March 2003 report summary also offered this explanation and concern:

> There is a significant backlog of casework samples that has been caused by a massive demand for DNA analyses without a corresponding growth in forensic laboratory capacity. These delays pose substantial barriers to using forensic DNA evidence to its full potential. Although the full extent of the problem may not be measurable (the nation has more than 17,000 separate law enforcement agencies that potentially could be retaining untested forensic DNA evidence), the problem of unanalyzed DNA is a serious impediment to effective law enforcement and denies justice to crime victims and the public. Based on National Institute of Justice (NIJ) staff analysis of preliminary figures relating to the backlog assessment, NIJ estimates that approximately 350,000 rape and homicide cases await DNA testing.

A third reason prosecutors and law enforcement officers are not asking for the analysis of DNA evidence to the extent that they could is because DNA evidence is often not considered or collected at the crime scene. Law enforcement agencies are overwhelmed with casework. Most do not have the manpower required to process all crime scenes as thoroughly as they would prefer. Many police agencies use police officers (including deputy sheriffs, troopers, etc.) to respond to crime scenes as "first responders," then rely on the same pool of officers to process the crime scene for evidence.

Regardless of whether police officers or civilian crime scene investigators process crime scenes, some police departments put minimum thresholds on the value of loss or damage before a department employee will respond. Some agencies will not respond to property crimes (burglary, vehicle theft, etc.) unless the loss is anywhere from a few thousand dollars to tens of thousands of dollars, depending on the particular situation. (The victim is often required to go to a local police station to fill out a report, or complete one over the phone.) Nearly every one of those crime scenes potentially has DNA evidence that might be the key to solving the crime, as well as many other crimes committed by the same suspect(s)—which would prevent additional crimes once the suspect is identified and apprehended.

This is where *CSI* comes into play as an important part of our society. I believe *CSI* is not only "educating" the public, but helping to prevent and solve crimes.

It's also shining a bright light on the fact that there are crime scenes that should be processed more thoroughly, evidence that should be collected but isn't, and evidence that should be analyzed in more detail but is not.

If prosecutors don't like it, if law enforcement doesn't like it, if the public doesn't like it, then I say—do something about it. But it does take time, and it takes a lot of money.

Many skilled employees are needed to run a forensic laboratory, and many more to process crime scenes and perform subsequent evidence processing. It takes a large amount of money to properly staff the labs we have and to fund additional crime labs. It takes a lot of money to buy state-of-the-art equipment to solve crimes and prevent many others. It will also take additional time in court to educate juries about forensic processes in criminal investigations. But it can and must be done.

The old adage, "Pay me now or pay me later," is quite appropriate here. Later the price will be higher, much higher, in more ways than one.

Before going on, it is important to mention that in stark contrast to the fears and complaints of prosecutors and law enforcement employees, some defense attorneys have complained that jurors who watch the CSI shows give unrealistic credit to the expert witnesses (CSI, fingerprint examiner, forensic scientist, etc.) and their testimony.

The CSI Effect—This Must Be How the Real CSI Does It

The second part of the CSI Effect is the idea that the viewing audience believes that all of the techniques and equipment used in the shows are representative of the things that happen in a "real" crime laboratory.

The CSI shows are not intended to be factual or educational television.

There are a lot of different types of equipment used in the CSI shows. For the most part, those items are used in real life, although the actual use of the equipment may vary greatly.

It is not that *CSI* does not make an attempt to preserve some "reality" in the use of equipment on the show. The case is actually quite to the contrary. David Berman, who plays Deputy Coroner David Phillips on *CSI*, is also the lead researcher for the show. Jon Wellner is David's research assistant, and has a smaller part on the show as Henry Andrews, a forensic lab worker. David and Jon have over 400 expert contacts throughout the criminal justice, law enforcement, forensics, and medical communities, whom they rely on to answer technical questions related to the show.

While no one at *CSI* attempts to pass the show off as "factual" or "educational," they do spend a lot of time conducting research to ensure that their story ideas are based on real-world events and procedures. The writers do a lot of their own research, but pass many of their ideas to David and Jon, who conduct further research into these ideas' feasibility. Their recommendations are given back to the writers, who still have editorial license to do anything they want to make the show "entertaining."

Imagine how boring it would be to watch a real AFIS (Automated Fingerprint Identification System) run through its paces for anywhere from five minutes to two hours or more. Also, the AFIS systems and other equipment used on *CSI* have some added enhancements to make them more visually entertaining.

In real life, crime scene analysts and LPEs often spend hours, even days, working on evidence in the laboratory in an attempt to locate, preserve, and recover fingerprints before the prints can be entered into AFIS. Some even take months or more.

In the episode "Mea Culpa" (5-9), Gil Grissom was on the witness stand during a new trial for a man convicted of murder five years earlier. He looked at the inside cover of a matchbook, a piece of evidence in the case, and saw something that made him temporarily speechless. What he discovered was a fingerprint (shown in red on the show; in real life, the print would have shown up violet) that he had not seen when he processed the item many years earlier. That scenario, and explanation below, is based on actual events.

Grissom had earlier used ninhydrin to process the matchbook for prints. Ninhydrin is a chemical reagent that is sensitive to amino acids, which are the building block of proteins. Amino acids are secreted from sweat glands, and sweat is a component of many fingerprints left on evidence. Ninhydrin can be used to develop fingerprints and to enhance bloody prints, and is often used on porous surfaces such as paper, cardboard, wood, and walls (painted with a flat paint).

The reason that Grissom froze on the witness stand when seeing the print was because the chemical reaction of Ninhydrin to the amino acids does not always create an immediate visible reaction. In some cases, it may take weeks, even months or more. In the episode, Grissom had apparently forgotten that possibility when on the witness stand.

When I worked as a CSI and processed items with Ninhydrin, I usually photographed the visible reactions and sent any developed fingerprints to the Fingerprint Section. But instead of booking the items into the Evidence Vault immediately, I placed the items in a plastic zip lock bag, and secured them in an evidence locker to be examined again a few weeks later. I often noted additional prints, which could then be photographed and sent for additional analysis, comparison, entry into AFIS, etc. Ninhydrin is just one of many different substances and methods used to develop or enhance fingerprints before they can be entered into AFIS or used to make a one-on-one fingerprint comparison.

It can take anywhere from a couple of minutes to an hour or more to enter a single fingerprint into AFIS. In some cases, the same print is entered multiple times with slightly different methods of encoding. Then, after the AFIS computer comes up with a list of "potential matches," or "candidates," a human LPE must compare the original print with the candidate prints. That comparison may take minutes, an hour, or several hours. Occasionally, it may take an entire day or more to complete the comparison of a single fingerprint, and the examiner may need to go through a long list of candidate prints before making an identification or determining that no matches exist under that particular search criteria. After a preliminary identification has been made, another examiner must conduct an independent comparison, or "peer review." Following that step, a technical or quality assurance review may be done by a third examiner or supervising examiner, followed by an administrative review.

Granted, there are exciting moments, when the end result of our procedures helps solve a major case. For example, identifying a murderer's print on a bloody gun found at the victim's apartment, finding and identifying a single sample of DNA that helps take a rape suspect off the streets before he rapes again, or getting an AFIS "cold hit" on a fingerprint from a brutal kidnap and robbery that occurred several years earlier. Capture those moments and you've got twenty seconds of great TV. Otherwise, you've got to improvise.

Even though I know and remind many others that *CSI* is not real, there have been a few instances where some of the procedures in the show went a bit too far, even trying my own patience. In one episode ("Bodies in Motion," 6-1) a body was discovered in the trunk of a vehicle. The body had decomposed to the point that we would call it "soupy." Just before fading to a commercial, Gil Grissom was shown holding a large roll of clear plastic (used to wrap cargo to hold it in place). "Car condom," he explained, and began to wrap the entire vehicle in the plastic. There are a LOT of things wrong with that procedure, and I was amazed *CSI* went that far. (Three things immediately come to mind: wrapping the vehicle in plastic may abrade potential fingerprints from the surface; some of the fingerprint residue and sources of DNA would likely transfer to the tightly wrapped plastic, rendering them practically useless when the plastic is removed; and bloodstains, gunshot residue, and other sources of trace evidence might also be disturbed or destroyed upon removal.) Minutes after the episode ended, I contacted Jon and asked him what they were thinking when they saw the script. He laughed and said, "Dave and I told them you wouldn't like it." Jon said they admit there are some things done for the sake of entertainment and visual appeal that even they would shy away from.

A colleague and I talked with David about some of the "impossible" methods they used to administer poisons, tamper with containers, etc., in some of the episodes. But David reminded us that there are times when the *CSI* staff feels the obligation to go to extremes to avoid "teaching" someone how to commit a crime that they might otherwise be unable to conceive or commit.

I've entertained questions about CSIs carrying guns, questioning suspects, and having access to helicopters. There is no end to the questions and the variety of "correct answers" I've heard and read from many who profess to know the "facts." The fact is this: Depending on which department you go to, some or all of those things are possible. Nothing here is certain but uncertainty. And the differences vary widely between departments within the same community or state, and from state to state.

Here are a few examples: The LVMPD CSIs are not cops (sworn police officers), but they really do carry guns (it is their option, and most do). North Las Vegas Police Department CSIs can carry guns and are a mixture of civilian (non-sworn, with no police powers) and police officers. The Boulder City, Nevada, police department has detectives who put on their CSI hat (so to speak) to process the crime scenes and evidence, then take it off to conduct interviews and arrest suspects. The CSIs in Reno, Nevada, at the Washoe County Sheriff's Office Regional Crime Lab are sworn deputies, with full police powers. Many of their other forensic lab employees are civilians. In Henderson, Nevada, CSIs are civilians who do not carry guns—but Henderson also has dozens of cops who process crime scenes, interview suspects, and make arrests.

Things are done much differently in the Western United States than in the Midwest and on the East Coast. There are thousands of different combinations of these scenarios throughout the US, and even more throughout the world.

I used to hear a lot of jokes from police officers about the CSIs on TV using helicopters. Right after *CSI* started, and I was new to my current department, we were working a case where aerial photos would have been helpful. A patrol captain joked about me not having "my *CSI* helicopter" available to take aerials. I called LVMPD from my cell phone and in about twenty minutes, a police helicopter landed in the intersection to pick me up. I'll never forget the look on many officers' faces when we lifted off and flew over their heads. I haven't heard any more comments about "my *CSI* helicopter."

The CSI Effect—All Crimes Are Solved in One Hour

The third part of the CSI Effect is the concern that viewers will be confused about the difference between the one-hour investigation they see on TV and what happens in real life.

I have always had a difficult time understanding this concern's origin, and why it is so pervasive throughout criminal justice communities, law enforcement, and forensics.

I cannot begin to count the number of times I've heard a member of law enforcement talking or laughing about the CSI shows and how ridiculous it is to show that crimes can be solved in one hour. I realize that to most people, this is simply a figurative reference to the speed that things are done on the show. Maybe to the ordinary viewer, the figurative interpretation is the case. But for some reason, David Berman and Jon Wellner receive a lot of comments from law enforcement employees complaining about what they believe CSI is telling the viewing audience, and those comments come from people who seriously think that the viewing audience believes the cases are solved in one actual clock-hour.

In "The Making of a Hit" on the *CSI* second season DVD, Zuiker said,

> "...we make some dramatic cheats and use some dramatic license in terms of how long DNA comes back or a tox [toxicology analysis report] comes back. Your DNA may come back, but it may take four days, tox may take three weeks. But it takes one scene in our show because we don't have time to say, 'Hey, audience, we'll talk to you next month and let you know how the DNA stuff worked out.' We take those time cheats to sort of move the story along...and we all know it takes more than forty-four minutes and fifteen seconds of screen time to solve a crime."

Do millions of viewers really believe major crimes can be solved in an hour or less? Why else would Zuiker feel it necessary to clarify with statements such as the one above?

But let's give the benefit of the doubt to the audience. Let's assume, for argument's sake, that the typical viewer believes that most of the events in a *CSI* episode can actually occur in, say, one work shift for a real crime scene investigator and for the detectives assigned to the case. At the very least, this appears to be the perception of many prosecutors and law enforcement employees. But upon close examination, many of the episodes shift from day to night multiple times. In "What's Eating Gilbert Grissom?" (5-6), the episode starts during the night shift and goes through two days and a third night shift. In "Viva Las Vegas" (5-1), the episode starts during the night shift and the sun rises and sets five times.

Let's look at the opposite case. In the episode "Paper or Plastic" (4-14), a robbery at a grocery store turned into a shootout, leaving five people dead, including a police officer. The entire CSI team worked on the investigation. The crime, which occurred in the evening, was depicted on television as being investigated throughout the night, into the next day, then into part of the next night.

Ironically, I was consulted during the writing of that episode, because I worked the original crime scene from which the story idea came. At approximately 4 A.M., I responded to an Albertson's grocery store where a man with a shotgun methodically hunted down and killed four employees, and critically wounded another. As he calmly walked out of the store and pointed the shotgun to his own head, he was confronted by police officers and eventually dropped the shotgun onto the pavement. Our entire CSI shift worked that scene, which had a significant amount of evidence to be documented, recovered, and processed. We cleared the scene about twelve hours later—ironically, in less time than it took the CSI team on television to complete their work.

Maybe it is the police officers, detectives, police supervisors, and police managers who contribute to this misconception. Do *law enforcement officers* have the wrong idea of the time it takes for CSIs to work a case? Are *they* just as guilty of believing what they are laughing about— that much of what the CSIs do for the investigation of crime can and does in fact occur in one shift?

On a "real-life" shift, an individual CSI can go from call to call, processing a couple of burglaries, maybe throwing in a robbery at a local "stop-and-rob" (convenience store and gas station) and making a quick stop at the hospital emergency room to take photos of the victim in a battery–domestic violence case. Another CSI may stop to help at some of those scenes, if available. Some crime scenes have little potential forensic evidence, and in other cases, there just isn't time to process a scene to the extent the CSIs would like, so they hurry through some of the processing.

But for many of the more extensive burglaries, robberies, kidnappings, and sexual assaults, the CSIs frequently spend an entire shift processing the crime scene. Sometimes additional time is necessary. Then, they return to the crime lab with bags of evidence that must be processed for fingerprints, DNA, blood, trace evidence, etc. This subsequent evidence processing may take days or weeks to complete, but the detectives and other police officers normally do not see the additional work. Do *they* know how long it takes to process evidence? Often, they do not.

Do they really know how long it takes to correctly process a homicide scene? Sadly, they often do not realize that either. Part of the reason for that misunderstanding or misconception is that police officers usually stay outside the scene while it is being processed, and maintain security of the perimeter. The detectives may leave the homicide crime scene as soon as they have interviewed persons in the area and the body is removed. CSIs often continue to work at the crime scene for several shifts, taking a "break" from the scene to attend the autopsy (which may tie up a full day), before returning to the scene for additional processing. (Many large departments have enough personnel to split the duties and locations between different CSIs.) The alternative is to have different squads or shifts of CSIs "tag team" the processing when manpower is available. In the meantime, the case's detectives, who usually outnumber the CSIs assigned, are pulling CSIs in different directions, trying to get help on *their* portion of the case—at a follow-up scene, a search warrant location, or where the detectives are interviewing *their* witness or suspect.

Many police officers, supervisors, managers, and detectives are not fully aware of the duties and capabilities of their own CSI or forensic lab personnel, nor the complexity of their jobs. Many do not even know what each specific forensic job classification or specialty does for their own department.

In a recent police department division meeting, a police manager was talking directly to his LPEs and referred to them as "the fingerprint identifier guys." Identifying fingerprints as belonging to a particular person is just a portion of their duties; LPEs usually have many other complicated and time-consuming tasks.

Sadly, this is not an isolated incident. Similar "misunderstandings" happen every day in crime labs throughout the United States. Without knowledge of and respect for the capabilities of the personnel in their own crime labs, how can prosecutors, police officers, detectives, and police managers understand and appreciate the major role the crime labs play in helping to fight, prevent, and solve crimes and save lives?

Could this group of professionals be partially responsible for causing the CSI Effect about which so many in public service professions complain?

Cultural Impact of *CSI*—More Crimes May Be Solved

CSI helps showcase some of the potential capabilities of a fully equipped, fully staffed forensic laboratory and coroner's office. It has given us a glimpse of what forensic science can do for us.

CSI has opened the eyes of a naïve, unknowing public. Now, the public is more aware of what a forensic laboratory, CSI unit, coroner's office, etc., are capable of doing. In fact, thanks to the show, many in law enforcement have a much better understanding of the capabilities of their own crime scene investigation units and forensic labs.

Many crime victims now know not to touch items before they call the police, because they know there could be some good suspect prints or DNA on something that the suspect touched. The only problem is these victims believe so much that we will always be able to recover that damning evidence that they seem to be more disappointed now than ever when we can't.

Victims who previously waited nervously in another room while we processed the scene now want to watch the CSI do his or her job. It isn't magic to them anymore. It isn't voodoo science. They expect positive results. They will not only tell us that they know a lot about our job, but also often try to tell us *how* to do our job.

In the past, victims often handled items touched by suspects, put things away, cleaned up after the crime while waiting for the police to arrive, or simply decided the cops wouldn't be able to catch the persons responsible. The CSI shows have (indirectly) educated the public to the point that we now have victims who are informed enough about certain aspects of crime scene investigation that they protect the items disturbed by the suspects. They even look for objects out of place or other tell-tale signs left by the suspect(s). More undisturbed evidence means an increase in the possibility of recovering identifiable fingerprints or DNA, thus solving more crimes.

Our prosecutors and jurors now expect to see more physical forensic evidence in court. Even when we have a taped confession, we are now expected to produce evidence the jurors can see and touch. CSIs and forensic scientists have a lot of added pressure, but their skills and abilities are increasing dramatically as a result.

As a result of the forensic technologies and capabilities demonstrated in *CSI*, I believe the public has a new, highly favorable view of our forensics community and a much better understanding of our potential capabilities.

Finally, high school and college students across the country, and around the world, are learning that science can be fun and meaningful, that math does have a usefulness outside of school, that biology and chemistry can help solve the crime of the century.

The CSI Effect, if it does exist, doesn't seem like such a bad thing.

Thank you, Anthony Zuiker.

Rick Workman is the criminalistics administrator for the Henderson Nevada Police Department. He manages the Forensics Laboratory, Crime Scene Investigation Section, and the Evidence Vault. He was previously a CSI with the Las Vegas Metropolitan Police Department.

He has consulted for numerous *CSI: Crime Scene Investigation* episodes, was featured in Court TV's *Forensic Files*, *Las Vegas CSU*, *Thrill Killings*, and in Lyon TV's series *The Real CSI*, in London, England.

Rick is a retired U.S. Air Force officer. He served in Desert Storm as the F-117A Stealth Fighter Commander for Maintenance and served as a defense nuclear agency technical inspector.

Rick is tasked with funding and building a Forensic Science Center (crime lab with evidence vault). Monitor the progress of the project at www.nevadacsi.com.

References

Commentaries on the Laws of England (1765-1769), Sir William Blackstone, Lonang Library, Historic Reference Works. Retrieved May 2006. <http://www.lonang.com/exlibris/blackstone/index.html>.

Innocence Project, Home Page. Retrieved 17 April 2006. <http://www.innocenceproject.org/>.

J. T. Baker Material Safety Data Sheets (MSDS). Retrieved June 2006. <http://www.jtbaker.com/msds/englishhtml/s4946.htm>.

Manual of Police Techniques, Third Edition. Paris: Payot, 16 Boulevard St. Germain, 1939. Quoted in: *An Exchange in Locard's Own Words (Part 1).* Retrieved May 2006. <http://www.modernmicroscopy.com/main.asp?article=63>.

Nielson Media. *Top Ten Primetime Broadcast TV Programs for Week of 11/07/05-11/13/05.* Retrieved May 2006. <http://www.nielsenmedia.com/ratings/broadcast_programs.html>.

Selenium, as Sodium Selenite, in the Treatment of Septic Shock. www.clinicaltrials.gov. A service of the U.S. National Institutes of Health. Retrieved June 2006. <http://www.clinicaltrials.gov/ct/gui/show/NCT00207844;jsessionid=3BF6AC179CDA81EDD22FF97096A28B57?order=9>.

U.S. National Institute of Justice, President's DNA Initiative, *Advancing Justice Through DNA Technology.* Retrieved May 2006. <http://www.dna.gov/basics/biology>.

Kristine Kathryn Rusch, back when she was editing the hardcover magazine *Pulphouse*, was the very first person to buy my fiction. I owe her a debt of gratitude for not only that, but for helpful and encouraging criticism concerning the story itself (including the inspiring words *Don't give up!*). I didn't, and thus began my writing career.

Her essay considers the thorny problem of whether or not the CSI programs are educating criminals, thus enhancing *their* careers. All I can say is that four *CSI: Miami* novels have certainly enhanced mine...and I might never have had the chance to write them if it weren't for her.

Thanks, Kristine.

KRISTINE KATHRYN RUSCH

Creating Criminal Masterminds

"Everyone learns from science.
It all depends on how you use the knowledge."
—GIL GRISSOM, "I Like to Watch" (6-17)

The episode "I Like to Watch," one of the best in *CSI*'s stellar 2005–2006 season, played with the entire idea of voyeurism. Cameras watched everything—obviously breaking the fourth wall. Reporters, following the team, asked the questions we sometimes ask, and at the same time, we saw the harried Crime Scene Investigators, trying to do their job in the media spotlight.

In *CSI*, however, the investigators do not fail.

CSI, remember, is fiction.

Excellent fiction. It grapples with societal problems from pornography to child abuse, but it also gives us a voyeur's-eye view of everything from a bullet invading a human skull to ways people in animal costumes have group sex. *CSI* is not about solving society's ills. It doesn't have an agenda like *Boston Legal* or even *Law and Order* does.

In many ways, *CSI* is a science fiction program. It focuses on the science—the oh-isn't-this-cool side of science. We can find a sliver of car paint, and track it to the year and model of a particular vehicle; we can use computers to see how many such vehicles exist in the Las Vegas area; and then we can inspect the vehicles that meet our criteria, finding the exact match.

CSI rarely worries about legalities—no one waits for a warrant, hardly any suspect asks for a lawyer before confessing all, and the CSIs themselves know which case they're working on and who might be guilty. In real life, crime scene investigators work on cases by number. They're asked a question—find a match for this fingerprint; see if this DNA sample matches that DNA sample—and they do so. They rarely, if ever, find out whether their work results in an arrest. Most often they learn years later, when they're required to testify in a trial.

CSI doesn't worry about the victims either. The victims are usually bodies on the autopsy table, whose flesh hides secrets just like the crime scene does. In fact, in *CSI*, the body is the secondary crime scene, often as cool as or cooler than the first.

Remove the science from *CSI* and the show simply does not exist. Unlike most other aspects of the show that are unrealistic (such as CSIs interviewing subjects, or the way the crime lab only handles a few cases at once), the science is spot-on, original, and fascinating.

It's no wonder that many of the *CSI* writers/producers once worked on *Star Trek*, another show that extrapolates from science. The programs have more in common than you might think.

The focus on science—fantastic science—in *Star Trek* led to cell phones that look like Captain Kirk's communicator. It also led to the first real doctor in space and inspired scientists the world over. *Star Trek*, as the show *How William Shatner Saved the World* amply demonstrated, became an inspiration for countless wannabe scientists, all of whom believed that if someone could imagine a transporter, someone else could invent one.

The focus on science in *CSI*—real, existing science—has inspired many teenagers to major in science in college. The attendance in forensic analysis classes at two-year colleges is up. Computer geeks and socially inept physicists aren't the media's only scientific representatives anymore. Now scientists can look like Jorja Fox or Marg Helgenberger.

In other words, you can be a scientist and be cool.

But not everyone who watches the show wants to catch criminals. Some people want to commit crimes. One of the major charges against *CSI*, its sister shows, and the non-fiction shows it spun off from is that they teach the average criminal how to avoid the law by destroying evidence. Thanks to these shows, the charge goes, everyone knows that DNA can be pulled from an intact hair follicle as well as sperm, and that a good dousing with bleach can destroy blood evidence.

The charge, actually made in "I Like to Watch," states that we're creating a subculture of criminal science geeks—people who commit crimes, snap their fingers, and say to themselves, "Aha! Grissom can solve this if I leave my newly purchased claw hammer beside the victim's caved skull."

Is the charge realistic? Is it true?

And is it something we, as connoisseurs of the mystery story in all its varied forms, need to worry about?

A Little History

In 1883, Mark Twain wrote what is arguably one of the first science fiction stories. In "A Thumb-print and What Came of It," Twain uses the brand-new science of fingerprinting to solve a crime. At the time Twain wrote the story, no police department had ever used fingerprinting. One of the proponents of the fingerprint method, Henry Faulds, wrote to various police departments to get them to adopt this method, and none of them had. In frustration, Faulds wrote an article for *Nature* describing fingerprinting. The article, which appeared in 1880, is thought to be the basis of Twain's story.

The mystery story came into its own in the nineteenth century. Edgar Allen Poe wrote his classic *Murders in the Rue Morgue*, introducing one of the first detectives into fiction. Arthur Conan Doyle did Poe one better and invented the most famous detective, Sherlock Holmes, shortly thereafter.

If the CSI stories resemble any classic mystery tales, it is the Sherlock Holmes stories. Holmes looks at tiny bits of evidence no one else can see, puts those pieces together, and comes up with a solution to the crime that seems obvious to him, but impenetrable to everyone else, including the narrator, Dr. Watson.

In CSI, we are Watson. Gil Grissom, Horatio Caine, and Mac Taylor are Holmes. They have sidekicks, who help with the work and sometimes put the cases together, but usually it is the team leader who assembles the final piece.

Arthur Conan Doyle was also the first to discover the problem with the investigative novel. Eventually, the story would get tiresome. Brilliant Holmes could walk into any crime scene and solve it. (So can brilliant Grissom.)

What, I'm sure Doyle asked himself, would make it hard for Holmes to solve his case?

The answer, in hindsight, is simple: Holmes needs to meet his match, and his match must be villainous. This criminal must be as brilliant as Holmes, in the same way as Holmes, able to thwart him at every turn. In the Holmes stories, it's Moriarity. In the early *CSI* episodes, it's the Blue Paint Killer.

Moriarity and the Blue Paint Killer share a trait in common: they are examples of the criminal mastermind.

Criminal Masterminds

The criminal mastermind is now a trope in American fiction. According to the fictional stories we tell each other, there are average crimes of passion, and then there are the bigger crimes, the harder crimes, the spectacular crimes. These amazing crimes are committed by the Moriaritys and the Blue Paint Killers of the world—and unless we have a Holmes or a Grissom, these crimes will forever be unavenged.

We Americans believe in the criminal mastermind. We have accepted this trope as truth so deeply that on September 11, 2001, our entire government (and much of the population) reacted as if a criminal mastermind were at work. We fully expected Osama Bin Laden's people (in the form of Al Qaeda) to attack *every* major city in the United States.

We grounded airplanes for days, and searched the passenger lists for suspicious people. We monitored the flow of traffic into every major city, and even stopped some cars from entering. We evacuated every single federal building, most state government buildings, and some local buildings. We shut down all roads going into our nuclear reactors and major oil and gas facilities.

We assumed Bin Laden's attack would escalate—because that's what our fiction has conditioned us to believe. Two of the most famous buildings in New York had fallen. Four planes were down. The Pentagon was burning. Thousands of people had died.

Of *course* we believed that Bin Laden would continue his attack. As a criminal mastermind, he would have to press his advantage—and the best way to do that would be immediately.

Fortunately for us, Osama Bin Laden is not Moriarity. He's not a criminal mastermind. He's a rich, well-educated, crazy, and charismatic criminal who spends most of his time in caves. In 2001, he had only a handful of followers, most of whom were incompetent young men who did not have the capacity to continue to attack the United States.

Is Bin Laden a threat? Yes, a continual one. But he's a threat the way that most criminals are. He will continue to commit his crimes until someone removes him from the streets.

He is not the intellectual equal of our great detectives or our great villains.

I mention this because Bin Laden is the closest thing we've had to a criminal mastermind in my lifetime. Most criminals are dumb, unlucky, hapless people. They turn to crime because they can't do anything else—because their imagination is limited or their education is limited, their circumstances are difficult or their options have narrowed (in their minds) to something illegal.

Studies have shown that the average IQ among inmates in America's prisons is less than 100 (100 being average). Granted, these are the folks who got caught. But, according to *Science News* (4/15/05), "available data...suggests that offenders who get away with their crimes fare no better on intelligence tests than those who get nabbed and convicted."

There are intelligent criminals—quite a few, as a matter of fact. But they tend to commit white-collar crimes: embezzlement, art theft, and money laundering. These people already take getting caught into account, so they commit either "victimless crimes" (crimes that theoretically harm no one except an insurance company [which, in the criminal's mind, isn't the same as a person]) or crimes that are, by their very nature, difficult to trace.

Most intelligent people do not *deliberately* commit low-level crimes, like robbing a liquor store or staging a home invasion, because they know they'll get caught. Intelligent people who do commit such crimes often lack education, are addicted to drugs, or have psychological problems.

The most common psychological problem among criminals is sociopathology. The criminal knows the difference between right and wrong, and *doesn't care*. Most sociopaths are charming and warm; they often work as con artists (also a job for the intelligent) and they just as often taunt the police. These criminals do kill, but usually as a part of a group (the mob, for example) or because they live in a culture that condones killing (some drug organizations).

Psychopaths are the ones that we worry about most. No one is real to the psychopath except himself. He is missing something—something has misfired in his brain. He enjoys inflicting pain, and he enjoys killing. He's often a violent criminal who commits a series of violent acts.

We know these people as serial rapists, serial murderers, serial child abusers. They don't care who they hurt, so long as they can enjoy the pain.

Here's the tough thing: All psychopaths are sociopaths on some level. They don't care about the law. But all sociopaths are not psychopaths. Most sociopaths are into beating the system, not into the violent (and often addictive/obsessive) act that entrances the psychopath.

None of the above categories breeds the criminal mastermind. The criminal with the low IQ may know that he'll get caught if he does something, but generally he trusts luck. These are the folks, remember, who rob convenience stores without wearing masks and look right into the security cameras. The reason so many of these folks are in jail is obvious.

Intelligent criminals are harder to catch, particularly if they commit white-collar crimes. If the embezzler were smart, he'd set a limit, and once he achieved that limit, he'd quit. But most embezzlers stay on the job, buy boats or large houses they can't afford on their salaries, and seem surprised when some forensic accountant finally catches up with them.

Often, white-collar crime comes from a compulsion, and in the grips of that compulsion the criminal can't stop. If the criminal stopped at a prudent time, he'd get away with it. And, in truth, a good percentage of embezzlers and other white-collar criminals do not get caught because no one knows that a crime has been committed. Sometimes the crime gets discovered years later, and sometimes it never gets discovered.

The folks who get away with embezzlement or other white-collar crimes aren't criminal masterminds either. They don't work at a high enough intellectual level to put them on the same level as Holmes or his modern CSI counterparts. These criminals are just cautious workaday folk who take a little extra for themselves.

The sociopath, on the other hand, doesn't have the same fear of getting caught. He tries not to, but it's the crime that interests him, not the covering of it. Sociopaths generally need to move to continue their schemes, and that's what makes them hard to catch. The American justice system is designed on the local and state level. Cooperation on the national level is only now coming into being, thanks mostly to computer technology.

But all those things that *CSI* ignores—all those legalities like warrants and jurisdictions, the slow, slow movement (and understaffing) of the criminal justice system—work to a sociopath's advantage. He can run his schemes from city to city, and state to state, and not get caught, no matter how many fingerprints he leaves on the scene, so long as he continues to move from place to place.

The psychopaths are the dangerous ones. Psychopaths never worry about being caught. They commit violent acts because that's who they are, not because they're playing some sort of game. They never even consider right or wrong. They don't ignore it; for them it does not exist.

And generally, they're dumb too. It's rare to have a smart serial killer. There are some who are smart like Ted Bundy and the BTK Killer. I suspect the Zodiac (who never got caught) was probably brilliant. And that's when we start having problems.

Even before *CSI* came on the air, the brilliant psychopath knew how to beat the system. The psychopath learns how to do this in order to continue practicing his sport, not because he's trying to outsmart someone. He knows if he gets caught, he can't kill anymore, so he avoids getting caught.

Some learn how to beat the system while in prison—prisoners are a wealth of dos and don'ts because they all went through trials. They were all convicted by their mistakes, and they talk about those mistakes.

Several psychopaths learn from the newspaper coverage of the crimes they've already committed. They discover that they left too much at the scene of their first crime. They learn how to capture their victims better, how to hide their trails, how to disappear into a crowd, by the things that the police release to the media about each crime.

A handful of really bright psychopaths study the same texts that the police study. It's estimated that a small percentage of people who take criminal justice courses are criminals learning the procedures. The textbooks are easy to get, and were even before the advent of the Internet.

High-end criminals subscribe to law enforcement magazines like *Forensic Journal*. They find kindred souls in the pages of *Soldier of Fortune* magazine, and they often hang out in spy shops, learning about the latest technology. The information is out there, and if you are a brilliant, dedicated criminal, you can learn everything that the *CSI* writers know, and probably as much as, or more than, some small town police departments know.

All the television shows do is make the information more accessible.

But will the criminals use it?

As I showed you, some already do in planning for a crime. But most aren't mentally capable of it. And the nature of crime itself makes covering one up exceedingly difficult.

Getting Away with Murder

All three CSIs focus primarily on the crime of murder. For some reason, we viewers find murder more interesting than embezzlement or carjackings. Murder even trumps kidnapping, which isn't logical from a storytelling point of view, since a kidnapping has a live victim who needs rescuing as opposed to a dead victim who doesn't even ask to be avenged.

Yet most of our mystery novels, and almost all of our mystery television programs, deal exclusively with murder, in all its variations.

In the real world, murder is a mundane crime. An estranged husband shoots his wife; a disgruntled postal employee shoots her boss; some young kid grabs his parents' gun from under the bed and shoots his little brother. Most murder cases are open and shut, often within twenty-four hours.

When you move away from rural and small-town America, murder becomes harder to solve. Murders occur in the middle of another felony, a mugging perhaps, or during a drug buy. And then the police must rely on informants and eyewitnesses, on investigations of the kind we see on *Law and Order*.

Usually those cases are closed within forty-eight hours.

It's the stranger-on-stranger killings that don't occur in the middle of a robbery or an obvious crime that are the hardest to solve. That's why folks like the Green River Killer can operate in the same vicinity for decades. The Green River Killer wasn't really smart, but he picked victims no one noticed when they were alive, so no one noticed when they disappeared. The bodies, which were dumped, weren't discovered for weeks. By then, most of the trace evidence was gone, the cause of death was often hard to determine, and the original crime scene had long ago been compromised.

The Green River Killer didn't learn this from *CSI* or from *Quincy* or whatever television show was on when he started. He didn't learn it from the Discovery Channel or even from *Forensic Journal*. His style of killing fit his pathology. He picked up prostitutes, took them to his lair to kill them, and then dumped them all over the Pacific Northwest. The only reason that detectives figured out what he was doing was because he didn't bury the bodies.

If he had buried them, he might still be killing to this day.

Police already know that the career criminals—the intelligent career criminals, be they sociopath or psychopath—learn from their mistakes. The police also know that these criminals learn from each other and some actually research police methods to avoid getting caught.

Most killers, however, are not of the serial variety. Most are the garden variety murderer, the person who kills someone else in the heat of the moment.

This killer strangles or stabs or shoots his victim, usually without a plan. Often the killing catches the killer by surprise.

Let's assume that our killer is a *CSI* fan. What does he do? First, he panics. After all, this is a person who is emotional enough to kill. He tries to imagine what Grissom or Stokes or Warrick would see if they came to the crime scene.

Generally, our killer will try to clean up. He'll be as sensible as possible. But he realizes—unless he's far away from civilization and the threat of being caught—that he has a time limit. The wife will come home, the co-workers will return from lunch, the neighbors will see suspicious activity.

So our killer will try to clean up quickly. Yes, he might use techniques he's learned from *CSI*. He might clean the blood with bleach (if there's bleach at the crime scene—because he'll know better than to go off and buy bleach at this moment). He'll contemplate moving the body, but he'll know he shouldn't use his own car, so he won't be able to move the body unless there is another vehicle available (although some killers have been known to use full-size trunks, like steamer trunks, which also aren't that common anymore).

Most likely, he'll try to remove all traces of his presence from the crime scene—fingerprints, footprints, possessions (unless he lives or works at the scene)—and then he'll go clean up. The really smart *CSI*-viewer-turned-criminal will clean up at his gym or in a hotel or at a gas station, where the blood evidence won't get caught in the shower trap. He'll dispose of the clothes he wore that day, including his shoes—and maybe even his glasses—in an untraceable way. He might give them to charity (using a St. Vincent's or Goodwill drop site in some parking lot somewhere) or he might toss them away in another town. He might bury them.

He also has to get rid of the murder weapon. He has to throw away the gun, or dispose of the knife. But, if he's a true *CSI* viewer, he'll know that he could be screwed if he strangled the victim with his bare hands because his grip could be measured, and his finger marks could be left in the victim's skin. (He'd be smart enough to clean off his victim's skin to get rid of DNA and fingerprints embedded in the oily flesh.)

The problem here is that the crime has already happened. And it happened in a particular way. The killer is playing catch-up. No matter how extensive his knowledge, he will miss something—or he won't have time to finish—or he won't be able to fix the problem (like the span of his grip in the bruises on the strangulation victim's neck).

I used to work for a forensic psychologist. I read countless police reports, typed up hundreds of interviews with criminals including murderers, and studied hundreds of psychological profiles. What became clear from all of this data is that murders are messy. *Crimes* are messy. They never go as planned. And they are rarely planned.

Think of it this way: You are reading this essay in some location. For the sake of argument, I'm going to assume you're reading it in your favorite restaurant while you gobble lunch before heading back to the office.

Try this exercise: Write down everything you touched from the moment you decided it was time for lunch to this moment. Be as accurate as possible. If you touched the top of the door handle coming into the restaurant, mark just that, not the entire handle.

Time yourself. See how long it takes to do this exercise. Write down each time you think "I'm pretty sure I . . ." instead of being positive.

Now try this exercise: Try remembering what you touched as you got ready for work this morning—or as you did some other routine task that you do every day. Add a few twists: Recall who you spoke to (even to nod hello) and write down their full names. Try to locate all the cameras in the neighborhood—not just the phone cameras or the security cameras, but the cameras on the nearby ATMs or the traffic cameras that hang near the stoplights or on highways to catch speeders.

Now account for all of this. See how you can eliminate—or explain—all of these traces of what you did to a detective who believes you committed a murder.

See how hard it is? And you're just sitting somewhere with a book in your hand. Imagine how tough it is when you're standing over the body of your best friend, your clothes covered with blood, and you have fifteen minutes until his wife gets home.

Criminals—even smart ones—make mistakes. Which is why so many of them get caught within forty-eight hours. Sometimes they don't get convicted, but they do get found.

Convictions are another matter, one with which *CSI* has only just started dealing. That wonderful episode, "The Unusual Suspect" (6-18), showed how the same evidence can point dozens of ways.

Crime scene techs are very good if they know where the original scene is. But they miss details, just like criminals do. And the average crime scene tech is as pressed for time as a killer is.

In the state of Oregon, where I live, it takes our state crime lab an average of four months to get something tested. As of March 1, 2006 (according to the *Oregonian*), the lab had a backlog of evidence in more than 600 cases that went back to May of 2005.

The backlog will only get bigger. The state, in the middle of a budget crunch so severe that it closes schools, is also laying off people in the criminal justice system, including crime scene techs and the scientists who examine the evidence.

Consider that, and the other things that I've alluded to above—the lack of time to thoroughly examine a scene; the competing jurisdictions; the fact that so much information, from fingerprints to arrest records, isn't available on a nationwide basis or requires a court order to examine—and the reason so many cases are not closed becomes clear. People either aren't caught (in stranger-to-stranger murder) or patterns go unseen (in serial cases) or obviously guilty defendants aren't convicted (in cases "solved" within twenty-four hours) because of understaffing, legal barriers, and impoverished localities—not because some criminal mastermind has studied the plots of *CSI*, *CSI: Miami*, *CSI: NY*, and all the forensic programs on TLC, Discovery, and A&E.

Shortly after *CSI* premiered, I went to a writers' conference in Denver. The Colorado State Crime Lab sent its information officer over to speak to us. In addition to showing us grisly photographs, describing cases, and showing off some equipment, the officer stated that he thought *CSI* hurt the conviction rates—not because criminals learned how to cover their tracks, but because juries now expected *all* labs to be equipped like the ones in the fictional Vegas, New York, and Miami.

Most labs can't even afford basic equipment, not to mention the high-tech stuff that so often shows up on those programs. Juries want to know why DNA wasn't tested in a routine murder, when the killer was caught holding the dripping knife over his victim. They want to know why the lab cut corners in the embezzlement case—not examining signatures, for example, or testing ink.

The Colorado information officer claimed—and I have seen no studies to back this up—that conviction rates were going down because our juries now expect crime scene techs to be as good as Grissom.

I think that may be an overstatement. But it has a lot more truth to it than the idea that a criminal, who has learned how to cover his tracks by watching *CSI*, will actually be successful in doing so.

Too many factors get in the way—and the largest, I believe, is that our criminal turned to crime in the first place. Study after study after study has shown that the criminal works outside society because something is wrong with him (be it economic or psychological)—not because he's trying to beat the system or because he's intrigued with crime.

Are there criminal masterminds out there? Maybe. But we won't know until we stop handicapping the Holmeses of the world by giving them inferior technology, small staffs, and underfunded labs.

The fact that we solve as many crimes as we do is, in my opinion, a miracle.

I suspect we'll solve more crimes in the future because of *CSI* and its counterparts, not in spite of them. With so many young people becoming interested in forensic science, criminology, or criminal justice in general, we're going to see a flood of interest in the high-tech part of the job in a few years.

The interest has even peaked for the laymen. In my state alone, people are asking why our crime lab isn't doing more. When they learn the answer is because of budget cuts, maybe they'll try to fund the labs the way they should be funded.

I see programs like *CSI* as a positive step. It gets lazy Americans interested in science again, and it shows us the possibilities. Maybe it'll even prevent a crime or two, as someone about to shoot his neighbor realizes he won't get away with it.

Maybe. Or maybe that's fiction as well.

The intriguing thing is...if *CSI* does prevent crime, we'll never know.

Kristine Kathryn Rusch is a bestselling novelist and an award-winning editor and writer, with two Hugos and a World Fantasy Award, as well as many other awards in science fiction, fantasy, romance, and mystery. Her most recent science fiction novel is *Buried Deep*. Her next is *Paloma*, which will appear in October. Under the name Kris Nelscott, she has just published the sixth book in her critically acclaimed Smokey Dalton series, *Days of Rage*. Her works have appeared in fourteen countries and thirteen languages.

CSI is very much a show of the twenty-first century. Here, Timothy M. Palmbach looks at how both techniques and the public's perception have evolved since the early days of detection—both on and off the TV screen.

TIMOTHY M. PALMBACH

CSI-Generation Juries
The Effect of TV on Juries
Predisposed to Scientific Evidence

FLASH BACK TO THE LATE 1950s, and picture yourself as a typical member of society sitting as a juror in a murder trial. Specifically, imagine being a juror on a case involving the hypothetical but unfortunately common scenario of a man with marital problems who is charged with the murder of his wife. You and the rest of the jury are made aware that the defendant had reported his wife missing, and that her body was never found. A circumstantial case unfolds, with presentation of crime scene analysis and physical evidence, and you must decide whether or not to send the defendant to jail for life based on that case, one based not on the testimonial evidence to which you are accustomed, but exclusively focused on expert testimony from an array of forensic scientists. You hear testimony that a small bone chip was identified as having originated from a cranial bone, and that the donor of such a chip would, with a reasonable degree of scientific certainty, be deceased. And, of course, a DNA analyst testifies that there was a statistically generated random match probability, suggesting that the defendant's wife was the donor of that skull bone. Oh, and by the way, the bone chip was found in the back of the defendant's pickup truck with the aid of a crime scene alternate light source.

While a *CSI*-generation jury would have no difficulty rendering a decision based on that type of evidence, it is likely that our 1950s counterparts would be confused, frustrated, and in search of some human being to stand before them and tell the whole, true story. The necessary requirements for a conviction are (and always have been) dependent on a jury's expectations, and those expectations have changed substantially during the last few decades. While the process has evolved, the end goal—learning the truth and delivering justice—has remained a constant.

"Who are you, who are you, who, who...I really got to know?" The Who and the producers of *CSI* are asking what essentially is *the* question in most criminal investigations. While it is an obvious end-game goal, does it matter how we arrive at the final answer? This question has been asked by investigators for decades, yet one can hardly claim that *Dragnet's* Joe Friday's approach to solving the caper from the 1960s mirrors our *CSI's* Grissom's method in contemporary times. But so what if Friday's and Grissom's methods differ?

On television and in books and movies, where it is as simple as solving a case with a solution predetermined by the author, the change in method doesn't matter. In reality, where the expectations, perceptions, and opinions of the jury interact with a complicated legal system and highly technical scientific procedures, "Who are you?" is not so easily answered. Thus, the dramatic changes in how we get a conviction today versus fifty years ago have more to do with the process, or what we expect in the way of proof. Many factors underlie these differences, but this discussion will address two key issues: the integration of new technologies in the war on crime, and public perceptions, expectations, and bias in response to a shift away from more traditional investigative techniques to those based in science and technology.

Let's walk through history and view the media's fairly accurate presentation of the changes effected by new technology and shifting public expectations. If we examine some notorious early cases, such as the trial of Sacco and Vanzetti in the 1920s, we find a trial stage set very differently than what we have become accustomed to in today's *CSI* world. It would be unfair to claim that the system summarily dismissed the value of physical evidence in those days. There was extensive testimony regarding firearms evidence associated with this case, however conflicting it may have been. Yet what was most noticeably missing was a big-picture view of all the evidence and crime scene observations. This process, commonly referred to as crime scene reconstruction, is a hallmark of today's trials and the television shows that represent them. In contrast, the Sacco and Vanzetti trial was heavily influenced by the political climate at the time and claims from countless witnesses, many of which contained more opinion than fact.

Looking at *Dragnet*, the *CSI* of the '60s, we see not a lot had changed in the intervening forty years. *Dragnet* worked not only as an entertainment medium enjoyed by that generation, but as a relatively accurate representation of the 1960s courtroom experience. "This is the city, Los Angeles. My name is Friday. I am a cop." What followed was a series of well-structured, deductive questions, designed to extract relevant facts from a variety of witnesses. Ultimately, answers led to predetermined follow-ups, which further focused a linear progression to solving the caper. So in any given concluding segment, to no one's surprise, viewers would be presented with the name of the only plausible suspect, and Joe Friday would disappear into the hazy city of Los Angeles until the next episode. If evidence (such as a fingerprint or footprint) was introduced, it often played a secondary role to the carefully orchestrated plot developed through the good, old-fashioned linear process of police work.

During this period and up until the 1980s, the public held tight to a basic understanding that the work of our courts was to evaluate a simple string of intriguing witnesses, which provided all the information necessary to reach a verdict. The media of that era supported and influenced this perception. If the essential facts could not be extracted by the sharp intuition of the likes of Joe Friday, then certainly the brilliance and flamboyance of an attorney like Perry Mason would get the job done. *Perry Mason*'s 1957 pilot episode, "The Case of the Restless Redhead," established a format that highly engaged the viewing audience, making it one of the longest running shows of all time. Mason waited until the waning moments of the trial to save his redheaded client from a homicide charge, using persuasive, passionate, and yet linear logic, and as a result the jury freed the innocent, and provided a means for truth and justice to prevail.

To some extent, life was much simpler under these standards. The incoming technology craze and rapid advances in forensic science over the next decades, while undoubtedly increasing our effectiveness in correctly solving more crimes, also changed our methods and introduced complications for investigators and jurors alike.

This major transition in forensic science began in the 1980s, increasing exponentially until it reached the point at which we are today. The transition was a move away from a format that emphasized confessions, eyewitness testimony, and good, old-fashioned police work, to a system that increasingly sought corroboration of information gathered through existing investigative methods, in addition to the new methods availed through forensic science. As more and more technologies were developed, validated, and implemented in solving crimes, even greater emphasis was placed on the analysis of physical evidence. Thus, the scientific process heavily impacted existing linear methods.

Today it is commonplace for juries to absorb days of testimony from a diverse variety of expert witnesses offering objective interpretations of evidence yielded by highly complex method and instrumentation. Before lunch, a juror could learn about DNA and the complex statistical analysis necessary to define the value of a random match, as well as how a defendant could be identified 2,000 miles away from the scene of a crime through a national DNA database (CODIS). Not only is this the likely script of a modern-day trial, but it is exactly what the jurors hope to hear. After all, we have become at the least crime scene enthusiasts, and often self-proclaimed experts. These perceptions and expectations have roots in both education and the influence of media. Forensic science as a discipline has been integrated into many venues. It is even being offered in America's high schools as a respected science elective. Concurrently, the tremendous success of countless works of fiction and primetime television shows have blown wide open the world of forensic science to the general public.

In decades past, Joe Friday directed witness-based "factual" cases to conclusion. In contrast, the 1990s' Grissom and gang knit together a poignant crime scene analysis based upon a multitude of scientifically based facts. And despite making some less than accurate Hollywood modifications, today's *CSI* investigators and their white-coat colleagues generally follow the process employed by most of today's criminal justice workers. Assuming this is true, if we study what we learn from an episode of *CSI*, it may give us better insight into the mind of the average juror deciding the fate of today's criminal defendants.

In the *CSI* episode "Invisible Evidence" (4-4), many of these modern perspectives are highlighted as the team incorporates both the use of forensic science and crime scene analysis to crack a case. The episode opened with CSI Brown testifying at a preliminary hearing in a rape/homicide case. Brown was presented with a bloody knife and explained to the court how testing of reddish stains on the knife and white towel in which it was wrapped established that the blood was consistent with the rape/homicide victim, Rachael.[1] Further, the knife and towel had been found in the suspect's car, and the suspect resided in the same apartment complex as the victim. But, oops, someone forgot to get a warrant to search the suspect's car. Therefore the judge ruled the knife and towel inadmissible, or as Grissom described them, "invisible evidence." In response (and somewhat in a state of desperation), all of the CSI team went on the offensive to uncover additional information which would prevent the judge from releasing the suspect. More pieces of the puzzle were collected, analyzed, and assembled. The defendant's fingerprint was found on a beer bottle in the victim's trash, and a foreign substance was discovered on both the "invisible" white towel and the victim's wrist. The substance was analyzed and found to be a high-end car wax used for commercial applications, which led investigators to a car wash, to broken tail light pieces found in the car wash, and ultimately to a DNA sample obtained from one of the car wash employees that was consistent with DNA obtained from the victim. Physical evidence won the case in every sense. Legal rulings related to the inadmissibility of the evidence forced this investigation to the next level. As additional items of evidence were recognized and analyzed, they provided a story. This story exonerated the innocent and identified the guilty.

Surprisingly, this sounds like nothing more than a high-tech version

---

[1] A little side note here: Brown stated that the match occurred through a CODIS (Combined DNA Index System) hit.... The ability to place the known profile of a homicide victim in a DNA database within days of her murder may indeed be of some dramatic value to solving the case in an hour; however, in reality backlogs and resource limitations would make that essentially impossible.

of Perry Mason. The methods are different, but the narrative form has remained the same. While *CSI* has done an excellent job of reflecting the scientific changes in modern justice work, it has failed to take into account the resulting differences in the courtroom.

CSI appeals to its millions of faithful viewers much the way any successful weekly television drama does: it uses a certain predictable schematic that the viewers learn to love. The case is solved by attractive people in slightly under an hour. With *CSI*, the plan goes somewhat as follows: Utilizing a variety of portable new technologies (alternate light sources, X-ray machines, chemical enhancement reagents, etc.), the high-fashion crime scene investigators search the scene for any potential physical or pattern evidence. Once a potential source of evidence is recognized as just that, crime scene processing begins. Next, documentation, including photography, videotaping, and sketch preparation, commences. To their credit, *CSI* personnel generally take necessary steps to collect and preserve the evidence, though this is not exactly a primetime sexy event.

Once basics have been addressed and evidence is transported to the dark, blue-hued domain of the CSI Forensic Laboratory, the real high-tech work begins.[2] Much to the envy of most, if not all, government-funded forensic science laboratories, the *CSI* team has access to the most modern, high-tech, and expensive equipment. Thus, their laboratory procedures are generally above reproach, and indeed inform us well as to just how far forensic science has come over the past decade.

Of course, the speed at which they obtain their results, the manner in which the results are reported, and the almost 100% success rate could use a reality check. For example, early versions of DNA analysis, known as Restriction Fragment Length Polymorphism (RFLP), required weeks to complete. Newer PCR-based methods can be accomplished in a couple of days. Yet, until emerging technologies such as microchip DNA analysis are implemented, the thirty second turnaround time depicted routinely on the CSI shows is only wishful thinking. Further, a majority of scientific procedures used by forensic scientists result in some form of data that may initially be uploaded for computer-based inquiries, but

---

[2] Another side note: How is it that they can see microscopic pieces of relevant trace evidence with lighting dimmed beyond the point where most of us could adequately tie our shoes?

will ultimately require careful evaluation by a competent examiner before any final conclusions are made. And they never make a mistake or obtain the all-too-often "inconclusive" finding. For entertainment sake, though, it's appealing and it works.

Suffice it to say, our current culture is teaching us much about crime scene investigation and forensic science. Some of that information is accurate and helpful to our understanding of our current criminal justice system, but other information is not. *CSI* has made us high-tech, instant gratification junkies. The influence of misleadingly simplistic representations of reality makes it a great challenge to evaluate a case as a member of a jury.

To begin with, what if, despite the best practices and expertise, a case concludes with little or no pertinent information garnered from the crime scene investigators or laboratory personnel? For example, let us consider a sexual assault case in which proper evidentiary samples were obtained correctly from the victim and forwarded for analysis. Further, let us assume that no investigative information was developed as a result of the testing. Even the best forensic science laboratories in America are able to identify intact spermatozoa in only approximately 30% of the submitted cases. And without whole sperm cells, obtaining a DNA profile is all but impossible. A case like this is likely to go to the jury based on "he said/she said," if it even gets that far in the system. In addition, despite great advances in detecting and enhancing latent fingerprints at crime scenes, a majority of the fingerprints obtained from crime scene searches are not suitable for comparison. This can be attributed to many factors, including poor quality surfaces, movement associated with the print placement, scene contamination, poor development techniques, adverse weather, etc. Based on the perceived ease with which *CSI* actors can find identifiable fingerprints, it is possible that a juror may infer a substandard performance by a crime scene investigator who was unable to get a good print, a judgment which could incorrectly affect his or her decision as to the defendant's guilt or innocence.

Another area in which we are misled by what we learn on *CSI* and in the pages of best-selling crime novels is in the appropriate value or relevance one should give to a piece of evidence. To gain a better understanding as to how forensic science is used to get the most out of a piece of evidence, let us consider what of this information can ultimately connect a criminal to the scene and what cannot. To their credit, some recent episodes of *CSI* have dealt directly with this reality. CSI Brown learned firsthand how his hard and scientifically reliable work could be excluded from the jury based on a judicial ruling for some tangential legal challenge.

A major point of contention between those who are practitioners in the field and those who portray those practitioners' work on primetime television relates to the manner in which the shows conclude their plots. Typically, after pieces of evidence and investigative facts have been critically analyzed, they are then strung together in a linear fashion leading to a concise summation. In the field of forensic science, this most closely resembles what is known as crime scene reconstruction. Crime scene reconstruction, done properly, is a scientific process completed in conformity with the "scientific method." Essentially, all sources of information—investigative, crime scene documentation, analysis of physical and pattern evidence, medical or autopsy data, etc.—are collected and evaluated, leading to the development of one or more sound hypotheses. This is followed by relevant and reliable testing.

The manner in which Grissom approaches his final few minutes of summation is indeed compelling, but often not conducted within the strict confines of a scientific method. These dramatic representations create a conclusion that assumes that the characters have arrived at the one and only one true theory. Properly conducted crime scene reconstructions often conclude with several potential theories. Of course, some of these theories may be more probable than others. For example, what if a trial involving the rape and beating death of a woman is based on facts that the defendant's fingerprints were at the crime scene, a vaginal swab obtained at autopsy developed a DNA profile consistent with the suspect's, a bite mark on her breast was consistent with his dentition, and contact bloodstains on his shirt were found to be consistent with the victim's blood? However, the suspect is her husband, who admits to engaging in consensual and spirited sexual intercourse the evening prior to her death, and claims that he lifted her beaten body from the stairwell and placed her on the hall floor so he could attempt CPR. The data supports two entirely different conclusions, including one which will likely acquit him. Yet, if he were a stranger to the home, the other would, in most cases, guarantee a guilty verdict.

Recall the *CSI* episode previously discussed. A bloody knife and towel found in the suspect's car was originally the building block upon which this suspect was charged with the crime, because there was a presumed connection between the suspect and the knife and towel in his car. But the knife and towel's presence in the suspect's car was later correctly interpreted in a manner that helped establish his innocence. The challenge for crime scene personnel and their colleagues is to objectively evaluate all of the data and consider any and all theories that may result from the reconstruction process.

Our extensive media coverage of high-profile real crimes often illustrates the complications of linking evidence to reliable conclusions. Recall the Scott Peterson murder trial, constructed mainly around a circumstantial case. One of the few pieces of physical evidence, a hair located on a tool found in Scott Peterson's fishing boat, was the subject of many legal arguments and much controversy. The prosecution wanted the jury to believe that this was a direct link between the victim, Laci, and an instrument under Scott's control that was used to help discard Laci's body. Yet, to determine whether that summation could be true, the underlying factors must first be evaluated. Although the hair was determined to be consistent with Laci Peterson's hair using technologies such as mitochondrial DNA analysis, statistical interpretation is still necessary to establish the likelihood that Laci was indeed the donor. More importantly, how exactly did the hair get there? Was it a direct or secondary transfer? So, in the final analysis, what significance does the hair evidence play in this case? In reality, the scientific process does not emulate a linear chain guaranteeing a concise conclusion.

Given the difference between the manner in which the CSI shows conduct their summation and the manner in which we expect our jurors to evaluate all of this evidence during deliberations, we need to further educate and clarify this process. Jurors cannot rely on the misguided perception that all the evidence presented will neatly and succinctly come to a single conclusion. Take, for instance, the mathematical product rule, which allows one to determine a probability given several independent factors. For example, what is the probability that the next person who walks past you will be a white male, with blue eyes and blond hair, carrying a brown attaché? If statistical data shows that there is a 50% chance of being male, a 20% chance of having blue eyes, a 35%

chance of being blonde, and a 5% chance of carrying a brown attaché, then the probability of this individual walking past you is .00175, or less than one in a thousand. But whether you're in a western U.S. ranching town or on Wall Street will alter the validity of that calculation. Quickly we see the problem with trying to utilize even a seemingly straightforward, established statistics principle to solve an investigative matter.

Jurors engaging in the scientific process must consider all potential variables and their relationships to one another. In many cases, this can become arduous and complex. There is a scientifically valid principle to simplify this process: Ockham's Razor. This principle (*pluralitas non est ponenda sine necessitate*, which means "entities should not be multiplied unnecessarily") was devised by fourteenth-century philosopher William of Ockham, and is generally interpreted to mean one should keep things as uncomplicated as possible, or in more colloquial language, "Keep it simple, stupid." Under this principle, specific concepts, variables, and factors that are not necessary to explain the observation or theory would be disregarded. Thus, Ockham's Razor becomes a very valuable tool in choosing among a set of possible competing theories. Undoubtedly a majority of us embrace this concept, if for no other reason than simplicity. And, as proven over time, through thousands of applications, it will likely lead one to an excellent, if not the correct, theory.

All jurors are the product of what they learn about the criminal justice system, through both independent education and the influence of media, authors, and producers. We have experienced a transition from a model strongly influenced by eyewitness testimony, interviews, and interrogations, and general investigative methods, to one which is highly dependent on sophisticated analysis of the crime scene and physical evidence. Perhaps as our culture is more influenced by a true understanding of the role of science and technology in solving crimes, we will be empowered to build upon what is good, and seek further avenues that lead us closer to a perfect system of truth and justice.

In 2004, **Timothy M. Palmbach** joined the faculty of the University of New Haven as associate professor and director of the Forensic Science Program. Prior to his tenure as director, Mr. Palmbach was a major in the Connecticut State Police where he was the commanding officer/director of the Division of Scientific Services for the Department of Public Safety.

While with the Connecticut State Police, Major Palmbach worked on assorted criminal investigations and processed over 300 crime scenes. He is co-author of *Henry Lee's Crime Scene Handbook*, published by Academic Press. He has also written numerous articles for a variety of forensic science disciplines and crime scene analysis, and lectured on the same.

One of the hallmarks of the CSI shows is strong female characters. But do they accurately represent the concerns and experiences of real female crime scene investigators? This essayist knows firsthand.

SHARON L. PLOTKIN

Many Faces

T IS VERY EARLY IN the morning and once again, I have seen a beautiful sunrise with a man who is not my husband. And as if this man is not enough, I share myself with several. Men who have seen me look my worst, in the filthiest conditions and in the most precarious situations. I attempt to maintain my femininity while drowning in testosterone. It's like putting lipstick on a hog. I am knee-deep in human filth, blood, and carnage and I am thinking of my hair, but distractions like these are only little snippets in the scheme of my life. Time and life's little surprises always put me back on track.

Twenty-one years ago, fresh out of high school and still under the rule of my parents, I chose education to be my pathway. I was young, vivacious, and knew that knowledge was power and with the support of my father achieved a graduate degree in criminal justice. Sixteen years ago, I put the road to my doctoral education on hold, deviated from my path, chose the road to motherhood, and began a family. My husband

and I did what every young couple does: build dreams and houses. A yard for the kids to play in and a place for us to grow old in meant everything. Eleven years ago, I put my family on hold and found a career—Crime Scene Investigations—definitely a hard way to earn a living. I struggled with my independence and grew apart from my husband. He was walking, while I was running. I sacrificed my marriage for a passion I knew I was born with: to seek clarity inside of chaos, answers where there are only questions; to choose compassion over hatred and look for truth despite lies. Reflecting back on my life after having done this for so long, I've come to understand that nothing comes easy. Every day, I wonder which mask I will wear today, which facet of my life will control the others: woman, mother, crime scene investigator, lover.

As I sift through brain matter, hoping to find the casing that will tell me the case is a suicide and not a homicide, I am absorbed. I find myself becoming one with my environment. I am a chameleon. I am determined, I am driven, I am not afraid. If the answers are here, I will find them. I will not allow fear, hesitancy, or gender to get in my way. The true struggle, however, is beneath it all. I am a woman amongst men. I am considered the weaker of the species. Haven't I proven myself a thousand times to those who watch my actions from inside air-conditioned cars? Didn't I perform difficult tasks solely on the notion that if a man could do it, so could I? Haven't I sacrificed so much to overcome the bias, being told, "How could someone as pretty as you do a job like that?" Isn't it true that having put a suit on for court makes me less credible than if I had worn my uniform? And as if my battle with my gender isn't enough, I fight another war within myself: being a mother.

As my cell phone rings, I rip off a latex glove at warp speed and struggle with the numerous items packed into my cargo pants, as if I were planning to hibernate for the winter, to grab the device before *The Pink Panther* theme ends. I know without looking that it is one of my daughters, wanting me to save them from their own private wars. The irony of it all is that I am currently standing amidst the end of someone else's war.

While I scrounge for the phone, I carefully step around the body, making a note to measure the firearm, perform the gunshot residue test on the deceased and his wife, remember to get the mashed potatoes and the whipping cream, call the school and explain to the coach why my child is missing swim class, and try to recover the bullet, all while telling myself I can do this—be a crime scene investigator and a mother—without breaking a sweat and out of earshot of the detectives. In all my years, I don't recall a single time I overheard one of the male detectives arguing with the school over a C on their child's report card, or making arrangements to carpool with other soccer dads to the game. I put my daughter's fire out and, since I have the phone out already, figure now's a good time to call the coach. Done with that, I'm back down on my knees without missing a beat, moving brain matter around to find the casing. Somehow, I don't think that most men would be willing to sift through brain matter and think it was worth it, but I always push myself to stay ahead of the game. I think back, with mixed feelings, to all the things I have done, the situations in which I have placed myself, the fears and obstacles I have overcome, all to keep up with the opposite sex.

Crime scene investigations are a male-dominated arena, run in the past by police officers. When I began this career my unit was comprised of Sean, a male police officer (who had been in law enforcement fourteen years doing crime scene), and two female crime scene technicians (civilian capacity). I was never told that women could do the job as well as men, just cheaper. We technicians were not part of the "inner circle" and did not know what it meant to put our lives on the line. To them, we were bored housewives with strong stomachs. But we weren't. Instead of choosing the police academy, we chose education, books instead of guns. The closest we got to the inner circle was marrying law enforcement. Wasn't it perfectly clear that crime scene was our passion, not enforcing the law? Didn't we enter this profession with maturity and objectivity, not overzealousness and the need to pound our chests for attention? We respected the law enough to marry within it, but it wasn't what we wanted for ourselves.

How many times was I told by the other two female crime scene investigators of the struggles they had to overcome to pave the way for me and other women? They fought plenty of battles, but I fought plenty of my own.

Unfortunately, with the estrogen coming from all angles, it was just a matter of time before Sean left the nest, leaving the unit to the hens. We were called the chicken coop, Charlie's Angels, and other nicknames, too many to count. There was even a magazine picture of three women dressed in thongs (back view only) with one of our three names over each female, sitting on the desk of a supervisor. Despite all this, I was never offended. This was the world I chose, and I knew that I needed thick skin and camaraderie to mesh in this career. Of course there were sexual undertones involved in working with the opposite sex; they were as much my fault as theirs. But the male detectives and police officers were also very protective while watching over me on crime scenes. I always hope this protection is because I do not carry a firearm while on duty and not because of my gender. I know what the detectives are thinking some of the time, but isn't that human nature? I want to fit in, I need to fit in. I don't stand on ceremony. I can laugh at the dirtiest of jokes and let my eyes wander like everyone else's. When I am bending over on a crime scene, I don't look back. When I am crawling around on my hands and knees, isn't my mind, too, conjuring up the raunchiest of things? I can handle all that. What I cannot handle is when ego and arrogance get in the way of initiative and talent.

While I am slaving away on this scene, hoping to finish it before the next sunrise comes, the detectives are eating, standing around, talking. Are the women still responsible for the dirty work? Do we really have stronger stomachs and longer spans of attention? Sometimes I think we as women have become so competitive that the only thing that ever holds us back is ourselves; that we have become our own worst enemy in the face of the conditions under which we serve.

Now, sitting here writing this, I wonder if I sound like I am stuck in the '60s, declaring my feminist independence, wanting to burn my bra (except I was born in the '70s). I asked myself: Do other women in my field feel the same way I do? I called some of these women as a personal research endeavor. I called Nat, who was a crime scene investigator for approximately ten years with a police department whose agency did not handle the casework for major scenes, such as police contact shootings and death investigations. She was very happy in her agency and, like others I spoke to, was being paid the same as her male counterparts, in contrast to private industry, where women are still being paid seventy-five to eighty cents on the dollar as compared to men in the same positions. Nat was blessed with a male supervisor who had always supported her in achieving the success she craved. He created and developed the unit approximately ten years ago and she was his first hire; maybe her success measured in with his own and he had a vested interest.

However, it was not until I spoke with Anna that someone was able to articulate my frustrations in words even I could comprehend. Anna, young, beautiful, and full of vigor, was hired as a civilian crime scene investigator for a newly incorporated city in a very ritzy and newly developed part of town seven years ago. When she first started she was told by some of the male officers in the department that she would either be known as a bitch or a slut. Fortunately, over time, since she was very happily married, she gave off an "I don't screw around" impression, while still managing to be nice about it. She was also fortunate to be the original crime scene investigator for this agency, so past history and practice were not an issue. What was and still is today a big crack in what appears to be a solid foundation is a small dilemma overlooked by many: gender differences. Anna felt that the old-timers were still living in the cave man period. Maybe we should keep our hair short, we joked; it would keep the men from dragging us around by it. Most of the men she works with are stuck in the era of women staying at home, raising babies. I was even told by the male crime scene investigator I worked with when I first started that the problem with kids today is that when women went to work the family order was destroyed. I'd love to know his thoughts on the energy crisis. Anna, who works with a male counterpart (also civilian), felt that she was always being treated differently than he. If he was screwing up at work, it was because he was going through a messy divorce. If she was having a bad day, she was temperamental. Anna and he are not only responsible for the crime scene work, but also for the management of the property room, and she is being paid slightly more than her male counterpart because she is deemed more organized and considered capable of cleaning up better than he.

As Anna continued talking, I could feel her becoming more animated about the subject. Being in police work gave us an outlook on men that most don't have the privilege to share. Women are seen as conquests. Whenever the new girl arrives (whether as an officer or crime scene investigator), it is as if we are back in the jungle, kicking up dirt, grunting, and pounding chests. We women thrive on the attention. But when we don't accept the man's conquest, the dejected male moves on. In the meantime, we have a job to do, and have to take into account their feelings while doing it. Sometimes I feel more like a juggler than the ringmaster. On top of that, we are no longer treated as well as soon as a new conquest comes in.

All we women really want is to be given attention with respect, and occasional acknowledgment. How many times has a man grown to success with the assistance of a great woman? How many times have I attended awards ceremonies where the detectives got Officer of the Month for the arrest of a serial killer caught by the DNA swab I did on a victim's breast? Where was the lead detective when we women were down on our knees processing the neck of a dead prostitute, in a room where a black light illuminated the entire scene, in search of semen and the sheets stuck together? Wasn't it the evidence yielded from her neck that gave the detective the lead he needed to solve the case? When women present ideas to men, men can't acknowledge that the idea derived from a woman for fear of appearing weak, and will present the concept as their own, whereas amongst themselves men will not only share in the credit for the concept, but have no fear of verbalizing its origination. How long do we as women have to placate the male ego to establish our own success? Haven't we gotten past that?

The real world is one thing; the world of Hollywood is often another. Listening to Anna, I wondered if television drama reflected the notions she, as well as the other countless women I have spoken to in my eleven years in this profession, have expressed—specifically *CSI*, the one seventy million people watch at least twice a week. As I sat down this past weekend for a *CSI* marathon, I found myself frustrated after watching only four shows. In hopes of remaining unbiased I asked my fiancé to watch a couple of the episodes with me, so that I could gain his perspective. He did crime scene himself many years ago, as an officer, and he is now a police lieutenant at the same police agency where I work. Immediately, he saw flaws in the interaction of the players, not appreciating the way that Catherine Willows and Sara Sidle, as well as Warrick Brown, were portrayed. The women looked as if they had just come from photo shoots for magazine covers, while the men appeared dressed for work. The women appeared to not be given the opportunity to take leadership roles, and though they demonstrated profound technical abilities, the men assumed the responsibility for many of the critical decisions and seemed to come up with the innovative and creative ideas. In two episodes (out of eight we watched) the women also could not handle the sights and smells at autopsies.

In the pilot episode, Holly, the brand new, still-wet-behind-the-ears crime scene investigator, ran from the autopsy room to throw up. As if that wasn't enough, she then got frightened by being locked in the cooler with several dead bodies and began to panic. Thank goodness for Gil Grissom, who saved the day and comforted her. I had been a crime scene investigator for approximately two weeks when I got my first call of a decomposing body inside of a dilapidated and un-air-conditioned house. The Halloween pumpkin on her porch stoop still sat there uncarved, and not only had Halloween passed, but Thanksgiving was right around the corner. When I drove up to the scene and all of the detectives were standing outside, I knew things had to be a little hairy. Some of the detectives were even wearing putrefication masks to keep the smell from assaulting their nostrils. The scene promised to be every bit as disgusting as I'd thought it would be, but I refused to empty the contents of my stomach while they watched. You never knew if someone would catch the moment on film or you'd walk to your desk the next morning to find it covered with motion sickness bags and spittoons. Besides, I always said if that was going to happen, I'd throw up in my shirt before I'd let anyone catch me.

Moments of Catherine Willows's life did reflect the constant dilemma that many mothers feel, including myself: watching someone else raise our children and having someone else share in their achievements. But worse than that are the trials and tribulations my children suffer because of my job. How many times have I put my girls through the ringer? If I handled a child's drowning that day, I put my kids in swim classes. If there was a child abduction incident, they were given new scenarios to work through, terrifying them. Fire scenes were especially exciting in my house; we would spend the next few evenings going through the exit plan and who was responsible for what. Thank goodness my children are older now; I don't think they could have handled much more. Watching Catherine go home to her daughter after handling a child sexual abuse case was heartbreaking. I knew that when her eyes filled with tears, as she hugged her daughter and told her she couldn't wait to get home just to tell her she loved her, that I had been there many times myself. If only more of these moments were captured on these CSI programs; in the episodes I watched, they were few and far between. We wouldn't want to show women being both competent in their work and emotional in their private lives, would we? The actors on *CSI* are only defined by their roles at work. But the work I do is defined by who I am, what I bring to the table.

Maybe America does not want to see our evolution, how we come to be. The problem is, after all, not only with the show's women. Why aren't the male characters depicted as fathers, or cradling divorce issues, or dumpster-diving in search of keys their spouses threw in the trash? But we as women are forced to make choices men are not. The sacrifices we make for work mean listening to our children cry on the phone, wondering why we are not home. The sacrifices we make for our children mean being accused of not spending enough time on our work.

When I reflect back on the decisions I made that brought me here today, I carry a heavy load. The time I gave away will never be given back. My daughters are who they are, clearly defined, by how much time I gave them. They are proud of me and I have instilled a strong sense of work ethic in them. They know that nothing worthwhile is handed to them. The sacrifices I made, I made because of the love and passion I had for the job. I love what I do and feel that being a crime scene investigator is the most exciting career in the job market. When I wear the uniform I am given an overwhelming amount of attention and recognition from both eager youth and wise elderly. Not everyone is cut out to do this kind of work, and I overcame a lot of fears and hurdles to become the person I am today. But after eleven years of doing this work, I wonder how many of my co-workers would define me any other way than as a crime scene investigator.

When we choose to be mothers it is not a sign of weakness or even a lack of commitment on our part. Work should accentuate our lives, not take them over. I want to be allowed to be emotional, compassionate, sexual, wise, attractive, sympathetic, athletic, aggressive, successful—to be a crime scene investigator, and a mother. Surely that is not asking too much.

Sharon L. Plotkin, MS, is a native Floridian with a twin sister who works as a federal agent. She has been employed full time in law enforcement as a crime scene investigator for almost twelve years for one of the larger police departments in Dade County, and is an adjunct professor who teaches in her field at several local colleges. She is soon to be married to a lieutenant at the same police department, with whom she shares two daughters and three stepdaughters (five teenage daughters in all). Her interests are reading, music, teaching, and travel.

I've always shared Grissom's fascination with insects, and apparently so does Ms. Engstrom. As Grissom himself might say, this essay bugs me...but in a *good* way.

ELIZABETH ENGSTROM

The Majesty of Maggots

GIL GRISSOM ALWAYS SEES THE big picture.

While the local police officers in some backward Nevada town stand around scratching their heads and staring at the headless corpse, Gil gets squinty-eyed, looking around at everything but the obvious. Then he pulls out a pair of tweezers, moves in close, and tenderly picks up a maggot.

A maggot!

Yuck.

Who among us can erase the mental imprint of the first time we saw something undeniably dead that seemed to be alive, it was so covered (and filled) with heaving masses of squirming maggots?

While endlessly fascinating to little boys (one summer, my brother had to make a daily pilgrimage to the vacant lot to check on some maggots' progress with a dead possum; he even made me go with him once), little girls tend to find maggots no less than gag-worthy.

I can't even eat orzo today.

While living in Hawaii, I once picked a friend up at the airport and took him back to his house. He had neglected to take out the garbage before he left for two weeks, and maggots were cascading out of the trash compactor, piled up in front of it, and spreading out across the kitchen floor.

I had never, I realized, gotten over the dead possum episode of my youth. I gagged and ran. (I'm certain that the human gag reflex when confronted with fly larvae is a good survival mechanism. Bugs are a good indication of food too past its prime to eat. In fact, until 1668, it was assumed that rotting meat *produced* maggots. Only when scientist Francesco Redi actually conducted experiments was it confirmed that maggots were from flies.) The thought of staying to help him clean up never once entered my mind.

The only time I ever saw majesty in a maggot was when I watched a time-elapse film of a dead animal—a dog, I think—rotting in the sun. Reduced to sixty seconds or so, what the maggots accomplished was a thing of beauty. I didn't see rice-like worms feeding, squirming, and oozing. I saw a sanitation system. They were efficient and effective in a dance of life and death and renewal.

Sheer poetry.

As with all things, bugs have their place in the great scheme.

I am a passionate gardener with huge compost bins. I keep red wiggler worms in a bin in my garage to eat my kitchen scraps. The worms take potato peels, celery leaves, and overripe melon rinds and turn it all into garden gold. I throw leaves and weeds and coffee grounds into an outside compost bin and out comes the most wonderful soil, thanks to sow bugs and worms and beetles and fungi and things I can't even imagine.

I know all about the value of digestive bacteria and the critters who slurp up what they leave behind.

Nature eventually recycles everything.

Maggots, though, aren't welcome in my compost (or anywhere else in my life), so I don't invite them. They're carrion eaters, so there are no meat scraps in my bins.

Ah, but even maggots have their uses. Clinical studies are now being performed in hospitals using medicinal maggots (!) to debride necrotic tissue, sterilize wounds, and stimulate healing. Doctors have known since the Civil War that soldiers who had maggot-infested wounds fared better in the long run than did those whose wounds festered and turned gangrenous. This idea fell out of favor when the miracle antibiotic drugs hit the market, but now we're turning back to larvae as perhaps the most efficient way to cleanse severely infected wounds.

And to a forensic entomologist, maggots are tools.

To Gil Grissom, *CSI* entomologist, they can be very revealing evidence.

Forensic entomology is one of the fastest growing sciences today, despite its humble beginnings in a now-famous murder case in 1235 A.D. China. A man was found murdered, slashed to death. When the local investigator had all the villagers bring their sickles to town and lay them upon the ground, flies were attracted to only one of the tools, most likely because of human tissue remnants. The evidence was obvious, even to the guilty owner of that sickle. Even then, bugs pointed the condemning finger at the guilty party. He confessed.

Actually, the first case of what we now call forensic entomology occurred near Paris in 1855, when the remains of a baby were discovered behind a plaster mantel in a house. The occupants were obviously under suspicion, but the investigator determined that the insects present on the corpse indicated the baby had died at least two years prior to discovery. The current occupants breathed a sigh of relief. They were cleared, and the previous occupants of the house charged.

Simply put, forensic entomology is the science of investigating insect activities as they interact with the legal system.

The legal system!

This definition surprised me. But then I remembered that not long ago I heard that "insane" is a legal term, not a medical one. That surprised me, too. I guess I'm still naïve enough to expect that science can still be practiced merely for the sake of knowledge. But the legal system has infiltrated every aspect of our lives and our deaths, and is now the driving purpose behind entire scientific disciplines.

The field of forensic entomology has been broken into three branches: The first is urban entomology, the study of insect infestations of buildings, such as termites, bedbugs, spiders, silverfish, carpenter ants, and such, and the pesticides that eradicate them. The second is stored products entomology, mostly the study of weevils, moths, mites, and beetles that infest and ruin stores of grain, corn, legumes (like beans, lentils, and peas), milled cereal products, flour, bran, macaroni and other pasta products, dried fruits, dried vegetables, cheese, and nuts. (These "pantry pests" spoil far more than they eat—10% of the world's stores of foodstuffs, and as much as 40% in some tropical environments.)

The third field of forensic entomology is medicolegal entomology, sometimes referred to as "forensic medical entomology," or "medicocriminal entomology" because of its focus on violent crime. This is the stuff of *CSI*.

The basics are this: Insects have a customary life cycle. Their habits are strict and their preferences are few. Carrion-eating blow flies (*Calliphoridae*) and flesh flies (*Sarcophagidae*) will infest a corpse within twenty-four hours, weather permitting. If there are open wounds, flies can arrive within minutes of death. It is on these carrion buffet tables that the female flies lay their eggs.

Carrion-eating flies generally go through three larval stages before pupating and emerging as adult flies. Each of these stages is brief and easily predicted, with factors such as temperature, humidity, and other environmental considerations factored in. Especially temperature. Maggots are cold-blooded; they don't grow well unless there's heat. (Case in point: my friend's garbage in hot, humid, tropical Hawaii.) Maggots hatch from fly eggs in large numbers and move around a corpse as a group, disseminating bacteria and secreting enzymes which enable them to consume virtually all of the soft tissue.

Investigators on a fresh crime scene can collect the eggs and incubate them to maturity to discern the age of the larvae and identify the species of fly (not easy—some microscopic differences in fly species produce significant differences in fly behavior). On more advanced cases (the ones where corpses have been allowed to ripen longer), several different types of larvae may be present, in differing life stages.

In what Grissom calls "linear regression," the time of death (or PMI, "post mortem interval") can be determined by the type and age of insects on the body. Examine what insects are present, determine their current life stage, and count backward to when the first eggs were laid (factoring in the ambient temperature), and you'll have the time of death.

It's not as easy as it seems. First of all, the first instar larvae, the stage that hatches directly from the egg, cannot be readily identified as to species. The second instar, or the next maggot stage, can only be correctly identified on occasion. And the third instar, or preputal larvae, the largest maggot stage and the most commonly observed, is only valuable to a researcher if it is collected and preserved properly. (Scanning electron microscopes are currently being used to refine maggot species identification.)

Next, there's the climate. Wherever there is a corpse, there are fluctuating temperatures—warmer during the day, colder at night. Rainfall, cloud cover, wind speed and direction, and relative humidity all have a bearing on the speed with which maggots develop. Not only do fly species differ from region to region, from habitat to habitat and from season to season, some come into their own in the coolest parts of the year, some flourish in the warmest parts of summer, some prefer the bright sun, some like the shade. After all the soft tissue has been consumed, the maggots leave and the beetles move in to pick the bones clean.

So it isn't just a matter of picking up some maggots and pronouncing the time of death. It's an extremely complex puzzle, right up Gil Grissom's alley.

It can be quite confusing.

Except to Gaia, who seems to have it all figured out. A place for everything, our Mother Earth tells us in myriad ways, and everything in its place. She has no problem knowing which bugs to send to a crime scene, and in what order.

There's something called the Gaia Hypothesis, which was formulated in the 1960s by a British chemist named James Lovelock. He believed that our planet functions as a single organism, maintaining conditions necessary for its own survival. Named after Gaia, the Greek goddess of the Earth, Lovelock's hypothesis postulated that the world is a completely self-sustaining entity. He has written a series of books on the subject, and his theories are popular in environmental classes all over the world. While still a hypothesis, the concept provides many useful lessons about the interaction of physical, chemical, geological, and biological processes on Earth, and endless fodder for intelligent speculation.

It's all about seeing the bigger picture.

I think he's on to something.

But let's get back to maggots.

Maggots. Horrible, grisly little critters.

And yet sublime.

Maggots and other insects cannot only tell crime scene investigators the time of death, but place of death. In "Grave Danger" (5-24), a particularly gruesome and suspenseful *CSI* episode directed by Mr. Gruesome Suspense himself, Quentin Tarantino, Grissom and company couldn't find Nick Stokes, who had been buried alive. When Nick was attacked by fire ants, they had their first real clue. Fire ants live in moist soils, not in the Las Vegas desert. The team found him buried beneath the damp earth of a commercial plant nursery.

Certain flies are typical only in urban areas. When Grissom found musket flies on a body left in the woods, he knew the corpse had been moved from the city, the original site of the murder, where musket flies dwell. "They're the first witnesses to the crime," he said. "They're perfect. They're doing their jobs, exactly what God intended, recycling us back to the earth."

Bugs are Grissom's passion. He has an "entomology collection," and even wanted to take a photograph of chigger bites for his "bite collection." I find this completely consistent with his character. He's the one who always seeks out, and finds, the larger picture, the way the details all relate to one another. He's the adult in charge, after all, and that means that he must have a wider view of everything: human nature, criminal behavior, co-worker relations, and the global consistency of insect activities.

I bet Grissom has a copy of Lovelock's book on his nightstand.

But let's set the larger picture aside for the moment, and get back to the grisly.

In 1994, Patricia Cornwell released a book called *The Body Farm*, alerting the world to an aromatic FBI "facility" in Knoxville, Tennessee, where on any given day, you can find dozens of human corpses lying about in the humidity. They are test subjects, and they are clothed and unclothed, buried and unburied, in the sun and in the shade, cooled, heated, sitting in a car, lying on metal shards. In many of the experiments, researchers are trying to duplicate crimes currently under investigation.

This is where the literal field research in forensic entomology is done.

By the way, if you want to donate your remains to the Body Farm, or the "Anthropology Research Facility" as it is officially called, you'll have to get in line. While at first they had to rely on unclaimed cadavers of homeless men, there is now a waiting list for those who name the Body Farm as their final resting place.

As creepy as all this may seem, it is in reality no different than the study of photosynthesis in a variety of plants, or the correlation of the phases of the moon to fish and animal activity. Everything has a system, and Gaia seems to know exactly what she's doing. We're just bumbling along, trying to catch up.

As much as we like the criminal aspects, the larger application for all aspects of forensic entomology is in civil court. Maggot-infested meat, for example, is a common complaint. Did whoever bought it leave it sitting on the counter too long before putting it away? Or did it really come that way from the butcher's counter?

In one landmark case, a 188-kilo shipment of marijuana was seized, and by plotting on a map the home turf of the sixty-one species of insects found therein, investigators were able to determine the country of origin, and the dealers were indicted not only for possession, but for international trafficking.

And then there's the very disturbing suit against a funeral home who failed to properly embalm a client. As the wake progressed, maggots began to stream out of the deceased's nose.

Not nice.

And just like with any new leap in forensic science, old cases are being reopened and reevaluated due to the new light being shed on entomological evidence.

Even so, knowing too much can sometimes be a confusing burden. There was a case of DNA being found so far away from a crime scene that it almost sank the investigation. Turned out to be fly specks; flies that had feasted on the deceased's blood had congregated by a window, as flies are wont to do, and their excrement included the victim's DNA.

For all the press forensic entomologists are getting these days, it's a pretty tiny universe of professionals, and they're rarely out in the field doing the fun stuff, like picking maggots from a slushy corpse. According to the American Board of Forensic Entomology, the most current worldwide directory shows only sixty-two forensic entomologists, with a mere dozen practicing in the United States. Thirty-three of the sixty-two work solely with the medicolegal subdiscipline, and five more say that medicolegal entomology is one of their specialties. The remaining twenty-four teach entomology or biology and/or are involved with research. Those working in the field spend most of their time training crime scene investigators to properly recognize, obtain, and preserve evidence. Then they review said evidence, render their findings, and regularly appear as expert witnesses in court.

Specimens are collected in the field by crime scene technicians, medical examiners, or forensic pathologists, but the skill to correctly identify each species of crime scene insect resides with fully qualified entomologists.

It's got to be a calling.

Perhaps we all have our callings. We each seem to fit, somehow, into our communities. And our families.

Perhaps we're a more integral part of Gaia than we know.

Salmon swim upstream to spawn and then die in order to feed the bears who fertilize the forests. And a salmon, it is said, can smell the difference between a worm from its spawning grounds and any other worm, even amidst all those billions of gallons of rushing river water.

The weather patterns of our planet would be vastly different if it were not cocked at precisely twenty-three degrees on its axis. Or if we had no moon. Perhaps Earth would be uninhabitable for life as we know it.

These things are not accidents.

And the expert housekeepers—the things that keep it all tidy—are the insects.

The fact that there are armies of arthropods ready, willing, and able to recycle our sloughed-off mortal remnants is no less of a miracle, and no less important a piece of our complex ecosystem.

What's fun about it is that we're just beginning to discover the beauty in its intricate dance.

The closer a thing is examined, the more exquisite it becomes.

And the bad guys? The despicable heathens who commit murder for no rational reason and then try to get away with it? Are they part of the whole ecological system too?

I don't know.

Personally, I think that of all the bugs that populate this planet, murderers are the ones that Gaia wants to swat.

She does not want the bad guys to get away with it, and she gives us all the tools we need to catch 'em.

We're just learning how to work with her.

Elizabeth Engstrom is the author of nine books and over 250 short stories, articles, and essays. She is a sought-after instructor and lecturer at writing conferences and conventions around the world, and on occasion holds riotous seminars on erotic writing for women. She is a regular contributor to Court TV's *Crime Library*. www.ElizabethEngstrom.com

While the CSI shows present us with forensic technology in easy-to-digest sound bites and vivid computer-generated graphics, sometimes it's nice to explore an interesting technology in a little more detail. For those of you craving a more in-depth explanation of fingerprinting, Doranna Durgin has the goods.

DORANNA DURGIN

A Quest for Identity: The Fingerprint in Its Natural Environment

A National Forensographic Presentation

SECRETIVE AND YET PERSISTENTLY PRESENT, the wily fingerprint wields an unexpected influence over the human condition…and yet its habits and needs are seldom taken into consideration. Now, lift the curtain of mystery over the remarkably hardy fingerprint by exploring its rich history, its favorite haunts, its various hosts, and the best methods for flushing it into plain sight.

• •

Under the hot Miami sun, two CSIs process a raised shack on the edge of the Everglades. The shack is obviously a popular make-out spot, replete with fingerprints and condoms both. Or perhaps it was a popular spot—it will take a while for the odor to fade. Until then, insect repellent can't begin to compete with the odor of decay.

One of the CSIs is young and Latino, with intense dark eyes now focusing on the task at hand—assessing fingerprint recovery from the worn, painted door of the shack. The other CSI, a neatly dressed blonde, ponders the railing, where porous wood adds challenge. "All right," she says. "Let's see what we can find."

. .

The Fingerprint

Discovery of the Fingerprint: A History

Although obvious to those who know where to look, the fingerprint is so sly, blending so well with its environment, that detailed observation and classification has been slow to occur. Most fingerprints go entirely unobserved, and under usual conditions this is the most natural and even desirable situation. Even now, most visible fingerprints are in grave danger from the cleanly among us, those who prefer the unnaturally smooth shine of an artificial surface. And yet, over time, there are those who have come to properly revere and preserve this important part of our social ecosystem.

Other cultures were way ahead of the West in this regard. In fact, in the Western part of the world prior to the mid-1800s, law enforcement officers still relied on cultivated memory to identify chronic offenders by sight. Photography helped, but appearances remained easy to change. Meanwhile, in other cultures, fingerprints were already recognized as significant. As far back as 2000 B.C. fingerprints were preserved in clay to mark important business transactions, most notably in barely B.C. China. Skipping ahead to the fourteenth century, Persia also found fingerprints quite handy for official documents—at which point a government physician finally made note that no two fingerprints were alike, not even those of identical twins.

It wasn't until the mid-1800s that fingerprinting was used in the Western world. One British official's whim—to impress a local Indian businessman with the significance of a contract by adding a palm print—led to the habitual palm-printing of all such contracts. Eventually the man pared that down to a couple of fingerprints, at which point he noticed that they could, in fact, be used to identify the fingerprints' host. By 1883, fingerprint identification was well known enough that

Mark Twain used it in *Life on the Mississippi* and then *Pudd'nhead Wilson*. At last, fingerprints were getting the recognition they deserved.

In 1902, the New York Civil Service Commission began systematic use of fingerprints to identify fingerprint hosts. A century later, we take fingerprinting technology and record-keeping for granted. From Superglue fingerprinting techniques to the Automated Fingerprint Identification Systems (AFIS), we expect criminals to be on record—or to find themselves there shortly after committing a crime. A current rough estimate places five to fifteen percent of the world's population on file in this manner.

• •

"With luck, some of these will be in AFIS," the blonde says, fastening the last tape on a makeshift clear plastic tent around the railing. Before sealing it, she places a test print on a plastic swatch and inserts it inside the tent where it will be visible. The young man, pausing in his own work, hands her the portable field warming plate and the Superglue. She arranges the plate and a tiny foil baking pan on the stairs, adds Superglue, and seals the tent around it all. A cloud of vaporized Superglue fills the interior. "Any minute now," she says, her gaze on the test print. They wait for the ridges to appear.

• •

A Life Cycle
Fingerprint ridges are formed young—even before birth of the fingerprint host—and they live in the limited environmental niche of the host's "friction skin," those areas of skin needed to grip surfaces. Each unique fingerprint leaves its mark on its environment using a number of physical formations, from bifurcations to dots to ridge endings and ridge shape variances. Not all fingerprints are complete...but any fingerprint the size of a dime contains enough individual characteristics to exclude it from belonging to any other than its actual host.

As time passes, the fingerprint bears the mark of its host's hardships in life, and can be interrupted by both temporary scars—minor injuries which heal smoothly, restoring the original pattern—or deep, permanent scars that leave the pattern forever disrupted. Warts come and go without consequence, while other conditions such as psoriasis can result in continuous shifting. There are also those very rare hosts who are born without prints, a characteristic that runs in families and is almost as identifying as a fingerprint itself. And finally, the patterns of aging fingerprints can flatten and crease. When the aging fingerprint leaves its mark, it is a declaration of its venerable status, and of survival in a difficult world.

Fingerprints are naturally neat and tidy entities and do not, as many people believe, generally mark their territory with oils. Just like the rest of us, they can be prone to leaving signs of the substances to which they've most recently been exposed—mud, paint, and sometimes more unpleasant substances—but otherwise mark their passage with substances from their eccrine glands—mostly water, with amino acids, proteins, polypeptides, and salts mixed in.

Most fingerprints are wily by nature, and they remain latent, or hidden—although in the study of fingerprints, any print left on an object at a scene of interest is termed a *latent print*. If a print is visible in some form of contaminant, it is called *patent*. *Plastic* prints are impressions found in wax, window putty, or similar materials.

The Fingerprint Environment

Classic fingerprint environments can be divided into two categories: porous and non-porous surfaces. Fingerprints will happily settle on any surface at least as smooth as its own corrugated ridges. Imitation leather, fruit, rocks, bed sheets, garbage bags... even human skin.

Non-porous surfaces such as glass or slick paper hold a tenuous print. Contrary to scenes presented in popular media, non-porous surface prints do not easily survive handling—not even handling meant to preserve those very prints. Wrapping a glass with a handkerchief or putting it in a plastic bag is almost certain to eradicate evidence of the fingerprint host's passage. Undisturbed, these marks can nonetheless survive many years. Porous surfaces such as rough paper products or unfinished wood hold a more robust fingerprint, and such marks have been known to last up to forty years.

All surfaces should be handled with the utmost care, and with no illusion that wearing gloves will protect existing fingerprints—they simply prevent the appearance of additional fingerprints.

Fingerprint Features

Fingerprint aficionados learn quickly that their chosen study is a matter of nearly microscopic detail that covers a number of features—patterns and minutiae of both level two and level three quality such as ridges, incipient ridges, dots, and pores.

A fingerprint pattern is the big picture, and is what the average amateur fingerprint aficionado can most readily recognize. Even those who care nothing about the exacting nature of fingerprint study can spot the various patterns, of which there are nine: tented, arched, whorl, right loop, left loop, double loop, right and left pocket loops, and the complex mixed figure (sometimes called "accidental").

Minutiae are the details in a fingerprint. There are level-two minutiae: big ridge details such as starting lines, splitting or bifurcated lines, and line fragments, and smaller ridge details such as a line unit (an isle of a ridge with only one pore), line fragments (two or more attached isles), eyes, and hooks. Even beginning and ending lines are characteristic in an individual print.

There are also smaller level-three details such as pores, incipient ridges, and lineshapes—the latter of which takes into account the way ridges vary in thickness, wavering and undulating along the edges. Incipient (or subsidiary) ridges, in the topography of a fingerprint, are lower than the primary ridges, barely rising up from the valleys between those ridges. How clearly they appear depends on the nature of the print—is it a robust print, showing every feature in detail to claim its territory? Or is it faint of heart, leaving only the merest impression of its passage?

Scars, creases, warts, and temporary damage are also important minutiae, and the savvy fingerprint expert pounces upon them with glee. As for pores…they can vary in number, shape, size, and position within the ridge, and perhaps merit deeper investigation. There is in fact a branch of fingerprint experts who have put forth poroscopy as an independent means of establishing the identification of the fingerprint host.

• •

Done dusting prints on the door frame, the intense young man eyes the door. "I think it should go to the lab. It needs to be fumed before I try to pull any prints."

The blonde is bent over the railing, applying a feather dusting brush with the lightest contact of her twirling brush. "It'll be hard enough finding a clear print," she agrees. "If we're lucky, someone leaned against it. The area around the doorknob—"

"It's going to be a mess." He eyes the hinges, assessing the difficulty of re-moving the door without damaging the prints.

She sets her brush aside on the paper holding the dusting powder and reaches for a ready stack of transparent lifting tape. "I might yet get a good one here. Give me a moment and I'll help you with that door."

· ·

The Fingerprint Expert

Background

Most fingerprint experts train for a minimum of several years under the watchful eye of experienced Latent Print Examiners before working un-supervised. After the successful completion of a six-hour exam admin-istered by the International Association for Identification, a fingerprint expert can earn the title of Certified Latent Print Examiner. Any finger-print submitted for examination to one of these experts can expect to yield its secrets. On the other hand, should a fingerprint end up in the hands of an ID tech completing a one-week latent techniques course or a self-taught ID tech laboring at a small department, it can confidently expect to remain a mystery to the world at large.

Superb fingerprint identification experts also follow a code of con-duct, whether it is of a formal nature or not. The ethical fingerprint expert presents evidence in a fair and impartial manner, without dis-criminating on grounds of race, beliefs, gender, language, or other social factors. They work within the limits of their professional competence, without exaggerating that competence to reach conclusions. And if they see a situation which may lead to injustice, they take action.

Conditions Supportive of the Fingerprint Expert

The expert fingerprint observer knows that certain conditions are neces-sary to fully appreciate and study the fingerprint in a manner that offers reliable, error-free identifications of their hosts. The basic environment needs to offer completely documented processes (which not only act as quality control, but allow review). The fingerprint expert must be fully and acceptably trained and regularly tested—and remain free of the political and judicial pressure that can allow bias to creep into their assessment of these remarkably individual prints. Errors in identification most often arise from an unhealthy environment where quality control has faltered and pressures create bias.

The process itself should only take place under certain basic conditions. The examiner should have as few links to the case as possible, so as to avoid any preconceived notions; ideally, the expert who collects the fingerprints from their environment should be excluded. The examination should be done in a quiet environment separated from other aspects of the investigation. And of crucial importance, the examination should be done in an uninterrupted fashion, reducing the likelihood that the expert will recognize factors from a previous session and subconsciously upgrade the significance of those characteristics.

Fingerprint Host Identification

Unlike most entities under study, either in their natural environment or artificially provided areas, the fingerprint has a worldwide range over all climes throughout the year—although sightings are rare in Antarctica and the northmost regions. Fingerprints are even associated with a range of host species, from human to primate to marsupial. However, the world's various countries evolved their identification techniques separately, and many still require different conditions for a positive identification of any given fingerprint. Some countries require a minimum number of matching features (or minutiae), while others, including the United States, rely simply on "expert opinion." These latter countries note that there is no scientific basis for establishing a minimum number of features; some identifications might require only a handful, while some, depending on circumstances, might require quite a few more. Whatever their differences in process, most countries do require verification by at least one expert.

Fingerprint Processing
There is an astonishing array of options for coaxing the fingerprint into visible form. Fingerprint collectors can divide processing techniques

into physical technique or surface type. Along with the basic porous and non-porous surfaces, fingerprint territory type can be broken down into glass or plastic surfaces, wet surfaces, metal surfaces, adhesive tape, glossy paper, and raw wood surfaces—not to mention cartridge cases. Fingerprints of the most desirable nature seem to find cartridge cases a natural gathering place.

Categorize fingerprint detection techniques by the technique itself, and you'll find yourself dealing with categories such as amino acid, sebaceous, eccrine, blood, fluorescent, post-cyanoacrylate, post-ninhydrin, and ultraviolet-induced techniques. There's also a separate category of non-destructive techniques that overlap some of these other categories, which is the preferred option for fingerprint aficionados everywhere.

• •

"They wiped it," the young man says with a certain fatalistic realization as he stares down at the well-fumed door in the airy fingerprint processing room. "The knob, the front edge of the door . . . it's a sloppy job, but it did the trick."

"They were in a hurry," the blonde observes. She has lifted only a few clear prints from the railing; they have not turned up matches in AFIS. The door is clamped in its original orientation; she moves closer and beckons to the young man. "Maybe too much of a hurry. Come look at this."

Ridge details, on the edge of a decorative panel. The tiniest smear of blood. The young man grins and reaches for his dusting powder.

• •

A Holistic Approach to Host Identification

Persistence of features throughout the fingerprint lifetime and uniqueness of those features are the foundation of all fingerprint study. Ridge-flow and minutiae come together to make it possible for the expert to identify fingerprint marks as having come from one and only one host. Once a fingerprint has indeed been noticed and coaxed into visibility for study, the holistic approach used in this identification procedure can be seen as a process of looking from the big picture to the small.

Initially, the expert observes the overall pattern configuration, noting the extant whorls. These are first-level observations, and they don't have sufficient uniqueness to stand on their own. They merely offer a basic categorization of each print.

Second-level minutiae are next observed—the specific ridgeflow, accidental features such as scars and flexion creases, and the location and type of ridge characteristics. Although scars and flexion creases are rarely used in the final identification, they have a place at this early stage of the process, allowing the expert to perform initial comparisons and sorting.

Third-level observations are used to support the second-level details, and include edgeoscopy and poroscopy. Experts are expected to take an identification to this level of precision.

At this point, the expert must go back to the big picture, assessing the clarity of the print and the comparison print before finally making the decision as to whether they share a sufficient uniqueness to eliminate the possibility of the print coming from any other fingerprint host. It is a subjective opinion, based on the expert's experience, knowledge, and ability.

Stages of Identification

The fingerprint is a complex entity; in order to fully appreciate its mysteries, there should be many stages of study, not limited to the initial identification described above.

The information stage allows for details to be detected and a record to be made of these details. The comparison phase allows an expert to begin true identification in comparison with prints on record. Here, differences as well as similarities are noted.

In the evaluation phase, the information from the previous phases is studied and weighed against margins of tolerance—that is, the differences that might normally expect to be found in prints created by the same fingerprint host under varying circumstances. Explanations for any differences are considered, and finally conclusions are drawn.

The work, however, is not yet done. The fingerprint is such a complex thing found in so many natural circumstances that conclusions are not to be taken for granted. Next comes a verification stage, via another expert. And should there be any differences of opinion, these must then be reconciled. After all, from the time fingerprints were first discovered and quantified, it has been recognized that look-alikes caused by distortions and by chance do occur frequently enough to be a factor.

• •

"We got a match?" the blonde says, sweeping her long hair behind her ear to look more closely at the monitor on which the crime scene fingerprint and the AFIS print of record have been displayed. The monitor also shows an unsavory character with poor grooming habits and a sneer, as well as a long list of drug-related offenses.

"Yeah, we got a match." But the young man doesn't sound happy, and she soon sees why.

"Only five minutiae in common," she said. Their print is, after all, smudged and distorted from its location on the sculptured, inset door panel. Lifting a clean print had been a tricky business. "And they're all first level. The DA might go with it."

"It's all we have on this guy so far." In the field, it was enough to run with. In court . . . not so much.

"Well, then," she said, straightening, her smile as serene as ever, "it's a good thing you brought that door in and fumed it. We'll just get that print again—and this time, let's use silicone to lift it."

• •

Back in the Field . . .

The savvy reader will have noticed that the old tried-and-true standby for fingerprint detection, preservation, and identification hasn't yet garnered much mention: dusting. So let's go back to the scene of the fingerprint survey, where our intrepid experts are discovering, preserving, and sending out samples for identification. They arrive in one of the fingerprint's many and varied environments, laden with gear, eager to locate and humanely collect their quarry—without smudging or erasing the often delicate prints. Contrary to popular belief, this does not immediately involve a jar of dusting powder, a spiffy brush, and lifting tape. It starts with a camera.

Pre-Dusting

Visible prints should always be photographed before all else, recording the fingerprint in its natural habitat. Prints tracked in grease, blood, paint, and the like can be photographed on the spot. A tripod is necessary; a macro (close-up) lens is preferable. A scale should also be included in the shot; the shot should be "head-on" to avoid distortion, and if there are difficulties with the lighting angles, at least one shot should be taken head-on regardless of the lighting issues.

Once the photos are taken, it's time to start fuming—not a reference to our even-tempered experts, but to the technical process. Superglue fuming of non-porous material is the most effective way to bring the wily latent fingerprint to sight, and then to preserve and protect it. Studies have shown that fingerprints preserved in this way have the best chance of surviving shipment and of being identified in the lab. Once fumed, the evidence requires no exotic shipping measures. Of course, these fingerprint collectors should be careful to avoid inhaling fumes or to expose their eyes to such fumes. This is especially the case if the expert is wearing contact lenses; exposure can literally glue the contact to the cornea. Fingerprint experts hate it when that happens.

The fuming itself is straightforward. Evidence is placed in a sealed container. It is not alone, however; it should be accompanied by material, such as clear plastic, that holds a recently deposited test print. A few drops of Superglue in a piece of foil placed on a coffee warmer are all it takes to initiate the fuming, during which the fumes settle on the fingerprint features, revealing them, coating them, and preserving them. But don't walk away—the process needs to be observed. The test print is a control, and when it develops, any latent prints will also be developed. Then it's off to the laboratory for identification.

Large items may require some ingenuity on the part of the print collector when it comes to creating a sealed enclosure, but otherwise the fuming proceeds in the same manner. Once the prints are developed, they are then dusted, photographed, and lifted. Superglue-fumed prints are robust, and can be powdered and lifted many times.

The Dusting

And at last, we approach the dusting, historically the first process used to make fingerprints visible to the naked eye. Fingerprint powders are available in several colors, and should be chosen to contrast with the background of the fingerprint habitat and the color of the lifter used; usually this is a black or grey powder. Fluorescent powders are available for use on multicolored surfaces, but require an alternate light source or UV light for the camera. Such lights are costly and can cause health issues, and must be used only by those with appropriate training and the correct protective clothing.

Fingerprint brushes come in fiberglass, animal hair, and feather versions. For overhead work or in situations where it is critical that the brush does not contact with the surface, there are magnetic wands and powders. To dust for prints, experts follow an exacting process:

First they check the surface using a test print; this tells the expert how amenable that particular surface is to harboring prints. They make sure there are no latent prints in the test area by brushing ever so lightly with powder. If the area is clear, it is wiped off and the expert donates his domesticated and pre-identified fingerprint before going to work with the powder.

Powder is never used directly from the container, which would contaminate it. Instead, a small amount is poured onto a sheet of paper; leftovers from this supply are discarded. The successful collector uses scant powder and a delicate touch, following the contour of the fingerprint ridges as they begin to appear (if not already revealed by fuming). A twirling motion ensures that the sides of the bristles do not contact and destroy the fingerprints. Overbrushing can also destroy the print, so an experienced collector stops twirling when the ridge detail is developed.

As with fuming, all developed prints should be photographed and then lifted. Unlike fumed prints, however, prints that have merely been dusted can be destroyed in the lift. It's important to get it right the first time.

Lifting devices come in many varieties. There are hinge lifters, lifting tapes, rubber and gel lifters, and various types of liquid lifting mediums—each has an advantage, depending on the situation. Hinge lifters and transparent lifting tape present the lifted print in its correct perspective. Rubber lifters reverse the perspective and must be reversed again using photographic techniques, but generally work better than hinge lifters. Transparent lifting tape works better for taking prints from curved or uneven surfaces; gel lifters are good for fragile surfaces and are excellent for use with dusted prints. Silicone and liquid lifting materials work well on uneven surfaces.

It should be noted that not all fingerprints can be fumed and/or dusted. Experts have an extensive toolbox for developing fingerprints, all of which were categorized earlier and most of which can only be accomplished after careful, exacting transport of the fingerprint to the lab.

Seldom observed in its natural habitat with the attention and respect it deserves, often endangered where its habitats overlap with dense human population—especially where glass is concerned—the fingerprint takes infinitely eclectic forms. Whorls and loops, ridges and minutiae and scars, lurking camouflaged in its environment or right out there in the open, it reduces the human condition of the fingerprint host to a single objective identifying factor.

• •

The blonde enters the print lab, papers in hand and distraction on her face. But when she sees the young man sitting at the computer with a satisfied expression, she stops beside him. "We got a match?"

He grins, transforming his normal intensity into something more youthful. "We did. A strong one. It's enough."

She smiles, and it turns whimsical.

"What?" he asks, not slow to see the change.

"What these prints go through sometimes, on the way from the crime scene to the courtroom. . . ." She shakes her head. "It's almost as if they have a life of their own."

• •

Doranna Durgin was born writing (instead of kicking, she scribbled on the womb) and never quit, although it took some time for the world to understand what she was up to. She eventually ended up in the Southwestern high country with her laptop, dogs, horse, and uncontrollable imagination; she writes across genres, with backlist in fantasy, tie-in, SF/F anthologies, mystery, and action-adventure/romance. You can find scoops about new projects, lots of silly photos, and contact info at www. doranna.net.

Don DeBrandt, as his essay explains, is a person I know well. The essay itself is his attempt to compare the science of forensics with the creative process of writing about forensics, which I think he does pretty well. If I do say so himself.

DON DEBRANDT

The Forensics of Fiction

WHEN I WRITE SUSPENSE FICTION, I write under the name Donn Cortez. For other projects—like SF, or comics, or essays—I use the pseudonym Don DeBrandt. This is the first and probably only time I'll get to use both for the same book.

So, let me take off my Donn Cortez-as-guest-editor badge and put on my Don-DeBrandt-as-essayist name tag. Although really, I should keep both on, because while this essay is non-fiction—and thus clearly in DeBrandt's domain—it's about the process of writing a *CSI: Miami* novel, which is Mr. Cortez's job. So, forgive me if the proceedings get a little schizophrenic.

Which, right off the bat, is wrong.

Schizophrenia refers to a psychotic break with reality. What I was trying to imply was more along the lines of Multiple Personality Disorder, which is entirely different. It's a common mistake, but not one a scientist can afford to make.

But then, I'm not a scientist.

I have no formal background in science, or even higher education. I enjoy books that use hard science, but I don't pretend to understand all of it. My usual emotional response to a highly technical explanation is first, *Wow, that guy really sounds like he knows what he's talking about,* and second, *I could never write something like that.*

Well, as it turns out, I was wrong again. By the time this essay sees print, I'll have written four *CSI: Miami* novels.

And this is how I did it.

1. Scene of the Crime

There are many approaches to writing a novel. Fortunately, the one I use duplicates in many ways the structure used in forensics investigations: you start with the crime, and work backward.

For my first *CSI: Miami* novel, *Cult Following*, I wanted an unusual crime. Something very appropriate to the setting, but unique enough that it hadn't been done before. My one visit to Florida was at the beginning of the rainy season; there were days when the sound of thunder started before dawn and went until after dark. When I learned that more people were struck by lightning in Florida than anywhere else in the U.S., I knew I had my murder weapon: death by thunderbolt.

Now I had to build a structure around it. Horatio and his team were going to be asking a lot of questions, and I had to have the answers. How can you kill someone with lightning? Who would do such a thing, and why? And most importantly, what sort of clues would they leave behind for my investigators to discover?

So I started to do research. I found out a lot of things about lightning, the physiological effects of electrocution, and Florida weather patterns. Every fact I learned was a support strut in the structure I was building, and influenced the shape of the plot. The facts told me what I could and couldn't do, as well as suggesting different directions to explore. It also gave me an ending—the same event that started the book would also come in at the climax.

2. DNA

DNA defines who we are on a genetic level. Every DNA pattern—and thus every person—is unique; even identical twins have genetic differences caused by environmental factors. Fictional characters have to be just as unique and distinctive as real people, but when I'm writing a book based on other media, the main characters have already been created for me. What I get to create is the secondary characters—and the bad guys.

In a mystery you often don't even know who the bad guy is until the end of the book—but I've always liked the idea of an epic villain, someone smart and ruthless enough to provide a real challenge for the hero. For *Cult Following* I chose—you guessed it—a cult leader. I made him highly intelligent, extremely good at manipulating people, completely self-centered, and a little psychotic. I wanted to give the cult idea an unusual twist, so I disguised it as a diet regimen involving vitamin shots—loosely based on an actual process—and gave it a celebrity spin by making it trendy, like the South Beach Diet. Not only is my villain cunning and amoral, he's got rich and influential people in his pocket—and he's *brainwashing* them. This is an antagonist skilled enough to match wits with Horatio and his team, and one that can bring political and media pressure to bear as well. Genetically speaking, he's descended from Jim Jones, Robert Atkins, and Bhagwan Rajneesh.

3. Ballistics

So I have a lot of facts, piled up like two-by-fours. I have my villain. I know how the book starts and how it ends—I just have to fill in the middle.

At this point, the book-as-building metaphor has to be abandoned, because a building is a static structure. A work of fiction has to *move*; it's more like a living, breathing creature than a toolshed. The research gave me—well, a pile of bones, and now it was time to string a few together with some muscle.

Muscles work by tension, by straining against something else. Fictional muscle is made of conflict—characters straining against circumstances, against themselves, against each other. When I'm brainstorming conflict, I see it in discrete scenes: Horatio chasing a criminal, Delko interviewing a suspect, Calleigh in a firefight. I jot those scenes down on 3" by 5" cards, and when I'm done I lay the cards out on a table.

This is my ballistics lab. The initial crime is the gunshot; now I have to trace the path of the bullet. Its velocity depends on suspense, its trajectory on the plot; because I don't want the path to be predictable, I have to change the angle periodically, having it ricochet off particular facts as I reveal them. Once again I work backward, setting up the major revelations near the end, then spacing out clues one by one toward the beginning. I look at the overall pattern, move scenes around, add or delete things until I have something that looks coherent and flows at a good pace.

4. Interrogation

They call it the interview room, but we know what it's for. This is where Horatio and his team ask suspects the hard questions, where they reveal the facts, call bluffs, and sometimes even collect physical evidence. On the show there are always a number of scenes set in the interview room, and I try to do the same. It's a very static setting, so little bits of business are important: people clearing their throat, moving a chair, sitting down or standing up. This is the place where the smallest details come into sharp focus.

This is also one of the best places to mess with the reader's head.

Mysteries rely on misdirection. You have to plant red herrings, pretend to lead a reader one way while actually going somewhere else. It's necessary to the structure, and the interview room is one of the best places to do it—because, of course, people lie. And *how* they lie and what they lie *about* can tell the CSIs almost as much as an honest answer.

I try to plan my misdirection carefully. Even in a book where you know the identity of the main antagonist, there's plenty of room for mystery. And in a forensic novel, the *how* is just as important as the *who*.

5. Trace

The CSI lab can identify a material from the tiniest thread or fragment. And knowing what something's made of is the first step to understanding how it got there and what it was used for.

The most important element of fiction is—always—the characters. And before you put a single word down, you'd better understand what *they're* made of. I've spent a lot of time studying the *CSI: Miami* characters, and they're basically structured as a family. Here's a brief rundown on how I see them and what makes them tick:

Dr. Alexx Woods: the mother figure. Stern, but loving. Alexx cares deeply about the bodies that pass through her hands, but she has a core of iron. She's like a lioness protecting her cubs.

Frank Tripp: the uncle. He's the beer-drinking, blue-collar regular guy who comes over to your house on Sunday to watch football. Likeable, dependable, tough.

Ryan Wolfe: the geeky younger brother. He idolizes Horatio, and tries his best to emulate him. He doesn't always say the right thing. He loves science because science is reliable; his obsessive-compulsiveness, though slight, still wants something on which it can count.

Eric Delko: the older brother. Smart, handsome, athletic. Eric's a Boy Scout at heart; he always wants to do the right thing. He goes out of his way to help people, but there's a little bit of bad-boy underneath; he knows how charming he is, and beautiful women are his weakness.

Calleigh Duquesne: the sister. Beautiful, smart, witty, with a playful sense of humor that just verges on flirting. Everybody on the team's just a little in love with her, but none of them would ever dream of asking her out. Her perfection is a little intimidating...and she can turn into a cold-eyed killing machine whenever necessary. If Alexx is a lioness, Calleigh is the Terminator—you don't want her mad at you, *ever*.

Horatio Caine: the father. Horatio is the heart of the show, and though he's a very complex character, the two primary influences that drive him are pain and science. In an early show, Horatio once compared himself to a racehorse, saying that "Some horses run better in harness." He then added, "Science...is my harness." And it is; while pain is what drives him—not just his own but that of others, pain he feels keenly—science is what he uses to keep those feelings under control. Without it, he would explode; the fury we can sense simmering behind those blue eyes would rage unchecked.

And Horatio knows that.

Horatio's compassion is more than just caring about others; it's the fuel that feeds his fire. "Guilt is good," Horatio said once. "It makes us stronger."

6. Autopsy

Beneath every pretty face is just another grinning skull.

But, as every medical examiner knows, those skulls all have their own unique characteristics that detail not just their owner's identity, but their history. The bones, the organs, the flesh itself, are all records of a life lived.

Though the focus of the show is usually on the suspects and what they may or may not have done, the investigators have their own pasts, their own history. Delko almost became a pro baseball player. Alexx grew up playing mom to a large group of siblings. Calleigh graduated from Tulane University. It's important to gather as many facts as possible about the characters and their lives, because what they've done and experienced gives insight into how they might react in any given situation.

However, I also have the opportunity to *create* history for these characters. This can be tricky; anything too pivotal or specific will probably be vetoed by the producers. Revealing that Horatio has a long-lost twin sister, for instance, will never fly. I've found the best approach is to take a plot thread mentioned in the show, and then develop it. Calleigh appreciates guns, so it's not out of the question she might have done some hunting. Wolfe was a beat cop, so I can mention some of his experiences on the street. Horatio was on the bomb squad, so he'll have firsthand knowledge of certain explosives. There's a wealth of directions to explore, as long as I do a little research beforehand—research which consists primarily of watching episodes on DVD, but also involves visiting fan sites on the Web. One of the best resources I found was a number of interviews David Caruso gave when the show first launched; he'd obviously spent a lot of time thinking about Horatio and what drives him, and his insights into the character were invaluable.

History is what lies beneath the skin. It's not always visible, but it's always there.

7. Transfer

So the major conflicts have been mapped out, and I've got a good feel for who the characters are and how they behave. The next part is something I only partially outline, because I find that some of the best of these kinds of scenes evolve organically.

One of the basic tenets of forensic science is Locard's Principle, which states that any two objects that come into contact with each other leave bits of themselves behind—or, as the CSIs call it, transfer. Forensics itself wouldn't be possible without this idea, and the interaction between the characters is just as fundamentally important as the interaction between the objects they study.

This is also one of my favorite jobs. Each of the characters has their own unique voice, and it's a real pleasure for me to put them together in a room and just let them talk. I've always had a good ear for voices, but I still double-check each line of dialogue carefully; I can actually hear the characters talking, and if one of them stumbles over a word, I change it.

In prose, a scene with only two characters works best, because you don't have to continually identify who's speaking. I like to switch around the pairings as much as possible, to let all the characters interact with each other and demonstrate the different relationships they have with each other. Delko and Wolfe have a sibling rivalry going; Calleigh treats Wolfe like her little brother; Alexx can be a little stern toward Delko and Wolfe. In my third *CSI: Miami* novel, *Harm for the Holidays (Part One)*, I paired Wolfe and Tripp up for an investigation because I thought their different styles would contrast nicely.

8. Fingerprints

At this point, I'm ready to start writing. Some writers hate doing outlines, primarily because they feel it handicaps their creativity—if everything's all laid out, there's no room for inspiration, right?

Maybe so, but no writer outlines *that* extensively. It's a road map of where you're going, sure, but there are plenty of routes to get there...and lots of interesting roadside attractions.

Secondary characters are a great opportunity to stretch creative muscles. Fortunately for me, Florida crime fiction has a long history of using oddball casts, so I have an excuse to come up with some unusual people: latex fetishists, heavily armed senior citizens, mysterious Cubans with KGB ties...and I create all of them on the fly.

No two fingerprints are alike; every supporting character should have their own distinctive style, too. That doesn't mean you have to devote a page of description and back story to every receptionist, beat cop, and witness—but it is a great way to have some fun, and entertain the reader at the same time.

Quirky characters can also wind up leading you in directions you hadn't expected, which is either a curse or a blessing depending on your word count. On the first book I actually found myself coming up short, largely because the story was so plot-driven it was eating up the outline faster than I expected. I wound up exploring a sub-plot sparked by one of the secondary characters—a Rastafarian plumber—and it led me to some very interesting places.

9. Technical Specs

So far, the process I've described is fairly standard for writing a novel. But the difference—the *essential* difference—between my previous fiction and this kind of book can be summed up in one word: *detailed scientific procedures*.

Okay, I know that's *three* words, but when it comes to forensics, it doesn't pay to skimp on the details. That doesn't always mean using three words when one will do, but it does mean those three words have to be accurate; if you're talking about AFLP, you better know it stands for Amplified Fragment Length Polymorphisms—*and* what they are.

Which I didn't.

As I said, I don't have a degree in science. How, I wondered as I sat down to start writing, was I supposed to research—let alone *understand*—the dozens of different scientific disciplines used by a CSI lab?

Google.

It was that simple. There was no way I could have written this book ten—even five—years ago, but the information available on the Internet today is *staggering*. No matter how esoteric or highly technical the data I needed was, all I had to do was type a few relevant words into a search engine and I was off and running.

The really interesting thing was, though, that along the way I turned into a sort of forensic investigator myself. Like a CSI, I'd start with the crime and work backward, learning the details as I went. I tracked down forensics databases, learned a few tricks for where to look for specific kinds of information, developed the skills to read a highly technical description and boil it down to something tighter and more easily understood. By the time I was done the first book, I was having a ball; I wasn't just doing research, I was *conducting an investigation*. It helped me grow as a writer and gave me a great deal more confidence in my own abilities.

10. Conviction

Different genres have different restrictions—not so much set-in-concrete rules as expectations the reader wants to have fulfilled. As with all literary conventions, half the fun is in finding ways to break these rules, but you can never lose sight of the fact that you're writing for an audience. Coming up with a clever way to confound everyone's expectations won't win you any new readers if you leave them feeling cheated.

There are two rules I try to follow when writing *CSI: Miami*. First, always remember that Horatio is the focus; despite an ensemble cast, he's the one at the heart of the story.

And two, always—*always*—give Horatio the opportunity to save someone. He doesn't always have to succeed, but he has to at least have a fighting chance. Saving people is what Horatio lives for, and his ability to accept the pain that comes along with that job is one of the things that makes him a great character. As long as I keep that in mind, I know I'm on the right track.

"And that, my friends," Horatio would say as he puts on his shades, "is a blueprint for murder. . . ."

Cue the theme song.

Don DeBrandt is a professional writer with eleven published novels, four of them *CSI: Miami* books. This is the tenth essay he's done for a BenBella anthology, and the first—and probably only—time he'll get two of his pseudonyms to appear in the same book.

CSI is the number one show on TV. Why?
Nick Mamatas analyzes the evidence.

NICK MAMATAS

You Care Who Killed Roger Ackroyd
Why CSI Is So Popular

A HOUSE I OWNED WAS A crime scene once.

It took months for me to get rid of a tenant who was consistently late with the rent—mostly because she had kids and I couldn't bear to throw them out into the cold of New Jersey's winter, and partially because I had hopes that she could turn things around. I couldn't have been more wrong; the ceiling in one room had collapsed thanks to a consistent leak, and she couldn't be bothered to tell me, not even to threaten a suit or as a reason to withhold rent. She just didn't pay and avoided my calls and visits and certified letters. And when she finally vacated the premises, owing me $3,600 and leaving no forwarding address or other information, she just left the doors wide open. That was a Tuesday.

By Friday, when I came to check out the place (and to be sure that she was gone), the house was ruined. The kitchen windows had been punched in and both back and front doors left ajar. The copper pipes of the baseboard heating registers had been removed, as had much of the boiler. Ironically enough, there was mail addressed to me—renewal for my homeowners insurance was coming up in two weeks. I called them, then the police, then waited in the broken building for ninety minutes—except for a side trip under the house, crawling in the dirt in the dark, to try to find the main water supply switch. I slithered out of the cellar door just in time to meet the cops, who weren't sure that I wasn't some criminal at first. The crime scene investigation was on.

The two cops looked around, *tsk-tsk*ed, and explained that drug addicts like to steal copper to sell as scrap for drug money. One of them might have had some sort of plumbing skills, given that the boiler had been taken apart too. They asked about the tenant, and when I said her surname, Owens,[1] one of the cops said "Owens!" excitedly. I looked at him, then glanced down at his badge and nametag: Owens. "Well, I don't know her or anything," he said.

Then the police left and a few days later I was able to retrieve my police report. The cops hadn't even gotten the number of units in the house right, and there weren't so many that it was difficult to count. That's the last I even thought about the police until months later, after I'd moved to California and had been playing phone tag with my insurance company for months. The insurance adjuster called me and asked for a faxed copy of the report one afternoon, then called me back first thing the next morning. (His East Coast morning, that is; it was 4 A.M. for me). "Have they caught the criminals yet, Nicholas?" he asked with all seriousness. I had to laugh.

And that's why we like *CSI*, and by extension, mysteries in general. In mysteries, the awesome power of individual genius, the limitless resources of the state, and, most important of all, a just universe, align themselves to find justice for ordinary people like you and me. *CSI* is the ultimate in mystery—no Dupin, no Holmes, no Nero Wolfe, could solve the crimes that the characters in the various CSI shows handle in an hour. The forensic detail goes far beyond drawing room ruminations, a study of the many kinds of ash left by local cigarettes, or even thinking, "If I were a stolen letter, where would I be hiding?" In *CSI*, science, which bedeviled so many of us in high school, is finally on our side.

In his seminal takedown of the detective genre, "Who Cares Who

---

[1] Names changed to protect, well, me, mostly.

Killed Roger Ackroyd?" which appeared in the January 20, 1945, edition of *The New Yorker*, Edmund Wilson explained some of the dubious pleasures of the genre of detective fiction. Reading *The Nine Tailors* by Dorothy L. Sayers, he found that "[t]he first part of it is all about bell-ringing as it is practiced in English churches and contains a lot of information of the kind that you might expect to find in an encyclopedia article on campanology" (59). And certainly, even one of the pleasures of today's mysteries—and especially its cousins the police procedural and the techno-thriller—is that we as readers or viewers learn a few fun little facts to talk about at parties.

Wilson's point, however, is that the crux of mysteries themselves are fairly ridiculous, involving as they do murders by bell-ringing, murders by pianos rigged with pistols, you name it. And they are, for the simple reason that complexity and obscurity allow for a plot. Most crime is like the crime I was a victim of: some guy wants drugs and grabs something that is convenient and unguarded to sell or trade for the stuff he wants. And sometimes, instead of unguarded money or merchandise, the poorly guarded will do, and that's when we plain folks end up facing a knife, a gun, or a gang. The universe doesn't feel very just under the lights of an ATM when a crook decides that your money is actually his after all.

It's no surprise that Wilson would find the pleasures of mysteries both incredible and silly. The universe is always a *bit* more just for those members of the reading classes able to make their mad money by placing ruminative essays about books in *The New Yorker*. Nobody jacks them up on the stoop of their brownstones, and I doubt Wilson ever came home to find his plumbing missing. "If I were seventy-five feet of stolen copper pipe," Wilson never ever thought, "where would I be?" For the rest of us, however, we've been in the grip of crime, or at least crime *hysteria*, since the Nixon administration.

But that's not what makes *CSI* popular on its own. Nearly a century past the golden age of detective fiction, we're jaded. The butler did it! It was an ice dagger, which then melted, eliminating the murder weapon! But as the Great Fear—of terrorists, of child-murderers, of racial and ethnic minorities, of the Villainous Outsider—has grown, so too has our sophistication. In this *fin de siècle*, the stakes and the complexity of our detective cases have to be pumped up to get us a good scare and an appropriate catharsis. From an episode of *CSI*, "Pirates of the Third Reich" (6-15), presented in summary form on the CBS Web site:

> Samples of both [the victims] eyes' vitreous fluid are taken to get an accurate reading for a T.O.D. In the process, they discover the woman's optic nerve has been severed on her right eye. The left one is still intact. Dr. Robbins has him clip both eyes and send them to the DNA lab where Wendy Simms runs a tox screen along with her normal genetic tests. She reports to Sara that oxycodone and chlorpromazine were found in both eyes. One kills pain, the other quells panic. It gets weirder: the dried-up eyeball belonged to someone else—a male. By the time the woman's autopsy is over, Dr. Robbins and Grissom are inclined to believe that Dr. Mengele may be working out in the desert. The victim has puncture wounds in all her glandular areas from large gauge needles. She also had a D&C, possibly for polyps, hyperplasia, or infection. Evidence also shows she suffered from necrotizing faciitis, a flesh-eating disease. However, it looks like the bacterium was directly introduced into her bloodstream to get at her internal organs, because her skin is fine.

Torn from today's headlines, to be sure! And the poor woman's bizarre death will not go unpunished. Warrants are issued, fifty CSI cadets pore over the desert to find more evidence, videotapes from sleep clinics are reviewed, etchings are stolen, spent condoms retrieved and sperm examined . . . you name it, it happens, up to and including a trap door that leads to a secret Nazi lair. And that's one episode. Pretty lurid stuff, and far more lurid and involved than any actual murders. "Bitch mouthed off to me and I don't play that shit," or, "We were drunk and fucking around, then it just happened," or, "He wouldn't give me his wallet," don't make for very good mysteries.

And the goal of the mystery is not verisimilitude, no matter the gritty "realism" of the corpses put on display or the authenticity of the scientific apparatus used (or the CGI used to make the audience go "Oooh" or even "Ew!"), but to provide the reader with a challenge in trying to guess what happened. As Wilson noted sixty years ago:

> The detective novel is a kind of game in which the reader of a given story, in order to play properly his hand, should be familiar with all

the devices that have already been used in other stories. These devices, it seems, are now barred: the reader must challenge the writer to solve his problem in some novel way, the writer puts it to the reader to guess the new solution (60).

Here in the twenty-first century, the number of devices used and discarded has grown to such a point that the rules adhered to by the Golden Age detective story writers have been thrown out the window. The Detection Club, founded in 1928 by Dorothy Sayers and other leading mystery novelists as a social club-*cum*-secret society-*cum*-in-joke, had, as part of its oath, a promise that that author's "detectives shall well and truly detect the crimes presented to them, using those wits which it may please you to bestow upon them and not placing reliance upon nor making use of Divine Revelation, Feminine Intuition, Mumbo Jumbo, Jiggery Pokery, Coincidence, or any hitherto unknown Act of God" (Giles). S. S. Van Dine, the once-famed but now nearly forgotten author who created the dandyish New York detective Philo Vance, was even stricter, denouncing love interests, teams of detectives, unmotivated confessions, secret societies or organized crime, or secret twins. Yes, well, forget all about that. This is television we're talking about, after all.

Instead of the clean, rationalistic lines of a Golden Age puzzler, *CSI* offers up its hypermodern equivalent. Crimes have gotten too complex to be handled by one man or woman, or through the wits God (or the author) have granted anyone. The rationalist method has been replaced by a scientific bureaucracy that never falters or errs—the only true obstacle to the solution of a crime and the arrest and punishment of the guilty is not the intelligence of the criminal, but the endless legalistic technicalities that keep some evidence from being admissible, or one room thoroughly searched, or a single wayward eyelash from being placed under the proper microscope. If only we all just had DNA samples taken at birth, there would never be any worry about catching a criminal, unless we also all took to slipping into four-limbed zip lock baggies when we wanted to bump off our neighbor. (But good luck disposing of your hermetically sealed plastic suit afterward.) *CSI* allows us to surrender our own agency, and to let the state and science take care of us, completely and forever.

CSI and the inevitable knock-offs (*Bones, Crossing Jordan,* and to a lesser extent the medical mystery show *House*) are the ultimate in wish-fulfillment. For all of us good American taxpayers, there is a nanny police state that uses nothing but objective and infallible means to keep society from falling into chaos. With infinite resources at its command, but no special demands made upon anyone except for the guilty, the nanny police state (staffed not by evil storm troopers or soulless techno-crats, but sexy, if flawed, individuals) keeps us safe. The detective nov-el was designed to not only let a reader match wits with the writer, but to give the reader an object on which to focus her hate: the murderer who, in Golden Age fashion, was never a petty criminal or some random boob, but an unexpected and often respected member of the communi-ty, much like the mystery reader herself was. In this new era, communi-ties have relatively few respected members, but there is still no room for the petty crime in the public psyche. So instead we go for baroque.

Imagine my experience with crime in a *CSI* world. I make a call and fog machines start up. Flashlights slice through the dark, beams cut-ting the confusion of mystery to ribbons. A stray fingernail, maybe even some dandruff is found…and a genetic test suggests that the individual may have a genetic propensity to Cooley's anemia. But wait, that's me! Cut to commercial.

After my genetic material is separated from that of everyone else who might have been crawling around the house, cops instantly and easily track down Ms. Owens and her three kids. The oldest, at fourteen, is the unfortunate "man of the house"; his eyes are wide with terror, but he still stands between the men in their nice suits and his poor, half-drunk mother. Finally, an attractive blonde pushes her way past her somewhat oafish male co-workers and charms her way past the boy and to the mother. The interview is inconclusive, and there are lots of close-ups of wrinkled Kleenex and murmuring in the background.

Later, three blocks away, a tiny sliver of solder is found by one of the forty cadets swarming over the greater neighborhood. It glows like life itself in the gaze of yet another flashlight. "I think we got something." Commercial. Buy a car, why don't you? Or a frozen dinner.

Yes, it is solder, but an obscure kind, mostly used in Latin America. The handyman is tracked down, thanks to the fact that only one hard-ware store sells the product, and careful receipts are kept. Did you see anything suspicious? the handyman is asked, while he is sweating, glistening, working on another job. Hear of anyone or anything? No, no, nothing at all...except that he knows he sometimes buys lengths of used copper piping from this scrap dealer downtown.

Barbed wire. A barking dog, froth on its lips. The owner—fat, disheveled, unshaven—isn't talking. But a bit of copper particulate, picked up from the paw of the dog—it was the dog's fault, for jumping on the cop, no warrant needed—does all the talking necessary. But is it admissible as evidence? Can we get a warrant?

After another commercial, the warrant may not matter, because another house has been hit! And it was the same place that the handyman had been working on before. But he has an alibi, namely the dried semen found in the cab of his pickup truck. He couldn't have been getting a ten-dollar blowjob from a local whore at the very same moment that he was uncoupling a furnace from a home heating system—not unless he's some kind of sexual superman. Haw haw haw.

There's a B-plot, too. Sexual tension. Someone has cancer, maybe. A cop almost wins the lottery. Anyway, as it turns out my tenant's oldest son had been following the handyman around, because he's looking for a father figure, and one of his friends is a crack addict who knows a plumber with a secret sexual fetish—he likes to wear ladies' shoes and stomp on the testicles of other men, and the crack addict had been the willing stompee for money, until one day when he managed to sneak a camera into the plumber's workshop/dungeon. Then the tables were turned, and it was blackmail. They work together to follow the handyman around and rip off any copper they can get their hands on, all to keep up with their drug-taking and ball-crushing habits. They sell the footage on the Internet too, as an extra thrill, and have made all sorts of money from their side gig. Money that, in a nice black briefcase, is presented to me so that I can make repairs on my house and rent it out again to some other, far more deserving, family.

And the poor woman with the kids...eh, who cares what happened to her? Nobody stole her furnace.

CSI is a scientific morality play. Though crime has been on the decline for nearly a decade, fear of crime has rarely been higher. In a world where an intelligence briefing entitled "Bin Laden determined to attack inside the US," issued on August 6, 2001, does nothing to thwart the attacks of September 11, we need to believe that somewhere out there, people are using science and reason to protect us. Few of us will ever fall victim to a neo-Nazi's attempt to develop a superhuman race by kidnapping us and performing illicit eye surgery, but given the generalized terror people feel over curly haired men with funny accents, myspace. com child molesters, and their own neighbors, you might be surprised at who worries about just such a thing.

And of course, *CSI* also offers, in spades, the secondary pleasure of a Golden Age detective novel. Wilson got to learn about bells and piano-tuning. In my notional *CSI* episode, you got to learn that people of Greek descent are especially prone to developing Cooley's anemia, and that crack addicts salvage and steal scrap to sell for drug money, and that there is yet another Internet perversion out there. It's cocktail party talk for the sort of people with whom I generally wouldn't want to have cocktails.

One thing I never learned, though: Who the hell took off with my furnace?

Nick Mamatas is the author of the Lovecraftian Beat road novel *Move Under Ground* (Night Shade Books, 2004) and the Marxist Civil War ghost story *Northern Gothic* (Soft Skull Press, 2001), both of which were nominated for the Bram Stoker Award for dark fiction. He's published over 200 articles and essays in the *Village Voice*, the men's magazine *Razor*, *In These Times, Clamor, Poets & Writers, Silicon Alley Reporter, Artbytes*, the UK *Guardian*, five Disinformation Books anthologies, and many other venues, and over forty short stories and comic strips in magazines including *Razor, Strange Horizons, ChiZine, Polyphony*, and others. *Under My Roof: A Novel of Neighborhood Nuclear Superiority* (Soft Skull Press) will be released in late 2006.

References

CBS.com. "Pirates of the Third Reich." *CSI Episode Guide*. 1 May 2006. <http://www.cbs.com/primetime/csi/episodes/615/>.

Giles, Mary Anne. "Dorothy Sayers: The Detection Club Oath." *Simon Fraser University English 383: Women Mystery Writers*. 1 May 2006. <http://www. sfu.ca/english/Gillies/Engl38301/oath.htm>.

Wilson, Edmund. "Who Cares Who Killed Roger Ackroyd?: A Second Report on Detective Fiction": *The New Yorker,* 20 January 1945.

Nobody can deny that the CSI shows are immensely successful—but why are they so popular? Bruce Bethke has a few ideas. . . .

BRUCE BETHKE

Alimentary, My Dear Catherine

I T'S A PECULIAR TRUTH ABOUT us humans: death both repels and fascinates us. While it's tempting to dismiss this as merely a predictable side effect of our being both mortal and cognizant of our own mortality, that explanation hardly seems adequate. On the one hand, we devote enormous amounts of time, money, and energy to the question of whether there is in fact some portion of ourselves that exists beyond the confines of our mere physical bodies, and if so, what happens to this immaterial component when we die. On the other hand, we also have a profound if somewhat disquieting fascination with *la danse macabre*—with the actual methods, appearances, and processes of death and decay, especially if the death in question is unexpected, untimely, and most importantly, someone else's. We routinely slow down in order to gawk at terrible traffic accidents. We queue up weeks in advance to buy tickets to view the plasticine people in Gunter von Hagens's traveling human taxidermy exhibit, *Body Worlds*. We even have a special term in the lexicon for just this sort of interest: "morbid curiosity."

It's testimony to the dedication of our emergency services personnel and the skills of our medical professionals that so very few of us ever get the chance to develop firsthand knowledge of either aspect of death (at least, such that we can talk about it later), and so we turn to vicarious experiences and the words of others in order to slake our thirst for knowledge. But which view holds the stronger fascination?

As Horatio Caine might say: consider the evidence. Every week, some sixty million Americans go to their church, temple, synagogue, or mosque in search of an answer to the first question.

And *three times* a week, between thirty and forty million Americans tune in to at least one CSI program, to spend sixty minutes in the close company of the second.

Let's make one thing clear at the outset: *CSI* is fiction. A cursory look at any major metropolitan area's police blotter should be sufficient to prove this. Factor out the deranged ex-boyfriends, estranged husbands, botched convenience store robberies, and young men involved in the retail illegal pharmaceutical trade, and homicides are rare crimes, with mysterious homicides being even more so. Factor out traffic accidents and the occasional "Hold my beer and watch *this*!" moment, and even unusual accidental deaths are, well, unusual. There are very few Lex Luthors out there, very few clever murderers who can be unmasked only by extensive scientific investigative work, and even fewer metropolitan police departments with the budgets to do this sort of work on a regular basis anyway.

But as Jack Webb proved long ago, a program about two guys who drive around and question witnesses all day long makes for dull TV, so a certain amount of dramatic license is permissible. The people of *CSI* live in the world of reality-*based* fiction, where DNA tests and toxin screens take minutes, not months; where scientific tests that don't quite exist yet in real life not only *do* exist but are admissible in court; and where civil servants routinely exhibit a level of self-sacrificing dedication rarely found in union employees. In this world, investigators occasionally use evidence-gathering tools that look as if they properly belong in the Ghostbusters' arsenal, poorly lit still-frames from security cameras in underground garages can be computer-enhanced to the point where you can read the appointment calendar on the suspect's Palm Pilot, and killers almost always confess when confronted by the evidence. More importantly, in this world more facts always mean less ambiguity, and Holmes's Law is as ironclad and absolute as the speed of light: When you have eliminated the impossible, whatever remains, however improbable, *must* be the truth.

Or in other words: yes, of course the investigators will discover that the reason there are two different DNA strands on the victim is because the suspect's left testicle is in fact his unborn, conjoined twin.

So, no more carping about these sorts of things, okay? *CSI is fiction*, and for the remainder of this essay we will examine it as such.

I'm often accused of overthinking these sorts of things. Sorry, but that's my job. As a professional science fiction writer I am required by the Fiction Writer's Code to periodically examine some hugely successful entertainment phenomenon with an eye toward answering the two most important questions: what is it that makes this thing so successful, and why didn't I think of it first? Sadly, the answer to the second question must forever remain unknowable, and so we will concentrate on the answer to the first. What is it that makes the CSI family of entertainment products—the original *CSI: Crime Scene Investigation*, and its progeny, *CSI: Miami* and *CSI: NY*—not only the most successful primetime television dramas currently running in the United States, but the most successful television programs in the entire world?

For make no mistake about it: CSI *is* the most successful television franchise in the world, eclipsing even the legendary *Baywatch* or *Dallas*. Every week during the regular season, one in ten Americans tunes in to watch at least one first-run show, with a commitment and dedication matched only by hardened chain smokers. More surprisingly, every week one million Dutch viewers also tune in, which is a remarkable audience for a foreign series airing in a nation of only sixteen million people.

Not only that, but every season, ninety million unique viewers—almost one-third of the entire American population—watch at least one new episode of a CSI show, and they're not alone. At last count, the original *CSI* series can now be seen in syndication in some fifty-three countries around the world, on every continent except Antarctica.[1] In some

---

[1] However, one does wonder what viewers in, say, Kenya, think of the nighttime action in the Miami club scene or on the Las Vegas Strip.

countries, simply being the guy who overdubs the voice of Gil Grissom has been enough to turn a local actor into a major star.

The original series has been running nonstop for six years now, and the spin-offs have been running for four and two years, respectively. The CSI concept has produced a total of 280 new episodes to date, with no sign yet of being anywhere close to wearing out its welcome, or as they say in television, "jumping the shark." So what is that special brand of magic that makes an episode of CSI no ordinary cops-and-corpses show?

Well, I can't presume to speak for anyone else, but I do know that for me the epiphany occurred on the night of Thursday, October 30, 2003. The show was the original CSI series. The episode was 4-6, "Fur and Loathing."

If this title doesn't ring any immediate bells for you, here's a brief synopsis: A man, dressed in a full-body raccoon suit, is struck and killed by a car on a dark stretch of highway. When Grissom and Catherine arrive on the scene, they discover that the man has not only been run over by a car, he's also been shot. The subsequent investigation leads the CSI team into the bizarre world of "Furries": people who dress in full-body fur suits in order to get in touch with their inner animal.

Of this episode, TV Guide said, "The writers at CSI have come up with some strange and kinky cases to investigate in the past (think the scuba diver in a tree or Lady Heather). But in this truly bizarre episode they've outdone themselves, which makes you wonder: do they have vivid imaginations or does stuff like this really happen?"[2]

Uncomfortable as it now makes me to admit this, I do in fact know the answer.

Stuff like this really happens.

You see, as a professional science fiction writer, I'm also frequently invited to attend fan conventions, or "cons." If the fans catch me in a good mood—and they're picking up all expenses—I may accept.

Some years before the "Fur and Loathing" episode aired, I accepted the invitation to be the Guest of Honor (GOH) at a con in a southern state, in mid-July. After I accepted, the con liaison added as if in afterthought, "Oh, by the way, we're also a Furry convention. Is this a problem for you?"

---

[2] TV Guide, October 26, 2003, "CSI Files."

Being considerably more naïve then than I am now, I said, "No, of course not."

Now, try to imagine yourself spending four days in a convention center hotel, in a southern state, in mid-July, at a sort of Demented Football Mascots From Hell convention, with several hundred people in full-body, head-to-toe fur suits. And you with what is apparently the only working shower and stick of deodorant in the hotel.

So when I saw Grissom and the CSI team trying to solve a murder at a Furry convention, I could only say: "Oh, *yeah!*"

Understand, "Fur and Loathing" converted me from being a casual CSI watcher to being a serious CSI fan, not because they were killing off Furries—that was merely an added bonus—but because it made it clear to me that the people behind this show were taking the time, doing the research, and making the effort to *get it right*. Having grown up watching the laughably bad depictions of counter-cultural types such as beatniks and hippies that prevailed on TV in the '60s and '70s, this program was something new, something different. They weren't just lifting a few visual style points and plugging in the same old stock-character stereotypes and situations, they were actually trying to reflect the existing sub-cultural milieu. They weren't simply plodding through all the standard cop show motions and chase scenes like dozens of other series scattered across the vast wasteland known as the past half century of television history; they were seriously trying to make it real. And in sharp contrast to the common repertoire of crusading-doctor-vs.-hidebound-bureaucracy clichés, they were actually trying to make the medical science *make sense*.

To appreciate how truly unusual these things are, let's take a look at some precedents.

In the world of television, there is a special word for TV series that are truly unique, original, and unlike anything the audience has ever seen before: "canceled." Ergo, most commercially successful series such as CSI are not genuinely original, but rather intelligent syntheses that draw on elements from earlier successful tropes.

In the case of CSI, we could probably spend several months trying to create a complete map of all the earlier sources and series it draws from, but in the interests of brevity I will try to narrow it down to the three earlier tropes that CSI uses most heavily: the detective story, the hospital drama, and the police procedural.

Of the three, the **detective story** is the oldest and most time-honored form. Sir Arthur Conan Doyle's Sherlock Holmes is generally considered to be the original prototype for the modern scientific detective, because he from time to time augmented his formidable observational and deductive powers with laboratory work, but the appeal of the exceptionally clever person who can ferret out hidden truths is far older than Holmes or even the scientific method itself. Stories of people who solve fiendishly difficult riddles and mysteries abound in heroic myths, trickster legends, and ancient folk tales from around the world. Clearly recognizable mystery stories can even be found in the Old Testament of the Christian Bible, in the Book of Daniel.[3]

Clearly, we've been entertained by tales of very clever people solving very tricky puzzles for a *very* long time, and in this regard, CSI functions as a classic detective drama. Each series features one exceptionally clever but somewhat quirky man—the gruff-but-lovable Gil Grissom, the tough-but-smart Horatio Caine, or the dedicated-but-troubled Mac Taylor—who, accompanied by his loyal Watson, never fails to entertain us, week in and week out, with his exceptionally clever means of finding the hidden truth behind some unique and peculiar mystery.

Watson, by the way, is an essential part of the formula. Since the actual work of observing, thinking, and deducing makes for dull television,

---

[3] To be fair, these stories are part of the Apocrypha. They appear in the earliest Greek versions of the Christian Bible right up through the King James Version, but were declared to be of dubious origin and deleted from most English-language Bibles beginning in the early nineteenth century.

In The Story of Susanna, a virtuous wife is falsely accused of adultery and sentenced to be stoned to death, whereupon young Daniel demonstrates his divinely inspired wisdom by taking up her defense and ordering the village elders to question again the two men who have accused her, only this time, separately. By tripping them up on seemingly insignificant but conflicting details in their stories, Daniel is able to prove that Susanna's accusers are lying. Susanna is freed, but her accusers, having both borne false witness and coveted another man's wife, become the guests of honor at that afternoon's stoning, thus proving that the idea of taking violent vengeance against false accusers is considerably older than even Clint Eastwood's *Hang 'Em High*.

Likewise, in The Story of Bel and the Dragon, young Daniel confronts King Cyrus of Persia, who insists that the idol worshipped by the Babylonians is a living god because the offerings left in the temple every night vanish before the morning. With King Cyrus's permission—and his life on the line—Daniel surreptitiously covers the floor around the altar with fine ashes, whereupon Cyrus seals the only known door to the temple with his personal signet. In the morning the offerings to Bel are gone, but the footprints in the ash clearly reveal the secret trap door that the priests have been using to enter the temple and steal the offerings for themselves. The worship of Bel comes to an abrupt and bloody end and King Cyrus bows before the God of Israel, thus proving that the "locked room" mystery is about as old as it gets.

Watson enables the lead character to both "think out loud" and from time to time throw out the odd red herring, to keep the audience from guessing the solution too quickly.

Herein lies the weakness of the classic detective story, at least as shown on TV. Since the actual work of solving puzzles is visually uninteresting, over time, the plots can't help but to become rote and formulaic, and the stories to rely increasingly on the lead character's "fascinating" personality and his witty banter with Watson. From David Janssen's Richard Diamond, through Peter Falk's Frank Colombo and Angela Lansbury's Jessica Fletcher, to Tony Shalhoub's Adrian Monk and Vincent D'Onofrio's Robert Goren, there is not one normal, happy, well-adjusted personality in the lot; and since the title characters in successful TV series are rarely allowed to grow or evolve in any significant way, this also means that in time the detective's "fascinating" personality is reduced to a catalog of signature shticks and nervous tics, and the witty banter takes on all the surprising qualities of the umpteenth replay of an old Cheech and Chong record.

When this happens—when the audience knows all the bits by heart; when the catchphrases become clichés, and the viewers would pay cash money to see, just *once*, an episode of *Starsky & Hutch* that did not end with a car chase, an episode of *Law & Order: Criminal Intent* that did not end with Goren having a near-nervous breakdown, or an episode of *Colombo* that did not end with the lieutenant walking away from the prime suspect, and then turning and saying, as if in absent-minded afterthought, "Oh, there's just one more thing—"

This is when the show jumps the shark, and for all practical purposes the series is over, even if the walking corpse manages to shamble on for another season or two. But somehow, a cumulative twelve seasons in, CSI has managed to avoid both the trap of the single indispensable character and the decay into self-parody, which suggests that there must be something more at work here.

So let's keep digging.

On another level, CSI functions as **hospital drama**. Not a doctor drama; that's a different thing, and doctor dramas typically suffer from the same weaknesses as detective stories. They quickly become too dependent on the audience appeal of the (typically) headstrong and irascible lead character, and once that appeal wears thin, the show is over. For example, I enjoy *House* as only a longtime fan of *Black Adder* can, but Hugh Laurie is the show, and on the day his quirks and quips cease to be entertaining, it's done for. There are only so many times you can watch the maverick renegade crusading doctor storm into his boss's office, slam his fist down on the table, and say, "Dammit, I know I'm right and you're wrong, and if you don't let me perform that risky new surgery (or use that new experimental medicine, or apply those new and lively leeches, etc., etc.) *right now*, that adorable kid in Room 312B is going to *die!*"

As I said, there are only so many times you can watch someone play that scene before you start saying, "So all right, kill the kid already."

In contrast, a well-crafted hospital show, like *ER* or *Grey's Anatomy*— or if you're old enough to remember it, *St. Elsewhere*—is very nearly actor-proof. Major characters may come and go (think of George Clooney's departure from *ER*) but the rest of the cast soldiers on and the series survives. The reason for this remarkable durability is fairly simple; it's because the Mother of All Prime-Time Hospital Shows is *General Hospital*.

Yes, *that General Hospital*. The soap opera. Go ahead and snicker if you must, but any show that has been on TV continuously for more than forty years and still draws an audience of over twenty million viewers daily is a cultural force to be reckoned with.

Once you accept the soap opera roots of the hospital drama, things become much clearer. Hospital dramas are ensemble shows, with complex and multithreaded plot lines. They're the dramatic equivalent to the variety show: in one room, we've got a team of doctors battling to save an aging grandmother with inoperable cancer; in the next room, there are the parents of a young accident victim wrestling with the decision to donate his organs; and when things start to get too tense, here's Topo Gigio and the Dancing Bears!

Or in CSI's case, a forensic lab work montage done as a short music video, with a pounding soundtrack and a lot of eye-popping close-ups and jumpy cuts between shots. Who knew that people in lab coats handling test tubes could be so sexy?

The scripts flip back and forth between short comedy skits, miniature dramas, and the further development of huge plot arcs that stretch over entire seasons, or in some cases, multiple years. In the hospital drama, it's the web of complicated and intertwining relationships between the cast members that keeps the show going, not the plot du jour. The *real* story that fans return to watch again and again lies in the professional disputes; in the feuds and friendships; in who's sleeping with whom, who's hoping to be sleeping with whom, and who was sleeping with whom last week but now has become their mortal enemy, immediate supervisor, and previous ex-girlfriend's new lesbian lover.

"Okay," you say, "that explains *ER*. But does this sort of thing really happen in Las Vegas? Miami? New York? Is CSI really, underneath it all, just a big-budget soap?"

Not entirely, but I do suggest that you take the time to ask a true-blue CSI fan to explain what's going on with Horatio's sister-in-law, Catherine's father, or Grissom and Sara's working relationship.

And when you do, make sure you're sitting in a comfortable chair, because you're going to be there for a long time.

The other weakness of the classic hospital drama is that it too readily bleeds over into doctor show clichés. No matter what else is going on, you just *know* they're going to find a way to save that adorable kid in Room 312B before the hour is out, unless it's *ER* and they haven't yet killed anybody else in this episode. But CSI neatly avoids this trap by the simple expedient of starting most shows with the adorable kid already dead!

In this way, CSI bridges the gap between the hospital drama and the **police procedural**. In this type of drama, the crime has already been committed before the episode begins, the story opens with the discovery of the crime, and the narrative typically focuses in a strictly linear fashion on the efforts of the investigators to gather evidence, interview witnesses, and determine exactly what has happened, why, and by whose hand.

Jack Webb's original 1949 *Dragnet* is the great-great-grandaddy of this entire trope, and for those of you too young to remember it, the show revolved around two plainclothes LAPD detectives and their strictly no-nonsense methods of working cases and solving crimes. Webb's Sergeant Joe Friday had little personality and no personal life—he apparently sprang fully grown from the brow of J. Edgar Hoover, and his deadpan delivery of "Just the facts, ma'am" became first a catchphrase and then a joke—but the original show had a long and successful run on both radio and television, and it spawned many imitators and three TV-series revivals.

If *Dragnet* originated the police procedural, the form reached its arguable apotheosis in *Law & Order*, a series which has run for sixteen years and spawned four spin-offs. *Law & Order* carries the police procedural to its logical final phase, the courtroom drama.

The problem with this concept is that, in the years since *Law & Order* first premiered, we've all seen far too many *real* courtroom dramas. The mechanisms and maneuvering of prosecution and defense are no longer all that fascinating. After watching, say, the antics of Johnnie Cochran during the O.J. Simpson trial, most of us have become perhaps just a tad jaded. By now everyone knows the verdict is not even the beginning of the end of the story; there will be appeals, and appeals of the appeals, and so on and so on, *ad infinitum*. A poll conducted today might well reveal that many Americans truly believe that a trial is a crapshoot, that facts and evidence have little or no influence on the judge and jury, and that the justice system is as likely to convict an innocent man or free a drooling psychopath as it is to produce genuine justice.

CSI avoids this problem by the simple expedient of never showing us the trial.[4] At the end of a CSI episode we know the *truth*, and more often than not the killer is led off in handcuffs. What happens after that, well. . . .

Consider this: the old *Dragnet* shows always ended with the perp walk; that is, with the perpetrator being marched out to center-stage in handcuffs, while a stern narrator intoned, "On March 3rd, trial was held in Los Angeles Superior Court. The defendant was found guilty on all counts and sentenced to three consecutive life terms in the California state prison system with no possibility of parole."

In twenty-first-century America, it is impossible to watch those old shows now without having the little voice in the back of your head add, "One month later, this conviction was overturned by the Ninth Circuit Court of Appeals on the grounds that Detective Friday did not have adequate probable cause for his initial search of the suspect's vehicle and

---

[4] Unless, of course, it's necessary to kick off the next story with a jailbreak.

did not properly Mirandize the suspect prior to the initial interview. Mr. Manson was subsequently released without bail pending a new trial, and was last seen in San Diego, driving a hijacked bus full of Girl Scouts toward the Mexican border. Anyone having knowledge of the current whereabouts of Mr. Manson is asked to call *America's Most Wanted* at 1-800-CRIME-TV."

Will CSI someday jump the shark? Yes, of course it will. Being television, it's inevitable. Personally, I believe CSI will be over on the day they expand the franchise just one spin-off too far. There are only so many shows you can do in any given city before the venue becomes stale, but as suburban sprawl and *Law & Order* prove, unlimited expansion is bad, too. Even now, there are rumors being bandied about in fan circles of more spin-offs in the future: of *CSI: New Orleans*, which probably would have worked before Hurricane Katrina; of *CSI: London*, said rumors even mentioning the choice of title music, which seems like an ominous sign. Therefore, in the interests of saving us all a lot of time and grief, I would like to cut to the chase right now. I've already written a pilot script for CSI's final jump-the-shark spin-off series, and it begins like this:

```
"CSI: DULUTH"


FADE IN:


TITLE SEQUENCE: Fast panning helicopter shot, harbor
MUSIC UP: "Now I'm a Farmer" by The Who
CREDITS SUPERIMPOSED OVER FAST CUT MONTAGE: Close-ups of
    crime scenes, more panning shots of harbor, snowmobile
    being hauled up through hole in ice, black bear walking
    down main street, Torvaldson's Ford pickup truck tearing
    back and forth across the only bridge in town.
MAIN TITLE CARD:
CSI: DULUTH
MUSIC DOWN.
END TITLE SEQUENCE.
```

EXT. A COUNTRY ROAD - DAY, SNOWY

An accident scene on the side of the road. Police vehicles
   are parked with lights flashing. CSI LIEUTENANT LARS TOR-
   VALDSON arrives on the scene in his signature Northland
   Edition Ford F-350 diesel pickup truck, towing a snowmo-
   bile trailer. He gets out of the truck, pulls on mittens,
   then pulls on elbow-length, orange plastic deer-gutting
   gloves over the mittens.

TORVALDSON
So what do we got here, eh?

Tall, blonde, beautiful CSI INSPECTOR INGE INGEBRITSON
   snaps a photograph of a tire track in the snow and then
   straightens up.

INGEBRITSON
Well, we got this dead guy in this pickup truck wrapped
   around this tree here, doncha know.

Young CSI INSPECTOR TORVALD LARSON emerges from behind the
   wreck.

LARSON
And there must be, like 20 or 30 beers here in the truck,
   for sure. Mostly empty.

TORVALDSON
Leinenkugel's?

LARSON
You betcha! Hey, this one's still full!

Larson cracks the cap on the unopened bottle and laughs as
   beer sprays everywhere.

LARSON
Ho boy, are *they* shook up!

DULUTH PD DETECTIVE SVEN OLAFSON emerges from the under-
brush. He also is wearing plastic gutting gloves over
mittens and carrying a shotgun.

OLAFSON
Found the gun. Remington, 870 Wingmaster. The safety's
off.

Olafson sniffs at the gun cautiously.

OLAFSON
Uff da. It's been fired.

Olafson works the action, ejects a fired shotgun shell,
catches the fired shell in mid-air and examines it.

OLAFSON
Federal, three-inch magnum load, number 2 shot. Steel.

Torvaldson takes his sunglasses off, cocks his head to one
side, and delivers his trademark faraway look.

TORVALDSON
The fools. When will they learn that drinking, driving, and
duck hunting don't mix?

Pause and hold for a long moment on Torvaldson looking
thoughtful.

INGEBRITSON
Hey there, what's this?

Ingebritson stoops, picks up an object hidden in the weeds.

INGEBRITSON
(loudly, to others)
I got something here. It's a camcorder.

Ingebritson examines the camcorder more closely.

INGEBRITSON
It's still recording.

TORVALDSON
So our victim taped his own death, eh? See if you can play
    it back.

Ingebritson fiddles with the camcorder a bit. There is a
    quick burst of rewind noise, then --

VICTIM (VOICE OVER)
(soft and tinny sound from camcorder)
Hey, Larry! Hold my beer and watch *this*!

Bruce Bethke is best known for his award-winning science fiction, but he does write the odd mystery story now and then. His interest in the genre is inherited from his mother, who, after she retired from teaching, actually did become a licensed private detective and spent several years working for a large investigative agency. Thus it is with some immediate familiarity with the field that Bethke assures us that, despite what you've seen on TV, serious capital crimes are almost never investigated, much less solved, by inquisitive but charmingly eccentric little old ladies.

Bethke can be contacted through his Web site, www.BruceBethke.com.

P.S. And Mr. Zuiker, if *CSI: Duluth* gives you a buzz, Bethke's agent is waiting for your call.

When I read this essay, I laughed so hard an atomic absorption spectrophotometer came out my nose. No, really.

ADAM ROBERTS

CSI: Camera Slams Inside...

Who Killed John Doe?

Here's a distinctive CSI moment. John Doe is dead. His corpse is laid out on a metal slab in the gleaming autopsy room. The crime scene investigator is clear about the cause of death: "fatal gunshot wound."

As soon as he says the words the camera *shows us* a bullet penetrating a human torso. But, no—that sentence hardly captures the visceral intensity of the way this act is shown to us. In fact, the camera *becomes* the bullet as it bursts through the victim's flesh: it *zooms* in, thrusts through the rubber and computer-generated imagery of muscles, organs, blood vessels. We see the slug *rip* through the body's tissue.[1] We see blood

---

[1] Incidentally, whilst we're on the subject: Isn't it a striking thing that the medical term for the material out of which our bodies are *literally made up* is the same as the generic word for *Kleenex*? That makes me think of myself as if I could barely withstand the impact of a lump of *nasal phlegm*, let alone a bullet....Personally I think this has gone on long enough....Cows are made of "tissue" too, but we call their stuff "leather" or "beefsteak." Why can't we humans enjoy a similar terminological boost to our self-esteem? I'm going to start a petition to get doctors to stop calling our body-stuff "tissue" and start calling it something like *krunkstuff* or *toughweave* or something like that....If I truly believed my body was made of toughweave, I'd feel pretty much invulnerable.

welling out, or perhaps some yucky yellow goo that represents the infection that follows such a wounding. We are *inside* the body.

Who killed John Doe? *We* did, of course; by ramming a movie camera into his chest and through his inner organs.

Have you any idea how much those things *weigh*?

Now I know what you're going to argue. You want to say that you didn't ask the CSI people to cannonball two hundred pounds of TV camera into the poor fellow. That won't wash, I'm afraid. You are guilty by association. You're the one watching the show, pushing up its viewing figures, egging the producers on to more and more elaborate modes of killing people off.

I am not being altogether facetious when I say this. Well, truth to tell, I am being a *little* facetious. Let's say 45% facetious. The other 55% is semi-serious. I believe that the reason why CSI is as successful as it is has little to do with actual science. It is something distinctly modern, something very early twenty-first-century.

Throughout human history there have been various strategies for determining a person's guilt or innocence. CSI dramatizes the procedures for determining guilt that make most sense to us in our technologically saturated age; but it's perfectly possible to imagine CSIs from earlier epochs that dramatize the science of their days just as effectively.

Take the Victorians, for instance. It was in the nineteenth century that the first professional police forces were established, when many of the strategies for fighting crime were first laid down, when crime fiction was invented. You wouldn't think of the Victorians as soft on crime, would you? Of course not.

Crime Scene Victorians

The Victorians thought of crime as something committed by a specific class of people: the criminal classes. Individuals from the non-criminal classes occasionally committed crimes, of course, but that was very much seen as aberration. The policing of crime largely was based upon the constabulary keeping an eye on "known criminals," people who by a strange coincidence also happened to be almost all of them poor, working-class men and women, immigrants, foreigners. Funny that. Victorians themselves certainly talked unembarrassedly of "the criminal classes" as almost a separate class of humans.

The most influential proponent of this way of thinking was an Italian called Cesare Lombroso (1835–1909). Lombroso believed that, whereas most human beings had evolved, the criminal type had *devolved*, and his or her criminality could be identified by what he called "atavistic stigmata," amongst which he specified: large jaws, high cheekbones, sharp or beaky noses, fleshy lips, sloping foreheads and over-prominent ears. Lombroso argued that criminality could be inherited from one's parents. He was crackers, of course; but his crackerishness didn't stop him having widespread influence on the criminology of his day.

Once you've decided that what you're doing is looking for a criminal type rather than trying to solve a specific crime, various strategies that would otherwise be dismissed as irrelevant come into play. In the nineteenth century, for instance, phrenology, the "science" of reading the bumps of people's skulls, was recruited into the service of fighting crime, as were equally dubious pseudo-scientific methods such as measuring the angle of a person's forehead-and-nose line—the more vertical the better, the more horizontal the worse. "Scientific" racism has its tangled and ugly roots in this soil—the Irish, for instance, were thought to be "naturally" prone to crimes of drunkenness and violence (although, oddly, not particularly sex crimes); people from the Far East were thought of as "naturally" devious and cruel. That all this was nonsensical boondoggle of the most specious sort did not stop it from being very widely believed.

CSI: Old London Town

Theme song: The Who, "Happy Jack"

SCENE: *A large London room in 1889. Glass cases and boxes of insects are located all around; at the center sits* Sherlock Holmes, *looking rather more rounded and indeed chubby than you might have thought: close cut hair, casual clothes.*
Enter Police Inspector Lestrade

Lestrade: You'll be pleased to hear, Mr. Holmes, that we have finally apprehended Jack the Ripper!

Holmes (*attending to his bug collection, not looking at Lestrade*): Have you, now?

LESTRADE: It is Sir William Gull, physician to the Queen herself. He has himself confessed to being the murderer of
half a dozen ladies of low morals.

HOLMES (*snapping on a pair of latex gloves as he stands up*):
I'm afraid, Inspector, that you have the wrong man.

CUT TO: *Sir William Gull, sitting in a police cell. The camera zooms rapidly and pans, swooping like a kestrel onto
the bridge of Gull's nose.*

HOLMES (*in voice over*): As you can see, the angle of his forehead and the purely Roman aquiline profile of his nose make
it scientifically impossible for him to be a murderer. [*The
camera lurches up, and then strikes cobra-like forward to
disappear into Gull's hair. It moves through the enormous-
ly magnified strands of hair as a panther might through the
long pampas grass of the South American uplands, until it
comes to a large, pale-gray lump rising out of the scalp*].
I also had Watson do a phrenological prominence assessment. The lumps on Gull's skull are scientifically incom-
patible with the skull of a murderer.

LESTRADE (*heartily*): Thank heavens for your scientific know-how,
Holmes! I'll order his immediate release. To think we nearly prosecuted the wrong man—and all because of a written
confession, the testimony of six eye witnesses, and finding
him with his elbows in the abdomen of a murdered woman!

HOLMES: Hey, don't mention it.[2]

---

[2] For no very good reason I feel that, at this juncture, I should mention Terry Pratchett's science of
retrophrenology, which he first described in his Discworld novel *Men at Arms*: "Phrenology, as everybody knows, is a way of reading someone's character, aptitude, and abilities by examining the
bumps and hollows on their head. Therefore—according to the kind of logical thinking that char-
acterizes the Ankh-Morpork mind—it should be possible to *mold* someone's character by *giving*
them carefully graded bumps in all the right places. You can go into a shop and order an artistic
temperament with a tendency to introspection and a side order of hysteria. What you actually *get*
is hit on the head with a selection of different size mallets, but it creates employment and keeps the
money in circulation, and that's the main thing."

Twentieth-century criminology, of course, has radically changed its philosophy about the proper way to address crime. It is now embedded in the legal and constitutional texts of almost all countries that individuals are never tried for *being a criminal*; they are always tried for *committing a specific crime on a specific occasion*. And quite rightly, too: this cornerstone of modern jurisprudence forces the police to acquire evidence that relates to the crime itself, rather than simply arresting likely looking individuals. It means that if a man is being tried for (say) rape, the prosecution is not permitted to mention previous convictions for rape he may have on his record. To do so would turn the trial into a matter of judging the individual's character rather than proving a crime.

But the older philosophy of criminology has died hard. There are, for instance, plenty of people who think that this is wrongheaded to keep suspects' criminal records from the court. If you were on a jury that convicted a man of rape, and then were told (as juries often are, post-verdict) that the man in question had previous convictions for rape, wouldn't you feel vindicated, as if this *proved* that you had made the right decision?

It's hard to deny that thinking of some people as prone to crime and others as "essentially" decent still informs a great deal of our thinking. It's not "scientific," but there are good reasons for it. It allows us, for instance, to be indulgent of our own lapses. Our fury at the other bad drivers on the roads reflects a belief that they are perennially bad drivers, and that they should be banned from the road for the safety and benefit of everybody else. But if *we* happen to drive badly—run a red light, narrowly avoid hitting a cyclist—then it is a merely *temporary* lapse that in no way reflects upon our broader abilities as drivers.

One of the strengths of CSI as a crime drama is that its focus is wholly upon the crime rather than on the character of the criminal. In any individual episode of CSI pretty much *any* of the characters could be guilty. This is the standard strategy of whodunits, you might say: a dozen or so characters, each of whom could plausibly have done it. Isn't that the point of a whodunit?[3] Of course, in most whodunits *motive* plays as large a part as the practical features of crime commission; the classical whodunit is as much about character as about ingenious solution to mystery. Here's one small example of what I mean from Agatha Christie.

---

[3] One question: why *dun*? Can someone please explain what's wrong with *done*?

I don't want to give anything away, but should you read a Christie whodunit, test out this rule of thumb. If there is a doctor amongst the cast list, especially a senior doctor—*he's your murderer*. Christie, it seemed, really didn't trust doctors.

To put it another way; modern whodunits don't tend to follow a Victorian physiognomatic notion of criminality. It would be hard to maintain dramatic interest if they did (eleven normal-looking people, and one with sloping forehead, large jaw, fleshy lips, and huge ears...ah! *he's* your man!). At the start of the standard whodunit all the characters could be guilty, but equally all could be innocent. A good whodunit is one in which, by the end, we understand why this one character was deceiving us about his or her actual nature; we believe that they were capable of the crime.

But CSI is much less interested in the character of the murderer, perhaps because with so much high-tech stuff to dramatize there's relatively little space in the show to develop such an interest. The character focus is shifted away from the murder suspects and onto the investigating team. We become involved in *their* interactions, their respective quirks and oddities (Warrick Brown's gambling addiction, Mac Taylor's insomnia), after the manner of superior soap opera. But the time given over to this characterization, combined with the time spent on dramatizing the scientific investigation and reconstructions of the crime, leaves very little space for developing the suspects as characters.

In a striking way this makes the show much more modern than many whodunits. The focus is always on a specific crime, and almost never on the unscientific business of the character of the criminal. This, I think, is what makes the show so distinctively modern; not the science labs and flashy visuals, but this simple shift away from character. It's why it is so hard to imagine a pre-twentieth-century version of the show. In those days the purpose of a trial was to use the "science" of the day (such as it was) to reveal the true nature of individuals.

CSI: Salem
Theme song: The Who, "A Quick One Whilst He's Away"

SCENE: *A seventeenth-century Massachusetts courtroom, packed
    with people, all dressed in black. An* EXCITABLE TEENAGE GIRL,

who clearly hasn't been sleeping too well, is at the witness stand. Her eyes dart hither and yon.

EXCITABLE TEENAGE GIRL (*pointing*): I saw Goody Hannigan with the devil! I saw Goody Moore with the devil! I saw Goody Richmond with the devil and she kissed his beard!

Enormous commotion in court.

REDHEADED WITCH SCENE INVESTIGATOR (*taking off sunglasses, putting them on again, standing at forty-five degrees to the witness*): And yet, Missy Hoggart, our scientific investigation has been concluded that Goody Richmond *must* be innocent. . . .

EXCITABLE TEENAGE GIRL: No! It's a lie! A lie!

REDHEADED WSI (*taking off sunglasses and gesturing at the witness with them*): My team conducted extensive dunking-stool tests upon all three suspects.

CUT TO *GOODY RICHMOND in dunking stool. As the stool starts to dip toward the water the camera dashes precipitously toward her terrified face. At the very moment that she is submerged the camera seemingly surfs the wave of pond water breaking into her open mouth, riding with it down her gullet and into her lungs.*

REDHEADED WSI (*gravelly voice over*): The testing was unambiguous. Goody Richmond took twelve pounds of pond water into her lungs and drowned, proving her innocence. The only conclusion we can draw, speaking scientifically, is that *you* lied. Now why would you do that. . . *unless you were a witch, yourself*?

CUT BACK TO *Courtroom. The commotion is even more enormous than before.* REDHEADED WSI *is walking toward the exit, his*

sunglasses back on his head, as two burly officers take
Excitable teenage girl *into custody.*

Excitable teenage girl (*struggling in the iron grip of the depu-
    ties, and crying out desperately*): I saw the devil! I saw
    the devil and he has red hair! *Red* hair!

Dodgy Science

I could fill the rest of this essay with examples of places where CSI gets
the science wrong, or where it presents cases as tied-up and watertight
when in fact no court in the land could possibly convict on the evidence
presented. But (a) there's not space for this, and (b) it misses the point
anyway.

In a celebrated original *CSI* moment, blue clay is poured into a knife
wound, and pulled out again as a perfect replica of the murder weapon. Now, if a corpse were made of close-packed damp sand this strategy
might *just about* work. But human bodies are not made of sand, close-
packed or otherwise. In fact, as anybody over the age of seven would
rush to point out, pouring blue clay into a stab wound would result in
blue clay worming its way through various inner crevices and rents of
the body. The resulting shape, assuming it could be extracted, would
look like an avant-garde hatstand, not a dagger.[4]

In the *CSI: NY* second-season episode "City of the Dolls" (2-9) a waitress was found dead in her apartment. The CSI team proved that she
was poisoned, and were able to pin the crime on her neighbor. The
murderer's motive was that he wanted her to die so that he could buy
her apartment and knock through to extend his place. A pretty slender
motive, it seems to me (there was no guarantee that he'd get the apartment, and no indication that he'd considered, say, just moving to a larger apartment rather than risking the death penalty for murder). But, as I
said, the show isn't strong on motivation and character. What I'm interested in here is the evidence the CSI team presented. They determined
that he had bought her some herbal teabags, opened them, put in some
arsenic, and then closed them up again. They knew this because there
was rosin dust in with the arsenic-teabag mixture. The neighbor was a

---

[4] This is not to rule out the possibility that a future episode of CSI will involve a murder committed by an avant-garde artist wielding his multi-pronged hatstand.

violin player. He used the rosin on his violin bow, and rubbing the stuff up and down the strings sent a near-invisible cloud of rosin dust into the air, to settle on surfaces—including inside the teabags, whilst he had them open to add the arsenic. The CSI team also showed, by obtaining his credit card receipts, that the suspect had spent $7.95. This was the exact price of the herbal teabags. Faced with this evidence the suspect broke down and confessed.

Open and shut, no?

Um? Is there any lawyer in the country (even Lionel Hutz from *The Simpsons*) who couldn't rip that evidence to shreds in *any* courtroom and before *any* jury? Is there any way, even in the land of the magically precise science of CSI, to link the rosin in the teabags with the suspect? Is there nobody else in New York who uses rosin? Is it possible to conceive that the suspect might have spent $7.95 on *something else*? Why did this guy break down and confess? Not because he'd been caught, but because the drama of the piece required things to be rounded off neatly at the end.

But I'm being picky; the exactitude or correctness of the science isn't really the point of either of these episodes. The criterion here is not reality, but a sort of corporeal *intimacy*. They are dramatic devices designed to encourage us imaginatively to enter into the world. The rosin dust makes us think more fully about things that normally don't occur to us—as do those scenes where firing a handgun is shown as dusting the hand holding the weapon with gunpowder residue. The blue clay is there for us to think of the body not as a sort of black box whose innards are mysterious, but as a physical fact with internal as well as external coherence. In both cases the show does its job: we take a little less for granted; we pay closer attention to the unconsidered consequences of what we do.

Modern criminology is not the first to consider *bodily innards* the way to the heart of mysteries. There are different sciences that certain historical eras have applied to those questions.

CSI Ancient Rome
Theme song: The Who, "Boris the Spider"

SCENE: Caesar *lies on the floor of the senate, his body a*

bloody mess. The SENATORS *stand around aghast.* BRUTUS *and the other* CONSPIRATORS *are standing a little way off, still holding their steaming daggers.*

LEADER OF THE SENATE (*eyeing* BRUTUS *nervously, and most especially the bloodstained dagger he holds in his hand*): The, er, dictator is slain. Clearly...um...a work of civic virtue has been performed here. It goes without saying that, that, there has been no crime....

SOOTH "CRIME SCENE" SAYER: I must disagree, honored patrician. We have brought the most recent scientific methods to bear on the problem, and guilt has been assigned! (*He is a short, dark-haired, rather punctilious man.*)

SENATOR: Look, there's no need for that....

SOOTH—CSI—ER (*loudly*): Beware!

CUT TO: *A goat. The camera performs a double-back somersault, spins around, and zooms to a tight close-up on a knife. P.O.V. then follows the knife as it stabs and slices through the neck of the goat, slicing it in one swift movement. The camera P.O.V. then goes inside the still-pulsing carotid artery, and swims piranha-like along this red tube. We swoop and jink through dimly lit inner cavities, and then pass through a series of minor capillaries into a dark space. A gash of light opens up in the darkness: it is the knife, cutting into the abdomen from outside. The camera rides the splurging, tumbling mass of viscera out into the sunlight. Fingers pick up and examine the liver and kidneys of the beast; prodding, holding them up. The camera follows a lobe of one glistening, red chunk of tissue as it is hacked off with a knife and tossed into a griddle. The smoke goes upward.*

SOOTH—CSI—ER: We performed a thoroughly scientific investigation upon the liver of a goat bred without a flaw. The omens pointed to *one thing* and *one thing only* as behind this attack in the integrity of our leader. (*He flings his arm out, pointing accusingly at nobody in particular.*) Arab terrorism! Two things I will never compromise...the integrity of the saying of sooths, and the defense of this country!

Dead Bodies

Why is contemporary popular culture so fascinated by dead bodies? It's not just the various CSIs, with their weekly parade of corpses. It's also *Six Feet Under*, five extremely successful seasons of which ran on HBO between June 2001 and August 2005. Every episode of that show began with a death; the main characters were morticians and funeral directors, and the arranging and disposing of corpses was the main business on screen. On *Six Feet Under* dead characters interacted with and chatted to living ones all the time—it was a show, in other words, about the way the living and the dead are actually in dialogue all the time. And there are plenty of other examples. On Showtime's *Dead Like Me*, a comic TV drama about a group of "grim reapers" working in Seattle, all the main characters are dead. ABC's *Desperate Housewives* is narrated by character Mary Alice Young, a dead woman. Think of *The Sixth Sense* (1999) with its slogan-tastic "I see dead people!" Or think of a best-selling novel like Alice Sebold's *The Lovely Bones* (Peter Jackson is presently in the middle of turning this into a movie)—a novel in which the whole touching, funny, sad story is told from beyond the grave by the main character, Susie Salmon.

Dead characters in popular culture are in itself nothing new, of course: think of all the zombie films and stories of ghostly hauntings you've ever seen in your life. What's different in these cases is that a fundamental shift has happened. Zombies are repellent, revolting; ghosts are scary, off-putting. In both cases, the point of films about them is to express our natural revulsion at the thought of death. We don't want to die; we want to carry on living. Death offends our sense of being alive. It's a taboo subject.

But the title of Sebold's novel is a significant thing. Her dead bones are, in their way, lovely. Instead of shying away from corpses, or from death, our contemporary culture, and our TV culture in particular, is increasingly drawn toward it. Why?

I'll tell you my theory. Previous ages, like the Victorian, also demonstrated a fascination with death, but this fascination was not with *corpses*. It was with the much more important process of *dealing with bereavement*: with funerals and the rituals of mourning; with what to wear and how to act; with how long to perform grief and at what point to restart one's life again. For them death was not so much a physical matter—or it would be more accurate to say that the physical features of death were the least important part of it. The Victorians believed, most of them, in a spiritual afterlife, and were content to dismiss the loved one to that unimaginable, non-bodily realm. All that was left were the social loose ends of the people left behind, and the Victorian protocols of mourning were designed to deal with that.

Do you know what I think? I think we don't really trust "spirit" anymore; most of us don't *believe* in a spiritual afterlife. Not in the bone. Of course there are many people, both those who are devoutly religious and those who believe in spirit-mediums, crystals, ghosts, and astral planes, who will disagree with me on this. But bear with me.

Ours is a material age. Science, our dominant mode of understanding the world around us, can only deal in *material* terms. Ghosts, heaven, and all such spiritual matters are outside its realm. And most of us, I think, find it hard to imagine what a spiritual world might be like *except in material terms*. If we think of dead people it must be in some way that interacts with our material universe; knocking on tables, speaking to us, things like that. A film like *Constantine* (2005) creates a *literal* material hell, just below the streets of San Francisco—devils that you can touch and talk to, an afterlife you can *feel* with your body's nervous system. Do you really think a spiritual dimension would be like that? Or is it just that we can't imagine anything outside our own experience of living in a bodily, physical, material way?

I think it's the latter. I think science has so far succeeded, even with people who think of themselves as "religious" or "spiritual," that we can only imagine death in physical and material terms. A corpse is a physical, material icon of deadness. That's where our fascination focuses now.

At the same time, we don't want to acknowledge all the implications of a radical materialism. Naturally, we want to live on past death. That's why wealthy people get their bodies (or their *heads*) frozen in cryogenic facilities—they cannot imagine any survival of death except the physical.

This is the heart of CSI's drama. It dramatizes death, which makes us anxious. But then it shows us, in various intimate ways, that dead people can still talk to us, still tell us things: tell us things like *this is how I died, this is what my life was like before, this is who I am.*

The beauty of the show is in showing us a way to have this conversation with the dead that doesn't involve spirit mediums or Ouija boards. Science has replaced spirituality, and its message is that death is not the end. This is the underlying rationale of the series. Its audience understands this, perhaps at a subconscious level. This is why CSI is so successful.

It says that our bodies will tell our story, even when we're dead. And because our stories will live on, then in a way we will live on.

Who killed John Doe?

Why not ask him directly?

Adam Roberts is a writer and academic from London, England. He prides himself on his collection of The Who albums. No, really, he's got a whole load of The Who albums, and a lot of the solo stuff that Pete Townshend did as well. Moreover, he once saw Townshend in the flesh, going into a fish-and-chip shop in Richmond, Surrey. If the producers of any further CSI shows need any advice on which The Who tracks to use on their soundtrack, they can contact him via Royal Holloway, University of London.

Katherine Ramsland wrote the excellent book *The Forensic Science of CSI*, which I turned to more than once in writing my own CSI novels. Here she offers an insightful analysis of not the science but the philosophy of each show's lead character.

KATHERINE RAMSLAND

IQ, EQ, and SQ
Grissom Thinks and Caine Feels, but Taylor Enlightens

WHEN *CSI: CRIME SCENE INVESTIGATION* spun off from Las Vegas to Miami and then to New York City, the writers took pains to make the programs distinct. The character of each city assisted that process, but among the calculated approaches was the creation of different temperaments for the three crime lab supervisors. Thus, Gil Grissom, Horatio Caine, and Mac Taylor, as early as their first appearances, demonstrate diverse methods of team leadership and, possibly without intent on the part of their creators, also represent different aspects of the human experience: head, heart, and spirit. (These characters may yet evolve, so this analysis centers on their most persistent features thus far.) For centuries philosophers have debated over which of these should lead life's dance, and if only Plato, Kant, and Descartes had watched *CSI*, they might have spared themselves the trouble. The answer is clear.

Each supervisor has a specific philosophy that influences his work.

Grissom (the head) adopts a mental stance, eschewing emotion to analyze crime scenes with logic, esoteric knowledge, and the scientific method; Caine (the heart) builds on this approach by not only analyzing crimes but also allowing empathy for victims to be his driving force; while Taylor (the spirit) not only thinks and cares but also enlarges his personal perspective by recognizing the part that crime investigators play in a complex universe. That is, we can imagine the three CSI leads as operating within expanding circles of light, with Grissom's the most constricted in focus: Grissom's sense of purpose manifests through the intellect, Caine's grows beyond that into compassion, and Taylor's expands even further to transcend personal limits and grasp how "it's all connected." Collectively, Grissom, Caine, and Taylor represent the ideal forensic scientist: passionate and compassionate, guided toward justice, purpose, and innovation. Grissom was a good start and Caine a qualified advance, but it's Taylor's sense of perspective, gained via searching for higher meaning, that moves the investigative enterprise into genuinely profound territory.

The Head

First impressions are calculated on CSI, so for our base of analysis, let's examine the introductory episodes for each character: Grissom encountered a perplexing suicide, Caine a kidnapped child, and Taylor a cross-jurisdiction homicide.

Grissom took a while to develop. In the pilot episode, Royce Harmon was found dead in his bathtub, with a gunshot wound to the chest and a suicide note recorded on a cassette. Grissom dutifully played the tape for Harmon's mother, who declared it was not his voice. That revelation forced the team to review the scene as a homicide staged as a suicide. Seeking more evidence, they found a fingerprint with latex flakes, but this had turned up only a docile latex parts dealer, Paul Millander, who used his own hand as a model, fingerprints and all. Anyone who purchased the part could have planted the print. (Grissom erroneously dismissed Millander as a suspect; Millander was certainly within that population.)

During this case, Grissom posed as a modern-day Sherlock Holmes, a popular fictional character famous for his ability to accurately deduce from obscure clues the direction an investigation should take. Holmes is emotionally detached and largely preoccupied with puzzles. He can read a lot from a first impression, and he is honing his power of observation at all times. As he tells his sidekick, Dr. Watson, it's not that he *observes* more than others do; it's that he *deduces* more, and that makes the difference in what he brings to a crime scene. To prepare himself to devise rich and informed hypotheses, he studies numerous exotic subjects. Grissom does the same, as Nick Stokes noticed in this episode, when Grissom pointed out minutiae about roof dust.

Like Holmes, Grissom prizes reasoned objectivity above all else, and when he dressed down Warrick during the Royce Harmon case in the pilot episode, he insisted, "There is no room for subjectivity." In "Pledging Mr. Johnson" (1-4), he criticized Catherine Willows's emotional involvement with certain cases. Even his mentoring style exclusively honors the intellect.

Although Grissom became increasingly intellectually oriented as the show continued, in the initial episode, he'd been on a date with a lab analyst, he smiled, acted a little crazy with Holly Gibbs, and even offered Holly compassion. In later episodes, we didn't see much of that behavior again. Rather, Grissom's associates noted his inability to engage appropriate emotions. When he had the chance during the first season to develop a romance with an attractive forensic anthropologist who showed an interest in him, he opted to focus instead on his job, from which he derived his ultimate satisfaction. Even in our initial impressions during the first episode, Grissom showed little regard for ordinary social protocol, as if he'd been buried too long in work.

Josh Berman, formerly executive story editor on the show and now an executive producer, comments on Grissom's personality, "I think Grissom is more comfortable in the lab and with dead people than with the living," he says. "He grew up in a quiet household, as his mother was deaf and his father died while he was young. Science provides answers and Grissom is most comfortable when the 'human factor' is not part of the equation. I think he's tried to take baby steps in his interpersonal relationships, but then he quickly retreats to the comfort of the familiar."

As a result, Grissom is the consummate scientist, preferring to throw mannequins in systematically diverse ways off a building rather than substitute a computer simulation ("I like to see it," he says in "Cool Change," 1-2); he's surrounded by various species of bugs, and he's dogged about sticking with evidence ("what cannot lie," as he calls it in the pilot), no matter where it takes him. So he follows the stereotype of the detached intellectual, fully engaged with his projects. (At times, he has failed his own ideal of relying strictly on scientific verification, such as when he erroneously accepted as science an unempirical method called graphology, which purports to "read" personality traits from a person's handwriting.)

In retrospect, we realize that Grissom's encounter with Paul Millander was yet another emphasis on his intellect. The latex dealer initially seemed to be only a distraction in this episode as Grissom dismissed him while trying to solve the crime, but because Millander was intelligent, clever, and intellectually strategic, later pitting himself directly against Grissom (placing his thumbprint over Grissom's as a challenge in the next suicide-in-a-bathtub case), it was clear from the first show that the writers considered Grissom's essence to be cerebral. His strength is his brain, so his key nemesis had to be "brainy" as well. By the second episode, Grissom had become the unit's head, literally, and as the series progressed, he evolved more clearly into the archetypal scientist buried in knowledge and scholarship. This was even juxtaposed with Horatio Caine's more emotional style in the episode that merged their efforts in a joint investigation.

So let's move on to Caine.

The Heart

When a child and her mother were kidnapped in Las Vegas and taken to Miami in "Cross-Jurisdictions" (*CSI* 2-22), Catherine Willows and Warrick Brown traveled to Little Havana to create a liaison with Caine's crew. It was this episode at the end of *CSI*'s second season that introduced the Miami team and revealed who Caine is.

His first scene presented him from behind as he stood apart from the team of official personnel coordinating a search for the missing child. While Caine was clearly a thinker, he had initially trained as a cop, not a scientist, so the show pitted his approach (action) against Grissom's (research). Yet Caine also has a special affinity with victims, and as the Miami-based series evolved, this feature gained prominence. Caine is deeply upset over what people do to others, especially to children, so he tries to view the world as the victim sees it and to make an extra effort to ensure they receive closure once a crime is solved. In this regard, he adds a dimension to Grissom's approach.

In this episode, Caine watched the team's activities and then walked in the opposite direction, as he believed a frightened child might do. He found her and, rather than signal to others her location, he sat beside her and remained quiet to correspond with her emotional aura. Before thrusting her into the urgency of the investigation, he showed respect for her concerns. Because he won her trust, when it came time to reveal the evidence she held, she delivered it to him. This attitude and behavior developed Caine as a man with heart—one who might dismiss Grissom's concerns about the corruption of "emotional involvement." While Caine does utilize logical analysis, his compassion adds greater fluidity to his investigative momentum.

Later in that same episode, when S.W.A.T. shooters took aim at a silhouette that they surmised was a killer in the act of attack, they ignored Willows's perception that the figure did not appear aggressive. But Caine heard her and responded. He recognized the possibility that an innocent person might come to harm, so he commanded a cautious and compassionate approach, even at the risk that the target might then complete an attack.

Giving Caine this introduction shows the depth of humanity that drives him, something that is not apparent in Grissom's early manifestations. While Grissom sides with knowledge, experiments, and factual evidence, Caine can tap into a wealth of emotional intelligence that lets him calculate the needs of the people his investigations involve. He's fully capable of the intellectual focus that Grissom applies but adds the extra dimension of compassion.

Emotional intelligence, popularly known as EQ and most often associated with psychologist Daniel Goleman, involves the ability to recognize emotions accurately in others and to effectively manage one's own. This allows for healthier social relationships, greater self-awareness, enhanced self-improvement, and increased generosity toward others. It provides a unique intersection of the heart and mind, balancing both for the most effective manner of living. When a situation requires compassion, such as when a parent loses a child or a co-worker needs some slack, Caine bends further than Grissom would, because even during an intense investigation that demands some distance, he ferrets out the golden moments of human connection.

For the third spin-off, similar to the way the Miami series was born, a crime in Miami with New York connections sent Caine to assist in a Big Apple investigation while helping his own. In the process, he passed the CSI baton to Mac Taylor.

The Spirit

A former marine, in *CSI: NY* Taylor occupies one of law enforcement's top—and busiest—positions. Yet he utilizes a more philosophical perspective than either Caine or Grissom, which allows him to work beyond his personal boundaries, both intellectual and emotional. That is, he adds yet another dimension, beyond both Grissom and Caine to the enterprise of dealing with good and evil: While Grissom focuses on solving crimes with an intellectual approach and Caine adds compassion for victims, Taylor sees meaning in bad things happening to good people, in a universe that offers both randomness and purpose. Thus, he achieves a certain perspective that offers him a greater range of options in solving his cases.

To illustrate their essential differences, if all three arrived together to a murder scene, Grissom would analyze it and apply science; Caine would analyze it but also offer comfort to the person most hurt by it; while Taylor would ponder how the diverse issues play out and consider what was most needed: analysis, comfort, or possibly something else not immediately evident. Grissom and Caine would both do what they do automatically (and do best), while Taylor might remain momentarily detached to consider more choices.

Taylor seeks to understand the full dimensions of criminal motivation, and as a law enforcement official in New York City, he's acutely aware of the losses sustained there during the most destructive terrorist attack ever made on the United States. Indeed, as a widower, he's experienced his own personal loss, which has forced him to confront life's complexity and to carry on with a deepened awareness of how much life can hurt. People may still end up dead or grieving no matter how they live: seemingly out of the blue on September 11, 2001, people going about their ordinary lives were disintegrated, burned, or forced to leap from high floors to the streets below. Their surviving loved ones had to come to terms with this horrendous event, and those who've managed best have formulated some larger purpose. Taylor is among them.

Spirituality is about connection. Sometimes that involves God and

religion, and sometimes just a commitment to human solidarity. It aris-
es from transcending personal boundaries. Experiments have demonstrated that consciousness occurs when the brain is fully awake, and the
more connected we are to others, the more "awake" we are to things beyond ourselves. A spiritual person can achieve a perspective that allows
greater vision and a broader range of choices than is available to those
who cling to restricted frames of reference.

Of the three CSI supervisors, Taylor is the most philosophical in this
regard. In fact, he's aware of the specific ideology that he applies to his
life and work, and in the first episode mentioned the profound thinker who has influenced him: Gabriele Veneziano, a theoretical physicist.
Since Veneziano's ideas relate directly to our understanding of Taylor's
approach to a crime scene, it pays to examine what this scientist proposed.

Veneziano was the father of "string theory," a conception of nuclear
particles and their interactions as one-dimensional vibrating strings that
he came up with in the late 1960s. Veneziano hoped to use this theory
to reveal the nature and behavior of atomic entities and thereby explain
everything in the universe. Like many quantum physicists, Veneziano
accepted the validity of Eastern as well as Western ideas. Eastern mystics have long considered the world to be organized according to religious principles through which everything is interrelated. Since this
truth is largely intuitive, these mystics try to bypass conceptual analysis to gain an undistorted experience of reality's quirks and complexi-
ties; they claim to achieve this through disciplined meditation. In the
process, they dispense with the linear abstractions so fundamental to
Western intellectualism and rely instead on suggestive metaphors that
represent indirectly the world's organic unity. To them, it seems obvious
that while we may need certain tools such as language and logic to focus
our attention, we should not confuse such tools for reality itself.

While Western scientists learned to appreciate that idea, especially as
the more mechanistic approach they inherited from nineteenth-century science proved inadequate, they nevertheless retained the theoretical
tools, taking full advantage of their potential for offering greater explan-
atory power. Throughout the twentieth century, the physicists developed one theory after another under the quantum umbrella, and string
theory, as an explanation of quantum particles, was among them.

Yet there were problems with this theory, so Veneziano failed to achieve his goal and his ideas fell out of favor. During the 1980s, however, it was discovered that the theory seemed to apply to the behavior of gravity in black holes, and string theory was re-invigorated, inspiring a "super-string revolution" that generated several versions of the theory. Then during the next decade, following the discovery that these diverse string theories converged into a larger theory scientists named "M-theory," which proposed eleven space-time dimensions, a second super-string revolution commenced. The impetus behind these efforts was to devise a single explanation for how it's all connected.

Taylor's appreciation of sophisticated physics indicates his grasp of both elementary and spiritual principles, i.e., his ability to keep perspective on any given situation from a broad vantage point that shows him how the parts interact and offers a range of choices for action. In his case, spirituality is not so much about religion as about the human ability to transcend the apparent reality of a specific situation. Indeed, the first shot of Taylor involved such perspective, as we viewed him from behind entering a crime scene, seeing the way into the room, the people already there, the room's size and furnishings, and the victim. And there were further hints of his attitude: Inside the building, he made everyone leave except a priest offering the victim last rites. Taylor respectfully waited for the holy man to finish, which signaled his spiritual side. No matter how urgent the situation, his actions seemed to say, it must be viewed through the lens of what most matters—something that is known best by those who comprehend a higher meaning.

Taylor exemplifies the notion of the "participant-observer," a term from cultural anthropology that denotes a person who engages in everyday living while also pondering its patterns. Participant observers do more than just make mental deductions about a situation; they constantly reflect on the big picture. It's as much of a God's-eye view on limited situations as any human can achieve.

At this point, Caine materialized to inform Taylor that he was there to investigate a double homicide in Miami that had connections to this incident. They bandied over jurisdiction and the death penalty, and Taylor was the one to step back to consider: he recognized that since everything is connected, if Florida gained custody of their killer, justice would be done in New York as well. He took the high ground and gave

Caine the nod, generously granting both what they wanted. Caine had a greater investment in claiming the case for the sake of the victim back in Florida, limiting his perspective to specific people and circumstances. For Taylor, justice for all eclipsed the jurisdictional lines and situation-specific issues. Background details in this scene emphasized his mystical approach: enduring paintings by great artists, the theme of "keys," and even the way high-rise Manhattan buildings joined earth to sky in the manner of cathedrals. In fact, the old morgue itself had a cathedral's arched windows.

Together, the New York and Miami teams solved both cases. As Caine left the city, he let Taylor take the credit, as if acknowledging that Taylor's generosity of spirit had placed him in a superior position. Caine had achieved his aim of getting closure for the victims' daughter, while Taylor's philosophy of connection was affirmed. This theme played out with Taylor in later episodes as well, such as when he informed a suspect in "Wasted" (2-12), being held because of evidence traced across several seemingly unrelated states, that, "It's a small world."

The fact that Taylor is a jazz musician emphasizes this connectivity as well. Jazz is an American-based improvisational art noted for its players' ability to merge simplicity with complexity. Like spirituality, it's about connection.

"The jazz player," says musician John Timpane, "must be master of her instrument and her performance. She must play for others, feel them, and play as she feels them. She must also be a master of technique, which means, among many other things, that she must have living resources within time, so that, if the music changes while she's playing live, she can go with it, do new things, explore. She must always be keyed in to the nuances of technique, tools, and language. The jazz player must be a slave of the emotions—she must know them, must know what moves, why it moves, where it comes from, where it goes, how it connects. And she must also be a slave of the body—she must accept its reactivity, its sexuality, its addiction to rhythm and sound. She must be a devotee to the body-in-rhythm, where the emotions and biology meet."

Whenever Taylor picks up an instrument to play jazz, it's a gesture that he's utilizing his full complement of resources in a connective rhythm that confirms his awareness of a universe larger than himself.

He can focus in an intellectual way when appropriate, use emotional intelligence, or adopt a spiritual approach that endows every situation with meaning and purpose.

But is this approach to crime analysis really better? Let's see what the philosophers say.

Reason vs. Passion

Many philosophers have based whole systems of thought on the notion that some human faculties (notably reason) are superior to others—notably passion. In fact, there is evidence that some intellectuals actually feared the damage that the "unruly" passions could do to systematic thought (and Grissom seems to be their heir). Reason, the dispassionate means for consideration of arguments and evidence, holds the grand position in Western culture as the way to truth. But a key question, then, is what kind of truth? Proponents of EQ insist that there are many types of truths, including intuitive realities that are better felt than analyzed and articulated.

But let's look at the tradition of rationalism, which prizes reason above all else. Socrates offered a vivid metaphor in which Reason is a charioteer managing the two unruly horses, Passion and Appetite. Following his ideas, the Stoics and Scholastics who opted for an intellectual tradition also viewed reason as the superior means of acquiring truth and living life. During the twelfth century, for example, French philosopher Peter Abelard advocated critical thinking above mere faith or religious authority. When considering a given situation or topic, he advised the use of a balance sheet of pros and cons, presenting all the known facts and using dialectical thought to move back and forth between the opposing lists until the right conclusion became evident. Many scholarly monks followed his example to claim that God had laid out the world in a logical design so that spiritually revealed truth is inherently rational: God simply makes sense. Other rationalists may not have agreed with the divinity of reason (or the reason of divinity), but the school of rationalism, which took many forms throughout successive centuries, believed in reason's authority.

On the other hand, Scottish philosopher David Hume argued that what we know comes from mental states or experience, and that morality is clearly a function of sentiment. Logic and reasoning can be too remote from life to adequately apply. "Reason is, and ought only to be, the slave of the passions," Hume stated, "and can never pretend to any other office than to serve and obey them." He saw that *both* approaches address aspects of human nature but *neither* exhausted the possibilities for truth.

Søren Kierkegaard, the nineteenth-century Danish philosopher credited with laying the foundation of existentialism, criticized the idea that humans could ever achieve complete objectivity. Who we are and how we live inevitably flavors what we think, so our style of being is part of our truth. When Grissom dresses down Warrick for "subjective interference," for example, Kierkegaard would say that he appears to have forgotten that no human being is completely objective and also still human. Only if we incorporate that awareness into our systems of thinking will we achieve an accurate sense of reality. Indeed, for Kierkegaard, passion was the key to life's momentum, including scientific activities.

Thus, rather than put the head and the heart in opposition, as if one must instruct the other, we must utilize both in proper balance. Overemphasis on either generates a certain amount of blindness. So to correct it and avoid tunnel vision, we may look to a term that no one has yet coined but which works well in this context: "SQ," or the measure of spiritual intelligence. A participant-observer could effectively utilize the contributions of both head and heart, noting when either is most appropriate, giving him or her the advantage. So let's get some perspective.

Pathfinders

The idea of objectivity as espoused by Grissom involves keeping the mind clear of emotional involvement, which could influence the interpretation of a crime analysis: if you care too much about experimental results, you might inadvertently create conditions that skew the results in a particular way, thereby interfering with the scientific process. Yet in reality, contrary to this approach, if you don't care at all, not much science is going to get done. The scientists who transcend a situation to understand that passion motivates the process while mental activity keeps it ordered, uncluttered, and organized are the ones who will likely make the greater contribution. They will see how it's all connected, utilize reason in its proper context, and channel their passions to fuel their drive to achieve their goal.

Throughout the 1990s and especially into the twenty-first century, the impetus toward integrating investigations with knowledge gained in the lab has been a priority. The application of "DNA fingerprinting" may have provided the impetus. When Sir Alec Jeffreys discovered how to map DNA in 1984, it was an alert detective seeking justice for two murdered girls who realized how this new science might help. He was right about the application, the killer was identified, and law enforcement has never been the same.

In fact, the history of forensic science is thick with scientists or medical men who saw the application of their work to the justice system and who stepped forward, despite resistance, to prove the value of science for crime investigation. Today, that same idea plays out on both sides, with law enforcement and science both looking over each other's shoulders to find or create the connection. As such, there have been surprising breakthroughs in cases that might not otherwise have been solved.

For example, in May 1992, investigators in Phoenix, Arizona, questioned Mark Bogan as a suspect in a murder but had no real evidence against him, except some scratches on his truck bumper that could have damaged a palo verde tree near the victim's nude body, and some seeds in the truck bed. Bogan's father's pager lay near Denise Johnson, who had been strangled and bound, but Bogan claimed that he'd had consensual sex with her before they had argued and parted; he claimed she had stolen the pager. Since the circumstances were suspicious but left room for doubt, the investigators would have to conclusively link Bogan's trunk with the damaged tree to make an arrest. Investigators wondered whether trees have identifying DNA the way humans and animals do. They decided to find out.

Dr. Timothy Helentjaris, a professor of molecular genetics, agreed to test the pods found in the truck. Using Randomly Amplified Polymorphic DNA, he compared the various trees in the area against one another and was able to match the crime-related pods from Bogan's truck bed to the tree with the gashes on the trunk. With this physical evidence, along with a witness report of a white truck in the area and other circumstantial evidence, Bogan was convicted of first-degree murder. An appeal challenged the DNA analysis, but it failed in 1995 and the conviction stood.

A similar meeting of minds (and hearts) occurred after the September 11, 2001, terrorist bombing at the World Trade Center in New York. Amelogenin is the major protein component of tooth enamel and it produces X and Y chromosome-specific products. Co-amplification of amelogenin with the loci used for short tandem repeat (STR) in DNA testing provides a type of gender-identity test. Even a small sample can be tested, which offered practical applications in the aftermath of the mass homicide. Some three thousand victims had to be identified, many of whom were in tiny pieces or incinerated down to bone fragments, and less than half of the more than 12,000 fragments that went through an initial screening process provided identifying information via conventional DNA technology. To improve the success rate, several laboratories tried out innovative techniques, and among them was one with improved sensitivity in amelogenin testing. The emotional impact of the attack had inspired scientists to use their heads in ways they might not have otherwise, and they were able to identify more victims for families.

Cold case squads, too, rely on knowledgeable professionals who also care enough to persist. Sophia Silva was kidnapped from her front yard in September 1996 and turned up dead shortly thereafter. Based on fiber evidence, police detained a suspect. Seven months later in the same area, a pair of sisters, Katie and Kristin Lisk, were also murdered. Based on the similar *modus operandi*, the police believed the cases were related, but the Silva suspect had been locked up during the Lisk incident. Conceding they might have been wrong, detectives on the Silva case asked the FBI to re-examine the fiber evidence, and the initial analysis turned out to have been incorrect. However, re-examination did link the two incidents. Yet the cases went cold until June 24, 2002, when a teenage girl reported a rape and provided an address. Police investigated Richard Evonitz, a convicted sex offender who had once lived near the Silva and Lisk crime scenes. Members of the task forces joined South Carolina detectives to search Evonitz's apartment. Fiber evidence collected there was consistent with the earlier cases' evidence, and a set of prints inside his car matched Katie Lisk, but before they could arrest him, he committed suicide.

In working on these cases, human beings are the key—people who care enough to go over and above what the job calls for, who are innovative and who seek justice for the victims. They're trained to think through a case and to obtain the knowledge required to solve it correctly. While they may find success by employing DNA testing or some other high-tech approach not available when the incident occurred, they can also gain from new perspectives—including admitting an initial analysis may have been wrong. Thus, thanks to the analytical functions of the mind, the motivation of concern, and the ability to employ alternate perspectives, cold cases even decades old are now getting solved.

As well, new ideas are being generated for future application. Computer simulation programs for diagnosing disease have become a new frontier for medicine, and are applicable as well to forensic medicine. "Virtautopsy," for example, produces a 3-D image of a body's condition, forgoing the need to cut and dissect. A combination of CT scans and MRIs can detect ailments and anomalies in the organs and muscles. For certain conditions, pathologists can go right to the heart, so to speak. The procedure eliminates the risk of destroying forensic evidence, such as a bullet trajectory path, and digitized images can be sent to other pathologists for consultations.

A computer technique called agent-based modeling is already assisting medical researchers to understand complex interactions within the human body. They're working now with simulated images of immune cells to watch how they direct an attack on an infection. The program gives each type of "player" a set of rules for its behavior and then puts different types into motion together on a computer screen to see what happens. The researchers can vary the environmental properties and apply a timeline to learn more about the effects on the interactions. The program's results inspire ideas for further laboratory tests just as an initial round of laboratory tests would, but can do so at a much faster pace. While this application is limited during an autopsy, since it requires living organisms that interact, it may offer insight on pathological conditions that accompany the death process, such as in a poisoning or for disease-based deaths that are difficult to diagnose postmortem.

Clearly, the forensic pathfinders are the scientists and investigators who think outside the box, joining their diverse activities in unique ways, and that means tapping into the head, heart, and spirit—our best resources. Collectively, Grissom, Caine, and Taylor show the benefits of working within a triad of logic, compassion, and spiritual perspective, but Taylor's approach—his broad application of awareness to evaluate a given situation for the most appropriate approach—has the best chance at avoiding the blind spots associated with too much or too little head or heart.

Scientists and investigators should take note: Before either discipline can benefit, or benefit from, the other, both must have knowledge of the other. Since unique applications involve painstaking work, the participants must care enough about victims, their families, and justice itself to see it through. Just as importantly, contemporary forensic personnel, whether investigators, technicians, or scientists, would do well to embrace the enlightened notion that "it's all connected," and let it inspire them to reach beyond their own field to seek new applications and investigative tools.

Katherine Ramsland has a Ph.D. in philosophy and masters degrees in both forensic and clinical psychology, and has published hundreds of articles and twenty-seven books, including *The Forensic Science of CSI* and *The CSI Effect*. For many years she taught philosophy at Rutgers University and now teaches forensic psychology at DeSales University. She also writes forensic features for Court TV's *Crime Library*.

The CSI franchise is renowned as much for its distinctive style as its cutting-edge technology. Here, Janine Hiddlestone puts each of the shows' different palettes under the microscope.

JANINE HIDDLESTONE

All That Glitters
Coloring Place and Identity in *CSI*

THE NEWS THAT JERRY BRUCKHEIMER, executive producer of two decades of big-screen, enormous-budget guilty pleasures, was producing a television series was greeted with mixed feelings. Any given Bruckheimer film is often spoken of in a tone of derisive superiority by critics and film-going intelligentsia alike, though mysteriously, possibly through some sort of celluloid osmosis, most members of both groups have still seen the film in question. He is a filmmaker who, along with his former partner, the late Don Simpson, has had substantially more hits than misses, a stable full of award-winning actors and directors, and has become a brand name that is a license to print money. But he also possesses a unique style, usually making his stamp on a film unmistakable. Whether it is the tense drama of *Black Hawk Down* or the campy adventure of *Armageddon*, there is always one constant and it is not the stuff exploding: it is the cinematic style and the trademark color saturation.

Color style has been an important part of the Bruckheimer recipe since early box office successes such as *Top Gun*. Revisiting these films now, the cinematography still looks fresh and attractive. The use of tints, bright vistas, and color-saturated skies has become as much a part of the Bruckheimer cinema experience as the innocuous ballad at the end of the movie. But the notion of bringing the distinctive visual style to the small screen was the least disconcerting aspect of the idea of Bruckheimer television. How was he going to manage a new action blockbuster every week? There was, of course, a simple answer to this quandary; he did not make an action blockbuster. It was too easy to underestimate Bruckheimer. He delivered a television show that was almost the polar opposite of his films—with the exception of the cinematic style and quality. That style and quality was an integral part of the story: as much a character as Grissom, as much a theme as following the evidence, and as much a plot device as the ideal of justice.

While the style delivered by Bruckheimer and co-executive producer Anthony E. Zuiker was apparent from the pilot episode of *CSI: Crime Scene Investigation*, an overall visual theme took a little longer to develop. Whether it was one of those happy creative accidents that occur over time, or whether it was through increasing confidence, identity, and budget, it was firmly entrenched before the end of season one and actively pursued in season two and in the creation of the two spin-offs, *CSI: Miami* and *CSI: NY*. Each has a thematic color and style that makes it almost instantly recognizable even without the regular characters. These themes reflected not only the geographic space, but also the characters, the crimes, the techniques, the storylines, and the subjective location of the show. What is also notable is that the colors—green, yellow, and blue—are not exclusive to their respective shows, but can be seen in all three. On occasion, an "outsider" dominates the style in a particular episode, without detracting from the show's individual theme. These colors, along with a recurring use of red hues (not surprisingly, given the content), tie the shows together as CSIs, anchoring a common thread to assure regular viewers that, despite the differences across shows, they are essentially still watching the same foundational concept.

It became obvious early on that the thematic colors were not simply an identifying marker, but also reflected meanings, ideas, and emotions. *CSI*'s green hues in Las Vegas are the color of fluorescence and the color of money: two essential aspects of Vegas. But it goes deeper than those obvious markers. For the crime scene investigators, the city is not a holiday destination, or a place of glamour and frivolity; their Vegas is one of darkness, seedy violence, and a soul-destroying greed. And it is also their home. For them, what happens in Vegas *really does stay* in Vegas. It is no coincidence that the show focuses on the night shift, as that is when it is all happening in Las Vegas, at least to outward appearances. In the windowless casinos it is perpetual night, a world lit only by fluorescence and muted colors, a visual situation repeated in the most utilized sets of the show: the lab. This creates a dualism that is constantly in opposition—it conveys a sense of both claustrophobia and safety.

From the very first episode, it was obvious that *CSI: Miami* had a different approach. The most startling difference was the brightness. *Miami* was a daylight show. Its bright wide yellow vistas were almost agoraphobia-inducing in contrast with Vegas's night. The show is bathed in a golden light, ranging from pale yellow to amber hues, and the "natural" colors have a travel brochure clarity: the white buildings are striking, the blue ocean enticing, and the greenery has a startling beauty. It is a place of hope, of obscene wealth and terrible poverty, of cultural diversity and racial tensions, of the constant flow of tourists, drugs, money, and spring break. It is a place where even the slums and the everglades look colorful and glamorous. While night exists, it is not the focus, not when the action really occurs: most of the interview rooms are bathed in sunlight (the lab remains in artificial light, but does not have the grainy grimness seen in Vegas). This does not suggest that Miami is devoid of crime; rather, its is an evil that does not require a cloak of darkness and instead revels with the tourists in the sunlight.

Perhaps fittingly, *CSI: NY* is not purposely set in day or night, but somewhere in between. Much of the show does appear to take place during the day; however, not only is this less obvious, more significantly, it is less crucial. Like the other shows, it reflects the city in which it is set. The blue echoes the perpetual twilight of life between high-rise buildings, where sunlight is fleeting and restrained by smog. The show has a darkness that is neither the nighttime darkness of Vegas nor the slightly lit darkness of the labs in Miami. It is almost a feeling (blue?): sadness, but not despair. New York is never despair, there is always some hope. Yet it is not a place of glamour and rarely one of happiness. The crimes themselves also seem less shocking, diluted by the blue hues, as if a city such as New York is so jaded, has seen so much crime and suffering, that the shock has worn off. That does not make the investigators any less diligent, or passionate, but it is as if someone has turned the volume down, and an occasional numbness shows through.

From the beginning of the original *CSI*, the tone was set. Director and production consultant Danny Cannon had been given his instructions: Bruckheimer wanted the motion picture "look," and recommended the right production designers to achieve it ("Cast and Crew Interviews"). Cannon knew that color would play an important role, though the idea of its thematic use was still in the future. The pilot for *CSI*, while made with the relative simplicity and awkwardness of most pilot episodes, introduced several devices that would become themes for the show. The green hue of the convenience store that was Holly Grimes's first crime scene, the startling first view of a wound tract, and chief investigator Gil Grissom's admonishment to Warrick Brown: "Concentrate on what cannot lie—the evidence." Holly, who had the dubious distinction of being the only investigator not to make it into the series, went, but the green, grainy hues subsequently became a mainstay, along with gut-churning but clever tours of bodies and injuries, in telling the story of each episode's crime. Grissom, while remaining eccentric, became more reserved and serious in the series proper, but his advice to Warrick became the contextual underpinning of the show itself, frequently repeated in various forms until it had become their credo. It was the visual style, however, that initially captured the attention and has kept the shows fresh.

Las Vegas was an inspired choice for *CSI*. Although frequently used by movies, its use is less frequent in television, and rare as a permanent setting. On the occasions it has been used, it is because of the casinos or the associated glamour, and many could be excused for thinking that these are the extent of the city. Do people go there for anything else? This issue was presumably high on the list of concerns the creators and writers had, but their approach was a novel one. They created a place that was eccentric and different and yet ordinary. Some crimes are a result of the "Vegas factor," while others are more universal. The first crime investigated, for instance, was a shooting in apparent self-defense against a home invasion (although it turned out to be the murder of a houseguest who had overstayed his welcome). But the Vegas factor does not necessarily refer only to crimes related to the Strip; scuba divers found in trees and a woman drowned in the desert have nothing to do with casinos, but they do reflect the theory that "nothing is too weird for Vegas."

William Petersen, who plays Grissom, has highlighted in interviews the differentiation between those who live there and the visitors, iterating that people do things in Vegas that they would never do in their own worlds. But he has also discussed Vegas's dark side: crimes are committed there that might not occur elsewhere ("Cast and Crew Interviews"). Marg Helgenberger, who plays stripper-turned-investigator Catherine Willows, believes that "there is a kind of desperate quality here [in Vegas] which works well for drama," but she too makes the observation that the traditional stereotypes of Vegas are not what the show represents—"We don't treat the town as if it is a character... we don't exploit the glitz or the casinos" ("Cast and Crew Interviews"). While the casinos are not consistently integral to the storyline, they are always there in the background, lurking like a dangerous predator at the perimeter of the investigators' lives. For at least two of the characters, the casinos have in some way caused them pain: Catherine associates them with betrayal and the revelation of her biological father, a corrupt casino owner, and Warrick's gambling addiction makes the casinos his serpent and forbidden fruit. It seems no coincidence that their occasional visits to the casinos, most often for work, are usually heavily saturated in green, reflecting the envy and greed that have caused them so much pain. Grissom regards the casinos with the same detachment he displays toward most locations, but he also has a surprising history with gambling. He revealed, rather matter-of-factly, in season three that he funded his first body farm in college as a master poker player, to the surprise of his colleagues, to whom he seems too "square" ("Revenge is Best Served Cold," 3-1). Sarah Sidle views the casinos with a barely veiled contempt, and the cheerful Nick Stokes considers them with an easy indifference—just part of the background scenery to the city in which he lives and works.

However, the casinos and associated industries cannot help but play a recurring, if supporting, role in a Las Vegas–based crime show. It is these places and the tourism they bring in that are the economic backbone of the city. Everyone knows someone who works at one. Victims and perpetrators, if not visitors, are often employees. The casinos also offer the opportunity to explore unusual aspects of society, as demonstrated by the episodes focusing on crimes related to the constant stream of conventions hosted by these venues. If the "little people" convention in "A Little Murder" (3-4) was not unusual (and sad) enough, the people dressed as animals living out their fantasies through their furry alter ego certainly meet all the criteria for weirdness. Catherine's surprise at being called to the scene of the murder and finding a grown man dressed as a raccoon on the highway was priceless enough, and even the unflappable Grissom looked bemused when the rules of the petting parties were explained ("Fur and Loathing," 4-6). However, while the murders may have been unusual, the motivations were the most time-honored of all: greed and jealousy.

With the exception of the aerial cinematography utilized to separate the scenes, there are few postcard-type shots of the sights of Vegas, and on the few occasions they are used, they are not meant to offer pleasant connotations. When Detective Jim Brass found and was forced to let go of his wayward teenage daughter, it was in front of the iconic Bellagio Hotel and Casino fountains ("Ellie," 2-10). It was one of the rare character- and emotion-driven scenes that at that point had appeared in the show, displaying a previously unseen side of a character and reflecting, though in a more dramatic fashion, the everyday problems of parenthood. Placing such a poignant yet universal scene in such an incongruous setting reminded viewers that, despite the glamour, it is not only the tourists that occupy Vegas.

There is little doubt that the coloration is used to create ambience and coerce emotion from the viewer. When pushed to extremes, there can be no doubt of its intent. Nowhere is this used to better effect than in the Quentin Tarantino–directed finale for season five and its sequel, in which Nick had been kidnapped and buried alive ("Grave Danger," 5-24, and "Bodies in Motion," 6-1). Nick's desperate situation, when seen through the green, was even more frightening, just as the same lighting made a bunker housing the eleven bodies of a Heaven's Gate–style suicide cult creepier still ("Shooting Star," 6-4). While coffins and bunkers may be obviously disturbing places, the green can make even a previously innocuous space feel that way. A home becomes a house of horrors, a luxurious hotel room becomes a seedy dive, a first class cabin on a plane becomes a place of fear-induced cruelty, and a previously "good" person becomes corrupted. The only space the green cannot infect is the morgue, which is always bathed in shades of blue; it is a place of peace and sadness, beyond the horror and suffering of the living world.

It is significant that the shows' use of place and color are reflected in the characterizations: Grissom, the intense scientist with his insect obsession at home amongst the green; Horatio, *Miami*'s unwilling golden boy; and Mac, *New York*'s haunted widower, as blue as his city. This technique becomes obvious with the introduction of *Miami* and its main character—Horatio Caine.

Rather than being diluted, Las Vegas's style, firmly in place by the season, was actually enhanced by the arrival of its spin-off, *Miami*. The *Miami* setting and main characters were introduced in a crossover episode, "Cross-Jurisdictions" (2-22), late in the second season of the original *CSI*. While investigating the death of a former police chief, and the kidnapping of his wife and young daughter, the evidence led the Las Vegas team to Miami and a new range of possibilities. The switch of location in the episode was startling in its intensity. The lurid grainy Vegas crime scene suddenly became a lush outdoor scene: wide angles, thick greenery, and bright yellow sunlight emanating from a wide blue sky. It was inviting, and a little unnerving. Vegas was never this clear and bright, even in the desert where the dust and the heat were grainy and overexposed. Night had become day.

It is unsurprising that by the time Catherine and Warrick arrived in Miami, it was night, and the two groups met in a sense of compromise, not only in relation to the case, but also their surroundings. A greenish tint seemed to adhere itself to the Vegas people and didn't lift until they were exposed to the bright sunlight. Catherine and Warrick looked as if they had landed on a foreign planet, and although polite to Horatio Caine and Calleigh Duquesne's confident friendliness, they were unsure of their Miami colleagues' methods. This was underlined within minutes of their meeting in a scene that articulated the *Miami* approach to solving the crime as clearly as Grissom did for the original *CSI* in the pilot episode.

> CALLEIGH: You got a theory how the mother and daughter ended up in Miami all the way from Vegas?
> CATHERINE: Well, we don't actually work theories, do we, Warrick?
> WARRICK: No, just evidence.

CALLEIGH: We're much more fanciful down here. Aren't we, Horatio?
HORATIO: I think that's a fair description.

And just in case this was a little too subtle for the viewer, it was re-iterated later in the episode, where back in Vegas, Brass, impatient for a break in the case from his end, complained to Grissom that in Miami they were pulling cars out of the water and finding bodies, while "you guys are flipping through textbooks." Grissom, not amused by the comparison, replied, "This is how I work!"

While the illumination was dramatically different, highlighted by the regular changes of location (Vegas has never seemed so drab and "green" as it did against Miami's yellow brightness), there was an effort to link the two places through the crime, particularly as it became increasingly Miami-based. When the child's escape from the kidnapper's car was shown in flashback, the inside of the car had an unmistakable green hue as she ran to the safety of the sunlight. Later, the nightclub was garishly green, while the evidence that had brought them there—honey—was a golden yellow. In a clever reversal of the color scheme, Horatio broke the news of the fate of her parents to the girl on the golden sand, and told her that an aunt was coming to take her home while beside her sat a bright new green spade and bucket. On leaving to return to Vegas, Catherine was almost disappointed to be leaving Horatio and Miami—after she'd gotten past her initial misgivings, there was an unmistakable chemistry between them—but arrived back in Vegas and reported to Grissom with a cheerful brightness, dressed more casually than usual, as if she had brought a bit of Miami with her. He complimented her tan, perhaps a little enviously, but she allayed his fears by making it clear that she was pleased to be back. The shows had gone their separate ways, and it was back to business as usual.

Miami, its brightness notwithstanding, is an altogether more serious show than the Vegas one. The dark-humored eccentricity that permeates many episodes, or at least scenes, in the original is notably absent in *Miami*. If anything, the bright vistas of *Miami* spotlight a sense of tragedy that is a recurring theme in the show. Whether it is the story of the desperate struggle of Cuban refugees, the follies of youth and the alcohol-fuelled antics of spring break, drugs, the massacre of families, or the recklessness of the rich and infamous, each episode demonstrates the best and the worst of human nature. Whereas in Vegas the investigation is about bringing closure, in Miami, it is about justice. It is not that these ideas are mutually exclusive in either show, but there is a preoccupation with judgment in *Miami* that is not often explored in Vegas. Miami, like Vegas, is a tourist destination, and a home, but is also more connected to the world outside the city. The insularity of Vegas is reflected in its claustrophobic camerawork, while the exposure of Miami through its proximity to the ocean and other countries and cultures is reflected in its panoramic technique. This is supported by director/producer Cannon, who confirms that the difference in method is purposeful, pointing out that, "Miami has a very different energy to Vegas. [It is] an international city. A metropolitan city" ("*CSI: Miami*: Uncovered").

This difference in mood and method is also recognizable in the characters. Horatio is a man on a mission—no matter what the crime. His emotional investment dominates every scene in which he appears, and his ability to communicate with both the victims and the suspects makes him a formidable force within the show. He takes every case personally—not as a puzzle to be solved, but as a wrong to be righted. He displays a quiet calm which can be gentle, or downright frightening. His character is perhaps best described by the actor who plays him, David Caruso. Caruso highlights Horatio's need to resolve things and bring people to justice, as well as his ability to connect with people:

> Horatio Caine is a man that has tremendous feelings for his victims and their families. He also has the opposite feeling about the perpetrator of the evil that we deal with. He is a gentle man, he is a kind man, but he is the last person in America you want after you ("*CSI: Miami*: Uncovered").

He is not content with just solving the crime, as that does not always lead to justice: he also wants answers for those left behind, something to hang on to in their darkest hours. It is as if, despite being the "golden boy," he lives in his own darkness and must constantly exorcise demons for which, though did not create them, he is in some way responsible. He will make any sacrifice necessary for family and friends, but he finds himself somehow unworthy of reciprocation. The loss of his brother, an undercover detective, whose apparent corruption and death is a recurring storyline, haunts Horatio; its resolution at the end of season three still failed to release him. This duality between the darkness within Horatio and the brightness of the location is echoed in the impenetrable dark glasses he wears outdoors as a prop to signify turning points in the case.

Initially, Horatio, with his open friendly face, red-gold hair, and nifty suits, seemed the opposite of Grissom's eccentric, sometimes nerdy, scientist, as different from one another as their locations were. There are other significant differences between the two men, including their approaches to solving crimes and dealing with the living, and their respective emotional investments. Grissom is also referred to almost exclusively by his surname, implying a bit of distance, whereas his Floridian counterpart is best known by his given name, implying a more casual openness. But it took only a few episodes of *Miami* proper to realize that the two have more similarities than differences. They are both very alone in their worlds, despite the admiration and affection of their friends and colleagues; they have cut themselves off (significantly, this may be even more true of Horatio than Grissom). They are great leaders, earning the respect of their colleagues and often their prey. Their meticulous patience and dedication to solving crimes have an obsessive quality that inspires their teams to greater heights. They are both deeply committed to their jobs, treating it more as a calling than employment, and both have a past they are unwilling to revisit. It is therefore no coincidence that these similarities are also shared by Mac Taylor, who leads the *New York* team.

The *New York* series was introduced in a similar manner as *Miami*. The episode, "MIA/NYC Nonstop" (2-23), took place during the second season of *Miami*, when an investigation took Horatio to New York to investigate a murder that appeared related to his current case. He (and the audience) met Mac Taylor at the crime scene in a poorly lit apartment bedroom. In a clever piece of shooting, the side of the room in which Mac stood was bathed in a blue-toned gloom while Horatio's had a subtle yellow (though shadowy) glow. It was fascinating to watch the yellow, bright world become a blue one as the colors gradually merged and New York took over. (This was repeated in reverse when Mac visited Miami in a later crossover: as Mac walked into the building, blue followed him down the corridor as he approached Horatio, who had gold light streaming behind him ("Felony Flight," 4-7).) Though he remained involved, Horatio stepped back in New York to allow Mac and his team to take charge in a manner that was not as obvious as in the Vegas/Miami crossover. This was a wise decision, as Horatio's charisma could have been a distraction from the introduction of the New York *CSI*. The producers probably felt more confident, as well; *Miami* had been a success—why wouldn't *New York*?

At first it seemed that *New York* would fit somewhere between the nighttime of Vegas and the daytime of Miami, and to some extent it does. Yet, despite the regular twilight style, it soon became obvious that day and night are of little consequence to the show, which depends neither on the New York vistas, nor the innumerable claustrophobic settings available. To assert that the first season was "dark" would be a disservice; it was downright gothic—the quintessential Gotham City. But Mac was no Batman (though he certainly brooded enough to qualify). In a reversal of Vegas and Miami, the New York lab is white, brightly lit, and spacious, contrasting with the crowded city outside. The only exception that first season was the morgue—a dark, damp-looking basement-type room—in which it was difficult to see anything. The change made for the second season, in which the morgue was in a room like the lab, arguably went too far to the other extreme: the crisp whiteness stripping the dead of their personality, interrupting the viewer's connection to them. Nevertheless, it did create a continuity with the theme offered by the opposition of this space to that of the city.

Nowhere in the other shows did a major character reflect the color theme better than Mac Taylor in *New York*. He is blue: in demeanor, in dress, and in pallor, most of the time. While neither Grissom nor Horatio could be called jovial, they seem positively giddy in comparison with Mac. Indeed, on the rare occasions when Mac smiles, there is little happiness behind it. It was eventually revealed that his wife died in the 9/11 terrorist attacks, a storyline that, according to journalist Kristine Huntley, was originally going to be explored in depth but was abandoned in preference of the more subtle approach. Problematically, however, the specter of 9/11 did seem to dominate the show at times during the first season; particularly, it seemed, through avoidance. As it did in many television shows set in New York, it became the elephant in the room.

Stella Bonasera is a good counterpoint for Mac, as Catherine is for Grissom, but the minimalist approach to character development throughout a good portion of the first season made the *New York* team appear bland and disjointed. In Vegas, the focus was the team. Though Grissom is the obvious lead, the emphasis on the team prevails, despite an unsuccessful and short-lived attempt to separate them into two groups. In *Miami* the team idea became slightly fragmented, with Horatio dominating the show in a way Grissom did not. The rest of the team was important, but definitely acted as supporting characters. This worked well in the different location, with Horatio never overwhelming the show but anchoring it as its center. In *New York*, the team had still less essence: it was not that the other characters did not have as much screen time as their Vegas and Miami counterparts, but that their development remained minimal. It was also not that Mac dominated the show (though putting an experienced character actor like Gary Sinise among talented, though vastly less experienced, small screen actors was bound to cause difficulties); indeed, it was the absence of a dominating factor that took center stage. The irony of the situation is that Zuiker wanted *New York* to be more character-driven than the other two, with less focus on the city and more on the investigators, to counteract shows such as *Law & Order* (Poniewozik 62).

The first season had teething problems—the approach, though not unsuccessful, did not have the power of its older siblings. It was not assisted by a poorly chosen time slot, and even as the characters began to mesh better and the plots strengthened, *New York* still struggled to live up to the franchise expectations. Some critics cited the show's "dark theme," or the characters, while others suggested that it had all been done before (Huntley). But what seemed to haunt the show was the location itself; the first two shows relied heavily on their locations, and those locations' associated themes. Perhaps New York was a poor location for the style of show, or the location was not used as skillfully as in the original and *Miami*. This was not for lack of trying, though, as demonstrated when Stella and Mac, frustrated by lack of progress in their respective cases, compared notes ("Creatures of the Night," 1-6). Although disparate, Mac attempted to use them to reflect the diversity of the city itself:

STELLA: Rats and rapists—worlds apart!
MAC: The city's the same.

Whatever the case, the producers made dramatic changes for the second season. Not least of these was changing the look of the show and increasing the focus on the team with the addition of new characters. The first episode of the new season, in trying not to be too "dark," may have gone a little too far in the other direction: it was downright "summery" in feeling, Stella wore a colorful tank top, and there appeared to be no real thematic look at all. But as the series has progressed, the blue has crept back into the show and a unique identity appears to be forming. Certainly the crimes have developed some quirky twists: a dead man wearing a diamond bra of his own design, death by swordfish, and an apparent fall/push from a bridge that turns out to have come from much further up in a case of wrong place, wrong time. And it certainly seems to be paying off, as *New York* has begun capturing regular top twenty spots in the Nielsens, or at least coming within close sight of the magic twenty ("Nielsen ratings, April 17-23").

CSI has become something of a phenomenon since Grissom offered Holly a chocolate-covered grasshopper on her first, and last, day. It has triggered a range of trends, including other criminal investigation shows and a rise in procedural gore (many shows now ought to contain a warning advising against eating), but also the use of thematic color tints, grainy and overexposed techniques to highlight characters, mood, and most commonly, location. Even aside from other Bruckheimer productions, such as *Without a Trace* and *Cold Case*—which use these techniques to great success—others, such as *Numb3rs*, *Blind Justice*, and *House* have also taken inspiration from the franchise, and the influence can be seen in individual sections of many other shows. Although the CSI franchise is an expensive trio of shows to make, those holding the purse strings are aware of their worth. John Morayniss, an executive vice president for television at CBS, was unequivocal: "We love the special effects, the Jerry Bruckheimer stamp on it; that dark and brooding look. Audiences loved the look of the show" ("Cast and Crew Interviews").

And of course, at the end of the day, it is what the "audiences love" that determines the health of a show. At the time of this writing, the original *CSI* remains the number one show in the world. The franchise avoids the political discussion and moralizing that often does not translate successfully overseas, sticking to the universality of evils such as jealousy, greed, and violence, but even so, the shows would have nowhere near the success they do without their distinct visual themes. Good writing, unique ideas, and superb acting are a crucial element of *CSI*, but this is not an off-Broadway show, it is television: the most powerful, competitive, and accessible medium on the planet; and also the most visual. All you have to do is follow the evidence. . . .

Janine Hiddlestone is a lecturer and tutor in politics, history, and communications at James Cook University in Australia. She has a Ph.D. in political history and has published on the place of war in culture and history, and how pop culture became the centerpiece of so much of the public's understanding—and misunderstanding—of events. She has explored the influence of technology on pop culture, and vice versa, and its pedagogical uses in encouraging students to develop an interest in political and historical issues. She has also attained infamy among her colleagues as a pop culture tragic.

References

"Cast and Crew Interviews." *CSI: Crime Scene Investigation* Season One DVD Set, Disc Six. Dir. Richard Lewis. CBS, 2003.

"Creating *CSI: Miami*." *CSI: Miami* Season One DVD Set, Disc Two. CBS, 2004.

"*CSI: Miami*: Uncovered." *CSI: Miami* Season One DVD Set, Disc One. CBS, 2004.

"Nielsen ratings, April 17-23." *Nielsen Media Research* April 2006. <http://www.nielsenmedia.com>.

Gough, Paul J. "*Idol* keeps Fox atop ratings race." *Reuters* 27 April 2006. <http://today.reuters.com/news/articlenews.aspx?type=televisionNews&storyid=2006-04-27T223948Z_01_N27344252_RTRIDST_0_TELEVISION-RATINGS-DC.XML>.

Huntley, Kristine. "*CSI* Files: Anthony E. Zuiker." *CSI Files* 6 April 2005. <http://www.csifiles.com/interviews/anthony_zuiker.shtml>.

Leopold, Todd. "Bruckheimer: the brand name in movies." *CNN.com* 12 January 2006. <http://www.cnn.com/2006/SHOWBIZ/Movies/01/11/jerry.bruckheimer>.

Poniewozik, James. "Crimetime lineup: How the slick show changed television—in part by dragging it back into the past." *Time* 8 November 2004: 62.

Matthew Woodring Stover is a notorious crank—or at least notoriously cranky. In this essay, however, despite throwing more than a few sacred cows on the barbecue, he manages to delve to the very heart of what the CSI shows are about—and why they matter.

Also, there's pie.

MATTHEW WOODRING STOVER

Vegas Rules, Miami Often Stinks, and New York Is (Apparently) Sometimes Mostly Okay

CSI: CRIME SCENE INVESTIGATION IS the most important program on television today.

Now that I have your attention—

It's worth noting that I am a notorious crank.

I have also been reliably informed that I am narrow-minded and arbitrary.

Readers of the following essay are advised to keep the foregoing caveats in mind, and to direct all uncomplimentary mail to BenBella Books, as—quite frankly—I only want to hear from people who regard the ground upon which I walk as Sacred Earth, and it's BenBella's fault my bizarre notions are included here in the first place.

There will, however, be pie.

So let's get started.

I'm no fan of *CSI: Miami*. I don't give a rat's ass who Horatio Caine's banging, what happened to his brother, what vendetta he's currently pursuing, or anything else remotely connected with his personal life, despite his borrowing his last name from the protagonist of my ongoing series of SF/fantasy adventure novels, and despite a certain sentimental Favorite Son attachment to David Caruso as the only red-haired dramatic leading man to have a successful Hollywood career since roughly Van Heflin.

I'm also unimpressed with *CSI: NY*, for the same reason. Though I've seen a couple of episodes that actually emphasized the detective work, in the (admittedly few) others I've seen there was just waaaaay too much character crap (probably because they have a couple of terrifically talented leads in Gary Sneereasie and Melina Kanyapronouncea-Greekname), and not enough about the case.

Case. Case case *case*. Crime Scene Investigation, remember?

Though I realize I'm going to be thrown out of the Serious Writer's Club for saying this, screw the characters. (The SWClub is a pack of boring old farts, anyway. I'll try not to let the butler pinch my ass on my way out....)

What was I saying?

Oh, yeah.

Who needs characters, anyway?

The original *CSI* doesn't seem to. Which is, believe it or not, what I *like* about it.

No quarrel with the acting, which is stellar. Or with the writing. Let's be clear on that. And sure, if I think long enough, I can come up with William Petersen's character's name...but not Marg Helgenberger's, or the pretty boy with the giant head and pencil arms...Eads? Whatever.

The point is, *I don't have to know.*

Who the characters are, as distinct individuals with personal lives beyond the parameters of the cases that they solve, is *functionally irrelevant*, which is not only really, really cool, it's vital to the existential weight of the show. It is precisely this which makes the show so important. The point of this essay is to explain to you exactly why that's so— and for the explanation to make sense, we'll have to detour through a couple side roads of PopCult CritThought.

Now, I didn't survey these roads, nor did I pave them (nor can I remember exactly who did, and I'm too damned lazy to look it up), but I've spent a good bit of time driving them. Be warned: I take the route pretty fast. Riding shotgun in the Stovermobile, you may find the ride a bit rough and the corners sharp, and there's a sudden stop at the end. I'd hate to send you through the windshield. Even metaphorically.

So buckle up.

Our starting line is the Village Green. I disremember who first put forth the idea that television is America's common ground—Edward R. Murrow, maybe? (Couldn't have been McLuhan, could it? I mean, he *was* the Electronic Global Village guy, but he was also Canadian, and what the hell have those politely frozen bastards done for pop culture since Shatner? Dan Aykroyd? Mike Myers? Celine Dion? Makes me shudder just to think about it....) Anyway, here's the point: In a nation that's three thousand miles from coast to coast and almost two thousand from border to border, commercial network television is still pretty much our only source of common experience, because (let's face it) most Americans are too ignorant for PBS and too cheap for the full-ride premium channels...and there's still never anything good on Saturday night, but that's another story.

What is the sole plausible point of congruence in the psychic lives of a Wall Street broker, a Montana ranch hand, a gay hustler in LA, a Southern Baptist deacon in Georgia, a shrimp boat captain in the Gulf, and a Saturn line worker in Tennessee?

What they watch on TV.

And what's the one show they might very well each watch every week? Yeah, you guessed it.

The most-watched show on television.

And part of why they can all find themselves engaged by this show is because it's not really about the lives of specific people in a specific place.

Las Vegas, for all its glitzy trappings, is the least-specific place in America; the victims in these cases either have been or, in the next episode or two, very likely will be members of any of those groups mentioned above, and the crime scene can be mountain or desert, lake or forest, shopping mall or urban jungle or...well, you name it, they've probably done it already.

Scott McCloud, in his brilliant, seminal work *Understanding Comics: The Invisible Art*, observes that the power of cartooning comes from abstraction—that the less "realistic" and individualized a character or place is represented, the easier it is for us to identify with it...because there are less signifiers that differentiate the character or place from who we are or where we are. You follow? The less real they are—the less distinctly individual—the easier it is to imagine ourselves in their place.

I don't want to see an episode where we meet Gil Grissom's parents and find out about his brothers and sisters and what kind of sports he hated as a kid. (Which is, by the way, the great thing about satellite TV—I can check the synopsis, even on reruns, and if there is such an episode, I'll never have to sit through it. Score!) I don't want to see where he lives, what kind of car he drives to work, any of that crap. I'm doing my best to forget his first name. I wish he could. Because he's the spine of the show, and I don't want him distracted.

In order for *CSI* to work—in order for it to be the Most Important Program on Television Today—Grissom needs to be exactly what he is: a *truth machine*.

Okay, that was a sharp corner. I'll run the Stovermobile back a few concepts and we'll take it slow.

There are essentially two contrasting ways of describing a genre. The way that is used by most critics is to describe a genre strictly according to the tropes and trappings: There are horses and six-shooters, so it's a Western. There are spaceships and blasters, so it's SF.

There are cops, so it's a cop show.

This process effectively illustrates what we all here already know: Most critics are idiots.

The proper way of describing a genre is by a combination of trope and *metathematic intention*. This requires brainpower above and beyond the capacity of your average critic, which is why you so rarely see it done.

To use an example near and dear to my own heart, let's take the original Star Wars trilogy. The idiot critics call it SF because of the aforementioned spaceships and blasters...but the entire trilogy's *metatheme*—the overarching consideration—is *the obligations of supernormal power* (specifically, will Luke use his Special Powers selfishly or selflessly), which is the metatheme of fantasy fiction from *The Iliad* to *The Amazing Spider-Man*. When we add the subordinate theme of *atonement with the father* (do I need to spell this one out?) we find that the original Star Wars trilogy falls squarely, as any student of Campbell will tell you, into the sub-genre of Quest Fantasy.

All genres (and sub-genres) have their characteristic metathemes and sub-themes—i.e., Romance is *the search for love*, and if we add a sub-theme of *the need for rescue from scary castles* we get Gothic Romance. This is where the idiot critics get themselves into trouble; by looking at metathemes we discover, for example, that two of the most success-ful "cop shows" of all time—*Hill Street Blues* and *NYPD Blue*—were not cop shows at all.

No, they weren't.

The metatheme of the cop show is *justice must be done* (which these days usually translates as *get the bad guys at all costs.*) *NCIS* is a cop show. *Hill Street* and *NYPD* weren't... they just used cop show tropes and trappings to present a metatheme of *the struggles of daily life*. And what genre, you might be wondering, deals with the metatheme of *the struggles of daily life*?

Its traditional name was Kitchen Sink Drama. These days we call it "soap opera."

Those shows were just soaps about cops. You knew it, too. You just didn't want to admit to yourself that you were addicted to a nighttime soap, you big softie. And for a nominal sum, mailed monthly in cash to me c/o BenBella Books, I won't rat you out to your wife. Or your girl-friend. Either.

Now you're wondering how I know you're a guy. I could pretend to get all intellectual and talk about the demographics of the *CSI* viewer-ship and the unlikelihood of the relatively few female fans of the show buying this book, except as a gift for their husbands or boyfriends—or multiple copies for those who have both—but I'm too honest for that.

Actually I'm just psychic.

However—like any other psychic—I am occasionally wrong.

Right now my psychic powers can sense your growing curiosity (per-haps impatience would be a better word . . .) regarding the ultimate des-tination of all these detours. Just hang on to your shorts. We're getting there.

The point about *CSI*'s genre is this: It belongs to a much older and more respectable genre than the mere cop show. *CSI*'s provenance goes back to Edgar Allen Poe.

No, not "The Cask of Amontillado" or "The Tell-Tale Heart" or any of the other creepy stuff your teacher made you read in freshman American Lit; on the contrary, Gil Grissom's literary ancestor is actually Poe's most influential contribution to American culture . . .

C. Auguste Dupin.

For those of you who haven't heard of him (*shame* on you!), you will likely be more familiar with his English grand-nephew-in-spirit, Mr. Sherlock Holmes.

"Oh, a *detective* story," you're thinking (see? Told you I'm psychic!). "That's really just another kind of cop show, though."

Except it isn't. It's a whole separate genre.

Yes, it is.

Look, you can argue all you want, but I'm never wrong. When I suggested otherwise above, I was being uncharacteristically (and dishonestly) modest.

As I mentioned earlier, the metatheme of the cop show genre is *justice must be done*. This often, as we've all seen, has very little to do with law, or even real detective work; it's not about discovering who did it so much as it is about bringing them to some kind of justice, often peremptory, or even vigilante. The roots of the cop show are actually in the Western, not in the police procedural, and it certainly has little to do with the classic detective story. The structure of the plot is *go get the bad guys*. *NCIS* is a cop show; *Wanted* is a cop show; many of the old "detective" shows were actually cop shows—*Magnum P.I.* springs to mind, or *The Equalizer*, or *Mannix* for us real old-timers. *24* is the current exemplar of the cop show.

What is *CSI: Crime Scene Investigation* really about? We know it's not about *the struggle of daily life* for the characters; it's as far from a nighttime soap as you're going to get in an hour-long drama. And it's not really about *getting the bad guys*, either; though bad guys frequently find themselves gotten, it's wholly a side effect of the primary process with which the show is concerned.

The same process, to (I hope by now) no one's surprise, used by Mr. Holmes and M. Dupin.

They examine the event in question, collecting clues that ordinary eyes have missed. They use those clues, in conjunction with witness testimony and skilled analysis, to *determine the facts of the case*.

You see it coming?

Not to *get the bad guys*.

To get the *truth*.

This is where the detective genre diverges from the cop genre; this is what makes the detective genre so existentially, even metaphysically, important, more so in fact than any other branch of literature.

Because the metatheme of the detective genre is *the search for truth*.

Detective fiction is the only branch of literature that asserts—insists, as its very foundation—that *nothing is more important than the truth*.

Real detectives—real in the genre sense, real like Holmes, Dupin, and Grissom, as opposed to Sipowicz or Belker—care about truth more than anything else. More than love. More than money or power. More than flag or country, faith or family.

Truth.

And the kind of truth we're talking about here is *useful truth*—truth as *fact*, the kind of truth that makes a direct difference in people's lives. Who did what to whom with what, and when.

Truth as the antidote for suspicion, and the cure for wishful thinking.

See where I'm going with this, yet?

One more detour, then we'll swing back to the Village Green for our Welcome Home party.

I believe it was Aristotle who, in a fit of massively over-complimentary gushing, described humanity as "the rational animal." Nietzsche had the right of it when he offered his classic correction: "Man is not the rational animal but the *rationalizing* animal; the primary use to which we put our reason is the justification of our prejudices."

As any scientist, mathematician, or philosopher will tell you, rationality is a skill: it does not come naturally, but requires training, and the conscious application of learned rules. What passes for reason in everyone else (including—perhaps especially—me) is another type of thinking entirely, which is generally referred to as "the voice of experience."

In actuality, it is a fund of stories each of us carries around in our heads. And we think by using these stories as touchstones, as mirrors, finding points of congruence between them and whatever circumstance or situation we're considering; it is the cumulative weight of these stories that gives us a feel for how a situation is going to work itself out.

This feel is what we call "a hunch," or "instinct." It is the psychic vector of all the stories we carry, both fact and fiction, giving us directions about how to live our lives and hints for what the future will bring.

These stories might be the tales we've told ourselves about our own lives; then we call them memories. They might be tales we've been told in school; then we call them history. Often they are tales of our parents' memories, or our friends'.

Often, believe it or not, they are tales from books, and films, and television shows.

This is why people who have lived lives close to the bone of whatever situation they are facing (say, a guerrilla war) will have a better instinct for what's going to happen than those who've only read about it—but those who've read a book by someone who was really in one, that evokes what it was really like (say, *The Things They Carried*) will have better instincts than those who've only seen *Rambo*.

Hey, there's the Village Green up ahead! We're almost home—see the banner? Wait...it doesn't say *Welcome Home*, it says—

MISSION ACCOMPLISHED

Does my butt look good in these *Top Gun* flight pants?

However—suspiciously similar to the more famous MISSION AC-COMPLISHED banner—we're not quite done here, as you might have noticed.

This is where I tie it all together for the Big Finish with fireworks, apple pie, and the brass band playing "The Stars and Stripes Forever."

Y'see, *CSI: Crime Scene Investigation* just might save our country.

Yes, it might.

You really need to quit arguing with me. Remember, I'm never wrong.

Here's the thing: America's current leadership thinks we're living in a cop show. Haven't you noticed? They keep telling us they're gonna *go get the bad guys* Dead or Alive, and they think that nobody cares how much they lie to us, how many laws they break, how many people they torture, or how many times they violate the Constitution...as long as they're *going after the bad guys*.

And they're sincerely puzzled that about 70% of the citizens of this country don't like it.

Hell, doesn't everybody cheer when Jack Bauer lies, cheats, steals, and tortures to *get the bad guy*?

But that's a cop show. And cop shows have nothing to do with the truth.

And *24* is *not* the Most-Watched Show on Television....

Lest you think I'm partisan, let me point out that the Democrats haven't found their way into the detective genre, either. Hell, they're still wandering wistfully on the moors, pining away for the lost romance of the New Deal, waiting for some new lover to *rescue them from the scary castle* of Republican domination....

Is it better to be merely pathetic and feckless than to be reckless and incompetent? I'm not the one to judge.

But I will tell you this: *CSI: Crime Scene Investigation* is the only program on the mass commercial networks whose message, every week, is that *nothing is more important than the truth.*

And it's the most-watched show on TV.

That's a message to *both* our political parties. Truth is what we're really waiting for, whether we know it or not. So what are *they* waiting for?

Grissom for President! Lookit them skyrockets, kids! Three cheers for the Red, White, and Blue!

Here's your pie.

Matthew Woodring Stover would prefer to be known primarily for his Acts of Caine novels, *Heroes Die, Blade of Tyshalle,* and the forthcoming *Caine Black Knife.* However—such being the way of the world—most of his domestic and international reputation rests on being the author of the novelization of *Star Wars Episode III: Revenge of the Sith.* His (entirely pretended) disappointment with this is assuaged by spending lots of Vader Money.

ELYSE DICKENSON

CSI Episode Summaries

CSI: Crime Scene Investigation
Season One

1-1. PILOT (Oct 6, 2000)

When a man is found dead in a bathtub with a suicide note, the case seems pretty cut and dry, but Gil Grissom has reason to suspect foul play. Nick investigates a tourist who was robbed by a hooker—in a most unique manner. Catherine and Warrick handle the case of a homeowner who shot an intruder, but the evidence isn't matching up. Meanwhile, Warrick is given the task of supervising new rookie Holly Gribbs, with tragic results.

1-2. COOL CHANGE (Oct 13, 2000)

A gambler wins $40 million and then falls to his death from a high-rise hotel. Grissom brings in junior criminalist Sara Sidle to assist in the case. Catherine must learn to work with the newest member of the team when Holly dies of her wounds. While Grissom receives an unwanted promotion, Warrick's gambling problems soon find him beholden to a judge.

1-3. CRATE 'N BURIAL (Oct 20, 2000)

Laura Garris, wife of a millionaire, is kidnapped and buried alive in the desert. The CSI team race against the clock to find her before she dies from lack of oxygen. Meanwhile, Catherine and Warrick investigate the tragic hit-and-run of a small child and find the driver. However, the evidence soon contradicts the man's confession.

1-4. PLEDGING MR. JOHNSON (Oct 27, 2000)

Something's fishy when the dismembered leg of Wendy Barger surfaces in a lake. Grissom and Catherine must backtrack the woman's movements, which may lead them to a fatal case of adultery. A college student found dead by hanging looks like a suicide, until evidence points toward possible foul play. Warrick seeks Grissom's help when the judge presses him to do something that could cost him his job.

1-5. FRIENDS & LOVERS (Nov 3, 2000)

The naked body of a young man is found in the desert after he attends a rave party. Another nude body—that of a woman who was buried a week ago—is found not in her grave but in a dumpster. Meanwhile, a young woman claims self-defense after she bludgeons in the head of a college dean.

1-6. WHO ARE YOU? (Nov 10, 2000)

Home improvements unearth a woman's skeleton buried in the foundation of the house. In order to determine her identity, Grissom brings in forensic anthropologist Teri Miller. When Nick finds a crucial clue in the case, it could cost him his life. Meanwhile, Catherine is faced with her ex-husband, who's been accused of raping of a stripper, and Warrick and Sara investigate an officer-involved shooting.

1-7. BLOOD DROPS (Nov 17, 2000)

The grisly mass murder of nearly an entire family in a suburban home has the whole team focused on finding the killer. Four family members were brutally stabbed to death while they slept. The only survivors are the two daughters: a teenager and a four-year-old girl who is too traumatized to talk.

1-8. ANONYMOUS (Nov 24, 2000)

When a dead body is found in a bathtub, Grissom suspects that a serial killer (from the "Pilot") has returned. Evidence leads Grissom to

Paul Millander, the quiet owner of a props factory, but it's very possible that the man is being framed. Warrick and Nick vie against each other to solve the odd case of a car crash which had no driver, just a passenger in the back seat.

1-9. UNFRIENDLY SKIES (Dec 8, 2000)

First class flying isn't what it used to be. A passenger dies violently on a small commuter flight to Las Vegas. The CSI and police encounter contradictory stories and conflicting evidence from the remaining eight passengers. They claim the man had a panic attack, but he also had footprints on his back.

1-10. SEX, LIES, AND LARVAE (Dec 22, 2000)

When a woman's beaten and maggot-ridden body is found abandoned on a mountainside, it seems that only Grissom's entomological skills can pinpoint the exact time of her death and convict her killer. Meanwhile, Nick examines a blood-stained car found near a bus station, and Warrick and Catherine investigate a painting stolen from a wealthy family.

1-11. I-15 MURDERS (Jan 12, 2001)

A thawed-out body found on a highway soon indicates that a serial killer is driving up and down the I-15 interstate, prowling for new victims. Grissom and Catherine soon realize the killer has another victim, and must quickly piece together the clues before she dies. Nick runs into prostitute Kristy Hopkins, the hooker who drugged her clients ("Pilot"), during a dispute with a security guard, and Sara and Warrick work a robbery-homicide case.

1-12. FAHRENHEIT 932 (Feb 1, 2001)

A man awaiting trial for killing his family by arson asks for Grissom's help in solving the case. He insists he's innocent and is sure that forensic evidence can free him. When a teenage "runner" is found shot to death in his car, Catherine and Nick discover that a family member may have contributed to the youth's death.

1-13. BOOM (Feb 8, 2001)

A security guard is killed when a bomb blows up in the lobby of a business office. Grissom must contend with Dominic Kretzker, a security guard and explosives buff who is eager to help—but is also a prime suspect. Nick finds himself under police scrutiny when he spends the night with prostitute Kristy Hopkins ("Pilot") and she is found murdered the next day.

1-14. TO HALVE AND TO HOLD (Feb 15, 2001)

A game of fetch with the family dog turns into a police case when the pet brings back not a stick, but a human bone. Soon the chopped-up remains of some poor soul are found scattered all over the desert. Clues lead the team to a very unlikely suspect. Sara and Warrick investigate a male stripper who died shortly after performing at a bachelorette party.

1-15. TABLE STAKES (Feb 22, 2001)

When showgirl Lacey Duvall is found face down in a swimming pool during a fund-raising party, suspicion falls on the husband and wife couple who insist they're house-sitting for Portia Richmond, a legendary showgirl from the 1950s who is reportedly on vacation in Europe. Warrick must face his own gambling demons when he's called to the homicide of a gambler who was shot dead, execution style, in a glass elevator.

1-16. TOO TOUGH TO DIE (Mar 1, 2001)

Sara becomes too personally involved in the case of a woman who was raped, shot twice in the head, and then left for dead. Meanwhile, Catherine and Warrick deal with the case of two neighbors who argue over a borrowed motorcycle—a fight that ends up in death and a claim of self-defense.

1-17. FACE LIFT (Mar 8, 2001)

A thief is found dead at the scene of a robbery. When fingerprints from the crime are analyzed, the CSIs are amazed to find they belong to those of a presumably long-dead kidnapping victim. Meanwhile, Sara and Warrick argue out precisely why a woman is now a charred corpse. Did the decedent die from an accidental fire, or was she the victim of spontaneous combustion?

1-18. $35K O.B.O. (Mar 29, 2001)

When a building collapse claims the lives of three elderly women, Catherine finds she must work with a district engineer whom she soon finds herself attracted to. Across town, a couple on their way home from a night out are carjacked and brutally stabbed to death. When a sudden rain storm occurs, the team frantically works to preserve the evidence.

1-19. GENTLE, GENTLE (Apr 12, 2001)

The wealthy Anderson family is frantic: their baby has been kidnapped. They are devastated when Grissom finds their child's lifeless body not far from the home, but pain soon turns to anger when the CSIs begin to believe that someone within the family was involved in the abduction.

1-20. SOUNDS OF SILENCE (Apr 19, 2001)

A young man is run over by a car and killed. Evidence soon comes to light that the victim, who was deaf, was also quite dead before the traffic accident. Blood evidence and the presence of lice help the CSIs hone in on the killer. Meanwhile, Catherine and Nick process the bloody mess at a coffee shop where five people were shot dead.

1-21. JUSTICE IS SERVED (Apr 26, 2001)

A jogger is found dead in the park from a savage attack by an unknown large animal. However, the animal had assistance, as several of the jogger's internal organs were surgically removed. When a little girl dies on an amusement park ride, Sara and Catherine investigate and the senior CSI becomes convinced that the child's death was no accident.

1-22. EVALUATION DAY (May 10, 2001)

It could only happen in Vegas: the police chase a stolen car driven by two scantily clad women and find the decapitated head of a freelance artist in the trunk. The CSIs soon find a body in the desert but realize it's not going to match up to the head: it's a gorilla. Meanwhile, Warrick is asked to help a young inmate who insists he has been falsely accused of killing a gang member in prison.

1-23. STRIP STRANGLER (May 17, 2001)

A demanding serial killer strangles his female victims, then takes the time to clean up the crime scene afterward, leaving precious little for the CSI to analyze. Grissom finds himself removed from the case when the sheriff brings in the FBI, and is appalled to discover that the feds plan to use Sara as a decoy to trap the Strip Strangler.

SEASON TWO

2-1. BURKED (Sep 27, 2001)

When the son of Las Vegas mogul Sam Braun is found dead in his home, the evidence at first points to a drug overdose. However, clues at the crime scene lead Grissom's team to deduce that the man was murdered. Suspects abound: family, enemies, even a gold-digging ladyfriend. Complicating the case is the fact that Catherine has known Sam Braun for her entire life.

2-2. CHAOS THEORY (Oct 4, 2001)
When co-ed Paige Rycoff disappears from a local university after calling a cab and leaving her luggage behind, unsavory facts about both students and staff begin to surface during the CSI's investigation. Did she run away with the professor with whom she had an affair, or did something more sinister occur?

2-3. OVERLOAD (Oct 11, 2001)
Grissom tackles the case of a construction worker who takes a fatal plunge at the work site—was it an accident, suicide, or murder? He needs to solve the case quickly as the sheriff is under political pressure to keep the construction project on target. Meanwhile, Nick and Catherine investigate the case of a young patient who died while undergoing an unusual therapy with a psychiatrist.

2-4. BULLY FOR YOU (Oct 18, 2001)
The team investigates two cases: In the first, a school bully is fatally shot in a high-school bathroom, and the suspects are plenty. Meanwhile, Nick and Sara have the horrid task of identifying a liquefied corpse found in a bag by a hiker.

2-5. SCUBA DOOBIE-DOO (Oct 25, 2001)
A tenant leaves behind a blood-splattered apartment when he skips out on the rent, and it's up to Grissom, Warrick, and Sara to determine where his missing girlfriend is and what the blood is doing on the walls. Meanwhile, Catherine and Nick get to solve the unusual case of a scuba diver's corpse (in full gear) found thirty feet up in a tree in the middle of a forest fire. Nick is leaning toward an old urban legend, but Catherine isn't.

2-6. ALTER BOYS (Nov 1, 2001)
Warrick and Catherine handle the case of an apparently healthy young woman who dies of heatstroke in a health spa's sauna, while Grissom, Nick, and Sara have a ready-made suspect in a multiple homicide when a man is found burying a body full of bullet holes—or do they?

2-7. CAGED (Nov 8, 2001)
Catherine and Sara handle the fatal case of car vs. train, which just might turn out to be a case of road rage. Nick and Grissom investi-

gate the death of a worker at a historical site who is found in a metal cage meant for rare books. Their only possible witness: an autistic co-worker.

2-8. SLAVES OF LAS VEGAS (Nov 15, 2001)

A young woman's naked corpse is found dead in a park's sandbox, but evidence indicates she met her death elsewhere. Clues of sadomasochistic activities lead Grissom, Catherine, and Nick to a fetish club. Sara and Warrick investigate the case of a man shot during a robbery at a check-cashing store.

2-9. AND THEN THERE WERE NONE (Nov 22, 2001)

Grissom's team investigates two dissimilar cases that just might be linked. Three women rob a local casino and get away with a quarter of a million dollars, but the witnesses all have conflicting stories when questioned. Meanwhile, a murder at a faraway mini-mart takes an interesting twist when fingerprints from a past case are found.

2-10. ELLIE (Dec 6, 2001)

A con man scams thousands of dollars out of a tourist couple, but minutes later, he's found shot dead in the casino's parking garage. The case becomes personal for Brass when evidence found at the scene implicates his estranged daughter Ellie, whom Brass has not seen in years. Warrick has the unenviable task of running the CSI when Grissom is off on a lecture and Catherine goes out of town.

2-11. ORGAN GRINDER (Dec 13, 2001)

An amorous couple's desires are definitely deflated when the hotel elevator opens up to reveal a dying real estate mogul on the floor. It appears that he died of natural causes; however, the CSIs figure out that he was poisoned and must track down people who received his donor organs.

2-12. YOU'VE GOT MALE (Dec 20, 2001)

The bodies of two young women are found stuffed into a culvert pipe at a highway construction site, and a trail of e-mail leads to a recently paroled inmate. A dead man is found out in the woods. Was he mistaken for a deer by another hunter, or was the shooting intentional?

2-13. IDENTITY CRISIS (Jan 17, 2002)

Serial killer Paul Millander ("Pilot," "Anonymous") returns, leaving yet another dead body with which to taunt Grissom. The case is even more difficult for Grissom to crack because Paul Millander is safely hidden by his identity as Douglas Mason, an honorable judge who deals with parking ticket violations.

2-14. THE FINGER (Jan 31, 2002)

A man with blood on his hands and one million dollars cash in his wallet draws attention from police when he's pulled over for speeding. Catherine soon ends up an unwitting participant in a kidnapping gone awry, in which the only lead to the victim is a severed finger. Sara goes on a date with Hank Peddigrew.

2-15. BURDEN OF PROOF (Feb 7, 2002)

A local body farm—where forensic scientists study body decomposition—has a sudden and unwanted increase in population when a murdered photographer's corpse shows up on the grounds. When a man's house goes up in flames, the CSIs discover clues leading to the sexual abuse of his fiancée's daughter.

2-16. PRIMUM NON NOCERE (Feb 28, 2002)

An unpopular hockey player gets into a fight on the ice, but when the bodies clear, he's been mortally wounded by a gash to his neck. Warrick and Nick investigate the supposed drug overdose of a jazz musician, which is complicated by the fact that someone cleaned up the crime scene before they arrived.

2-17. FELONIOUS MONK (Mar 7, 2002)

When several Buddhist monks are slain in a monastery near Las Vegas, the suspects are numerous, as the monks' presence was not welcomed by the local townsfolk. When a killer makes a deathbed confession involving the murder of Catherine's best friend during her exotic dancer days, Catherine discovers that her old mentor may have tampered with evidence.

2-18. CHASING THE BUS (Mar 28, 2002)

A tour bus on its way to Las Vegas crashes, leaving multiple injuries and fatalities in its wake. Grissom's entire team, including a novice Greg, are called out to process the scene and determine the cause: was it driver error, a tragic accident, or was the bus company owner looking to save money on maintenance costs?

2-19. STALKER (Apr 4, 2002)

A young woman is savagely murdered in her apartment, but it wasn't a botched robbery. The killer took time before he left to color her hair. When a clairvoyant shows up claiming knowledge of the killer, he is able to provide clues that the killer actually lived in her apartment, in the ceiling. While following the evidence, Nick is nearly killed.

2-20. CATS IN THE CRADLE (Apr 25, 2002)
A woman is found stabbed to death in her home and the only witnesses aren't talking: they're her cats. Was a neighbor who hated the cats responsible for the murder? Meanwhile, a woman narrowly escapes death when a pipe bomb hidden in her engine explodes, destroying her expensive car.

2-21. ANATOMY OF A LYE (May 2, 2002)
When a child burns himself in the park just playing in the dirt, the police discover a lye-covered corpse buried in the ground. The autopsy shows the man may have been struck by a car and taken days to die. Evidence for the hit-and-run leads the CSIs to a lawyer, who is more concerned about his "stolen" car than a dead man. Meanwhile, Nick investigates the case of a woman who drowned in the desert.

2-22. CROSS-JURISDICTIONS (May 9, 2002)
Pilot for spin-off series *CSI: Miami*. When an ex-chief of detectives is murdered in a lurid fashion at his home, and his family is nowhere to be found, the trail of evidence leads the team to Miami. Catherine and Warrick meet up with Horatio Caine's team when the wife's corpse is found wrapped in plastic with her eyes glued shut.

2-23. THE HUNGER ARTIST (May 16, 2002)
The mutilated and partially decomposed body of a woman is found under a freeway overpass. She was hardly homeless—a day planner discloses Botox injections and more, and the woman turns out to be a high-paid fashion model. Unfortunately, that career came at a very high price. Meanwhile, Grissom realizes that his hearing problem may be affecting his ability to perform his job.

SEASON THREE

3-1. REVENGE IS BEST SERVED COLD (Sep 26, 2002)
When a renowned gambler drops dead in the middle of a high-stakes poker game, it doesn't take Grissom long to figure out it wasn't from natural causes. Meanwhile, Nick and Catherine investigate a "fast and furious" death of a street racer out at an abandoned airstrip in the desert.

3-2. THE ACCUSED IS ENTITLED (Oct 3, 2002)
A young woman is found dead in the hotel room of a popular actor, and

Grissom and his team have their work cut out for them when the actor's lawyer hires Grissom's former mentor, Philip Gerard, to find mistakes in the case. Unfortunately, Gerard is good at his job. Meanwhile, Sara's on/off boyfriend, emergency worker Hank Peddigrew, returns.

3-3. LET THE SELLER BEWARE (Oct 10, 2002)

A house sale turns sour when prospective buyers find the owners still at home—but dead. Suspects abound, including the realtor, who just may have been robbing his own clients. Sara investigates a cheerleader who was eviscerated on a high school soccer field.

3-4. A LITTLE MURDER (Oct 17, 2002)

Grissom investigates the case of a dwarf who apparently committed suicide at a Little People's convention that's in town, but the CSIs suspect it may actually have been murder. While at the site of a home invasion, Catherine is attacked by an intruder.

3-5. ABRA CADAVER (Oct 31, 2002)

The team tackles two cases: Nick and Catherine try to piece together clues left behind when a singer from a popular band apparently ODs while on tour, even though he'd supposedly gotten off drugs years before. Grissom, Warrick, and Sara investigate the case of a volunteer who disappears during a magic act, and soon discover that not all is as it seems.

3-6. THE EXECUTION OF CATHERINE WILLOWS (Nov 7, 2002)

Could Catherine's work have inadvertently put an innocent man in prison? Over a decade ago, Catherine's testimony helped put John Mathers on death row for the rape/murder of several young women. New DNA evidence is now granting the man a stay of reprieve. Complicating matters, another girl at the exact same college is murdered in the identical fashion.

3-7. FIGHT NIGHT (Nov 14, 2002)

Grissom, Sara, and Warrick investigate the brutal world of boxing when a boxer abruptly dies in the ring after a nasty fight. Meanwhile, Nick investigates a "smash and grab" at a jewelry store, which may be more than a simple robbery, and Catherine must determine who gunned down a gang member in a parking lot.

3-8. SNUFF (Nov 21, 2002)

A film developer calls the cops when a "snuff" film turns up in the latest batch of processing, but while the woman's identity in the film is unknown, the CSIs are determined to find out where the film was made. Meanwhile, Grissom investigates the death of a young man with Down syndrome, whose fire ant-covered skeleton was found stuffed inside a large box.

3-9. BLOOD LUST (Dec 5, 2002)

A taxi driver accidentally runs over a teenager who steps in his path and pays the ultimate price: he is beaten so badly by a mob that he dies. However, the team soon discovers that the car may not have been what killed the youth. Also, a man is found shot dead. How is he related to the taxi death?

3-10. HIGH AND LOW (Dec 12, 2002)

Some skateboarders encounter an impediment to their fun: a body lands on the concrete. Did he jump or fall from the building, or somewhere else? Also, a man is shot to death in a parking lot.

3-11. RECIPE FOR MURDER (Jan 9, 2003)

The team ends up dealing with bad food in this episode: First, a chef from a local restaurant ends up as part of the hamburger in a meat-packing plant, and soon it turns out that more than cooking was going on in the kitchen. The second case is a young woman whose disturbed personal history makes her a perfect candidate for suicide—or murder.

3-12. GOT MURDER? (Jan 16, 2003)

The team deals with some people who take a while to die. First, a car salesman dies—twice. Then, a woman thought to be dead shows up alive, but then turns up dead, and some very disturbing facts about her family come to light during the investigation.

3-13. RANDOM ACTS OF VIOLENCE (Jan 30, 2003)

When a child of Warrick's former mentor is killed in a drive-by shooting, Warrick lets his emotions wrongly lead him to assume a suspect is guilty. A second case involves the CSIs entering the world of cubicle dwellers as they look for clues into the case of a man who lay dead for hours before his geeky computer programmer subordinates noticed anything was amiss. And all of them had plenty of motive to kill their boss.

3-14. ONE HIT WONDER (Feb 6, 2003)

Catherine investigates a peeping Tom who is now breaking into women's apartments and terrorizing them. Sara reopens an old case in which a colleague's husband was murdered, but the killer was never apprehended. Meanwhile, Grissom's hearing problems worsen.

3-15. LADY HEATHER'S BOX (Feb 13, 2003)

Ninety minutes. Grissom runs across the dominatrix Lady Heather ("Slaves of Las Vegas") again when two murders have a connection to the woman: they were her employees. Catherine becomes personally involved when her ex-husband, traveling with their daughter, crashes his car and vanishes. Sara is in charge of the investigation, but Catherine wants quicker results.

3-16. LUCKY STRIKE (Feb 20, 2003)

This episode revolves around the kidnapping of the five-year-old son of a professional basketball player who is visiting Las Vegas. Another case, quite odd, involves a man who stumbles out of his car and dies—from a wooden stake rammed into his head.

3-17. CRASH AND BURN (Mar 13, 2003)

An elderly woman plows her car into a crowded bar during happy hour, killing herself and injuring several patrons, including Sara's boyfriend, emergency worker Hank Peddigrew. However, as the case is investigated, Sara uncovers some startling facts about Hank that could destroy their relationship. Grissom quickly decides that a woman's death by carbon-monoxide poisoning was no accident.

3-18. PRECIOUS METAL (Apr 3, 2003)

The world of robotic sports is put under the microscope when a badly decomposed body is discovered in a chemical waste drum. Grissom and Warrick investigate the death of a newly married man whose body was found in an alley.

3-19. A NIGHT AT THE MOVIES (Apr 10, 2003)

Catherine and Grissom go to a dingy art theater to find out why one patron ended up stabbed in the head with a screwdriver. Across town, the badly bruised body of a teenage boy is found shot to death in a bullet-ridden warehouse, where over one hundred rounds were fired from every conceivable angle.

3-20. LAST LAUGH (Apr 24, 2003)

A despised comic drops dead on stage, apparently after drinking tainted water. Elsewhere, a fifteen-year-old boy dies in a convenience store after drinking the same brand of water. Brass re-opens a woman's accidental-death case after seeing the deceased's husband enjoying himself in a flashy new sports car with an equally flashy new date.

3-21. FOREVER (May 1, 2003)

A horse trainer is found dead in the cargo bay of a private 747 jet, which is carrying a dozen well-heeled passengers and a prized race horse. Meanwhile, in a brutal section of Death Valley, Warrick and Sara investigate the apparent suicide of a fifteen-year-old found underneath a bedspread. Later on, a girl's body turns up half a mile away.

3-22. PLAY WITH FIRE (May 8, 2003)

A woman is found strangled to death in a small press box at a high school football field, and evidence points toward a convict who is still behind bars. At the lab, disaster strikes when an explosion destroys DNA evidence for a case, and leaves both Greg and Sara injured. In a shocking twist, the explosion might have been caused by one of their own.

3-23. INSIDE THE BOX (May 15, 2003)

Three masked bandits steal something from a bank's safe-deposit box in a daring heist during which a police detective is shot and killed. This case hits home for Catherine when the evidence leads to casino owner Sam Braun, who has been like a father to her. Also, Grissom's hearing gets progressively worse, forcing him to finally seek help.

SEASON FOUR

4-1. ASSUME NOTHING (Sep 25, 2003)

Part 1 of 2. The investigation of a woman found in a hotel room with her throat slit turns into a double homicide when clues lead the CSIs to a second body—that of her husband. The investigation is jeopardized when something Nick said turns up on the local TV news station.

4-2. ALL FOR OUR COUNTRY (Oct 2, 2003)

Part 2 of 2. Suspects in the double homicide case are eliminated, but only because they're found dead as well. Soon the evidence trail leads Grissom and his team to suspect that a police officer may have been involved. In another part of town, Catherine and Sara probe the death of a college student found dead in his bathroom.

4-3. HOMEBODIES (Oct 9, 2003)

The teams tackle three cases: The mummified remains of an elderly woman are found locked in a closet and evidence indicates she was alive when she was trapped in there. The discovery of a handgun in a yard is mysteriously linked to the shooting death of a bounty hunter in another part of the city. And Nick and Sara deal with a family who denies that a breaking and entering occurred, even though evidence of the crime is undeniable.

4-4. INVISIBLE EVIDENCE (Nov 13, 2003)

Grissom's team has only twenty-four hours to find new evidence in a murder case when, in court, a bloody knife that Warrick found at the scene of the crime is suddenly declared inadmissible.

4-5. FEELING THE HEAT (Oct 23, 2003)

Heat claims several victims on a sweltering day in Las Vegas: A baby is tragically found dead inside a locked car. Nick and Sara must determine where a young woman died before she was washed ashore at a lake. An out of shape "couch potato" is found dead inside his sweltering house and Warrick must determine what killed the man.

4-6. FUR AND LOATHING (Oct 30, 2003)

It's not unusual for a driver to dodge an animal on a road at night and then have an accident, but this time, the animal was a man dressed in a raccoon costume, and the car smashes into an eighteen-wheeler. The man turns out to have just left a convention for "furries"— people who dress up as animals—prompting Grissom and Sara to look for suspects there. Meanwhile, a convenience store employee is found dead inside an industrial freezer.

4-7. JACKPOT (Nov 6, 2003)

CSI coroner Dr. Robbins receives a head in the mail. It seems a dog found this severed head in the small town of Jackpot, Nevada, where Grissom soon finds himself. He finds the headless body, but also encounters resistance from the local sheriff, who may know a lot more than he's saying. Catherine confronts her father after she receives an unexpected gift from him.

4-8. AFTER THE SHOW (Nov 20, 2003)

When a beautiful model vanishes, everyone is trying to find her, but despite the blaring media attention, she remains missing—until a man calls 911. While Catherine is positive she's found the woman's killer, he has yet to confess. Making matters worse, both Nick and Sara believe whichever one of them solves the case will be promoted.

4-9. GRISSOM VERSUS THE VOLCANO (Dec 11, 2003)
A musician's girlfriend is found dead in her bathtub, and it wasn't from slipping on a bar of soap. The CSIs suspect murder and zero in on her close circle of friends. Meanwhile, a bomb explodes at the front entrance of a popular hotel on the Strip. While terrorism is first and foremost on everybody's mind, the clues instead lead to a school science fair.

4-10. COMING OF RAGE (Dec 18, 2003)
A fifteen-year-old boy is found brutally beaten to death at new housing construction site. The evidence soon leads Grissom to the boy's friends. Across town, Nick investigates the odd case of a woman shot dead outside her home while her husband and ex-husband were having a fight nearby.

4-11. ELEVEN ANGRY JURORS (Jan 8, 2004)
A hung jury finds itself under deep suspicion when one of their members drops dead during the final deliberations. Meanwhile, a woman reports a murder—three years after it occurred—prompting Nick to seek new evidence.

4-12. BUTTERFLIED (Jan 15, 2004)
Grissom puts his life on hold to investigate the chilling homicide of a woman found murdered in her home who bears an eerie resemblance to Sara. When the team widens their search perimeter into the alley, they find the dismembered remains of a man whom they'd pegged as their prime suspect.

4-13. SUCKERS (Feb 5, 2004)
During a lavish party at a Vegas hotel, a priceless seventeenth-century Japanese samurai sword seems to be stolen from a vault right under everyone's noses. An art heist leads the CSI team into the bizarre underground society of young blood-drinking goth devotees.

4-14. PAPER OR PLASTIC (Feb 12, 2004)
Officer Fromansky ("All for Our Country") returns and is a prime suspect when a grocery store robbery goes sour and people die in the ensuing shootout. Grissom must set aside his personal feelings toward the officer, who opened fire in the store after his partner was shot.

4-15. EARLY ROLLOUT (Feb 19, 2004)
When a millionaire and his wife are ruthlessly gunned down in the driveway of their supposedly safe gated community, Grissom's entire CSI team

pulls together to solve the mystery. The prime suspect is a former business associate of the victim who apparently had lots of motive.

4-16. GETTING OFF (Feb 26, 2004)

A dead man in clown make-up is found tossed aside in a junk yard, but his murder is no laughing matter. Meanwhile, the brutal stabbing death of a motorist in a drug-ridden area town discloses that the man worked for a drug recovery center.

4-17. XX (Mar 11, 2004)

A bus carrying prisoners from a woman's correctional facility is having problems: it's losing body parts. The CSIs must literally piece together the scattered remains of a woman who was tied to the vehicle's undercarriage. While Catherine heads up that investigation, Nick and Grissom probe the death of a multiple-stab-wound victim.

4-18. BAD TO THE BONE (Apr 1, 2004)

The CSIs are astonished when a huge, intimidating man is found beaten to death inside the men's room of a casino. It's not his death that's surprising, but that their prime suspect is a slightly built man. He's the apparent owner of a run-down motel that is hiding the secrets of past crimes.

4-19. BAD WORDS (Apr 15, 2004)

A young girl dies tragically in a house fire, but was it an accident or arson? There's definitely a sore loser at a local gaming tournament: One of the participants is found dead with an "S" tile stuck in his throat.

4-20. DEAD RINGER (Apr 29, 2004)

During an annual law enforcement road race, Grissom finds a dead runner along the road. Meanwhile, Warrick and Sara investigate the apparent murder-suicide of two police officers in a hotel room. In both cases, all the suspects turn out to be their fellow cops.

4-21. TURN OF THE SCREWS (May 6, 2004)

A day at the amusement park turns to terror when a roller coaster flies off its tracks, claiming the lives of six people. Everybody is demanding answers for this tragedy: was it simply poor maintenance, or did somebody want another person dead?

4-22. NO MORE BETS (May 13, 2004)

When two gamblers beat the house by using science and win a six-figure sum, their elation is short-lived: Their bullet-ridden bodies turn up later, shot execution-style. Grissom is forced to take Catherine off the case when it turns out that the casino is owned by her father, Sam Braun.

4-23. BLOODLINES (May 20, 2004)

On her way home from work, a casino employee is beaten and raped. Fortunately, she survives the attack and is able to identify her attacker, but the DNA evidence refutes her testimony. Grissom and his team are determined to unravel this mystery, and the shocking conclusion of the case is not what anyone could have expected.

SEASON FIVE

5-1. VIVA LAS VEGAS (Sep 23, 2004)

Greg gets his first taste of fieldwork when Grissom brings him along to a fatal shooting at a nightclub. Across town, Catherine must determine who is responsible for the death of a stripper found in a hotel suite. Warrick deals with a man electrocuted in his bathtub, while Nick and Sara dig up an "alien body" near Area 51. Meanwhile, Chandra takes over Greg's role in the DNA lab.

5-2. DOWN THE DRAIN (Oct 7, 2004)

A severe thunderstorm reveals the badly mangled corpse of a man in a city's storm drain, and further examination of the tunnel uncovers human bones that just may belong to a murder victim. The CSIs focus their investigation on the surrounding neighborhood and canvas old cases to determine the bones' identity.

5-3. HARVEST (Oct 14, 2004)

When a teenager goes inside a convenience store, her twelve-year-old sister is abducted from the parking lot, leading the CSIs on a race against time to get the girl back alive. Meanwhile, Catherine's daughter Lindsey is picked up by the police for hitchhiking. Warrick is attracted to Greg's latest replacement in the DNA lab, but her personality could be a problem.

5-4. CROW'S FEET (Oct 21, 2004)

When a woman is found dead in a hotel room, and her body is covered in bizarre skin lesions, the authorities fear the worst. However, it's not an infectious disease but the result of a strange anti-aging treatment at an expensive health spa. Meanwhile, Grissom, Greg, and Sara investigate the death of a man who apparently died in his house during a fumigation.

5-5. SWAP MEET (Oct 28, 2004)

A well-off neighborhood has a lot to hide when one of the women is found dead in a fountain following a party where married couples swap their spouses. Across town, Nick and Warrick investigate the murder of a man found in a closed video arcade and, with the aid of a crime scene clean-up man, unearth more than they bargained for.

5-6. WHAT'S EATING GILBERT GRISSOM? (Nov 4, 2004)

The "blue paint" killer from "The Execution of Catherine Willows" returns. It's been nearly two decades since a serial killer began stalking a Las Vegas college, and now Grissom believes the man may be at it again when body parts are found. However, the pattern is different from before, suggesting a copycat killer.

5-7. FORMALITIES (Nov 11, 2004)

An expensive and private high school homecoming party is disrupted when a teenage girl is found murdered, and the investigation indicates that another girl was abducted as well. What the CSIs find shocking is that the abducted girl's father thinks his daughter staged the whole kidnapping to get attention.

5-8. CH-CH-CHANGES (Nov 18, 2004)

In the show's 100th episode, a woman who was pulled over by the police is found horribly mutilated and murdered just miles down the road. The autopsy reveals a startling clue: the woman was once a man. The team soon delves into the world of transgenders to find out who committed the gruesome killing.

5-9. MEA CULPA (Nov 25, 2004)

When a fingerprint mysteriously shows up on a crucial piece of evidence during a murder trial, Ecklie puts Grissom in the hot seat, as this oversight makes the lab look bad. Meanwhile, when a gun from a fatal shooting misfires in the lab, Sara and Greg find out that it was tampered with. As the cases come to a close, Ecklie uses the mistakes to split Grissom's team.

5-10. NO HUMANS INVOLVED (Dec 9, 2004)

A boy has been shot to death and the crime scene cordoned off, and when Greg goes into a nearby alley, he discovers the emaciated body of another boy stuffed into a dumpster. Meanwhile, Catherine, Warrick, and Nick go to the county lockup to investigate the beating death of a prisoner in an overcrowded cell. After Warrick accuses a policeman of sloppy procedure, Catherine calls him out for what she sees as unprofessional behavior.

5-11. WHO SHOT SHERLOCK? (Jan 6, 2005)

The chief suspects in a shooting death turn out to be people who pretend to be Dr. Watson, Prof. Moriarty, and Irene Adler. It seems the victim portrayed Sherlock Holmes, and converted his basement into the sleuth's famous dwelling. Grissom starts the case, but lets Greg finish it. Warrick and Nick must determine if a man found inside a wrecked vehicle died in an accident or was murdered.

5-12. SNAKES (Jan 13, 2005)

The CSIs come across a particularly gruesome crime: a woman's severed head, with a baby rattlesnake stuffed in the throat, is found inside a newspaper dispenser in a Spanish-speaking area of town. It appears that her murder may be linked to a local style of music that glorifies crime. Meanwhile, evidence indicates that the shooter of a man in a casino parking garage may be wheelchair bound.

5-13. NESTING DOLLS (Feb 3, 2005)

The bodies of two young women covered by tar are found by construction workers at a new housing development. The CSIs discover that both were Russian mail-order brides and were abused. Sara takes the case personally and is reprimanded by Ecklie, who tells Grissom to deal with her. Instead, Sara opens up to Grissom about why the case has angered her so much.

5-14. UNBEARABLE (Feb 10, 2005)

When a hunter is found mauled to death in the mountains by a bear, it appears to be a tragic hunting accident—unless you know Kodiak bears are not native to Nevada. Also, someone has removed the bear's gallbladder. A wealthy young woman vanishes soon after meeting a friend at a bar where a male patron took an unusual interest in her.

5-15. KING BABY (Feb 17, 2005)

When a prominent Las Vegas casino owner is found dead on his driveway after falling from the balcony of his mansion, Ecklie brings in Grissom's team to help wrap up the high-profile case. This doesn't sit well with Catherine, whose team was first to respond. Soon the investigation reveals that the man had more enemies than he could count, and a startling secret that he kept hidden from everyone.

5-16. BIG MIDDLE (Feb 24, 2005)
A badly mutilated body is actually the victim of a shotgun blast, which leads Catherine and Warrick into the world of high-stakes sports betting. Meanwhile, Grissom, Sara, and Greg try to unravel the case of a man who was crushed to death in his hotel room. They soon discover that he was friendly with some heavyset women in town for a convention.

5-17. COMPULSION (Mar 10, 2005)
When a flight attendant is brutally raped and stabbed to death in her hotel room, the CSIs match it up to a five-year-old cold case with a similar M.O. Across town, Catherine investigates the death of a twelve-year-old boy who was beaten to death in his own bed while his parents slept in a nearby room.

5-18. SPARK OF LIFE (Mar 31, 2005)
A fire in the countryside claims two victims: one on the road and another a stargazer killed by a fireball. However, as Grissom processes the scene, he finds a third victim—who, although badly burned, is still alive. In town, a five-year-old girl drowns in the family swimming pool and her parents are found dead inside the house.

5-19. 4 X 4 (Apr 14, 2005)
Four cases occupy the CSIs in this episode: Grissom probes a hit-and-run collision involving a stolen vehicle. Warrick investigates the death of a model at an automobile show. Nick tries to determine how and why a dead boy was left on a city bench. And Sara and Greg try to piece together clues in the mysterious death of a bodybuilder in his own home.

5-20. HOLLYWOOD BRASS (Apr 21, 2005)
In this Brass-centric episode, the detective goes to Los Angeles to help his estranged daughter Ellie—who is now a prostitute—find her missing friend. Unfortunately, that friend ends up dead, prompting Brass to enlist the aid of Warrick, who is in town for a convention, as well as the local police department.

5-21. COMMITTED (Apr 28, 2005)
In this extremely tense episode, Grissom and Sara investigate the brutal murder of an inmate at a state mental hospital. While the hospital is full of patients quite capable of committing such a crime, the CSIs soon realize that there are members of the staff who are suspect as well. During the investigation, Sara is attacked by an inmate.

5-22. WEEPING WILLOWS (May 5, 2005)

After a hard day at work, Catherine meets a man at a bar and has a drink, which leads to flirtation and a kiss, but when she wants to leave it at that, he boils over with anger. Later that night, she's called back to a case with Grissom at that exact same bar, and the man who hit on her is now a suspect in the murder of another woman. Meanwhile, Mia has contamination issues in the lab.

5-23. ICED (May 12, 2005)

Sara and Greg go back to college when two freshmen are found dead on a sleeping bag in a dorm room. Another case revolves around a dead man who was blindfolded and found in the middle of a crop circle outside of town. There are no footprints leading to the body or from it, so where did the body come from?

5-24. GRAVE DANGER (May 19, 2005)

This special ninety-minute episode was directed by Quentin Tarantino. Grissom and his team have only a limited amount of time to find Nick, who has been abducted and buried alive by a man who holds a grudge against the department. With time ticking down, the kidnapper delights in tormenting the team as well as Nick.

SEASON SIX

6-1. BODIES IN MOTION (Sep 22, 2005)

Grissom tackles the case of a gas main explosion that apparently claimed the lives of two people who died in a trailer. Catherine and Warrick investigate the homicide of a high-priced stripper whose corpse was found in a low-rent area. During the course of that investigation, they find even more bodies, and Warrick drops a bombshell on Catherine: he got married.

6-2. ROOM SERVICE (Sep 29, 2005)

Nick and Warrick probe the mysterious death of a movie star who'd spent the night partying with a woman in a luxury hotel room. Meanwhile, Grissom and Catherine investigate an accident victim who just may have been murdered, as well as the shooting death of a Laotian man and a cabbie.

6-3. BITE ME (Oct 6, 2005)

A distraught husband claims to have found his wife's body after she fell down the stairs, but evidence begins to mount that it was no accident, particularly when it comes to light that his previous wife died in nearly the same manner. The CSIs also discover the man has been seeing another woman with a peculiar fetish.

6-4. SHOOTING STARS (Oct 13, 2005)

When a man's battered and bloody body is found in a backyard, the search perimeter widens into the desert where the team discovers an abandoned underground military bunker—which holds an even more alarming discovery: the bodies of eleven cult members who committed suicide by ingesting poison.

6-5. GUM DROPS (Oct 20, 2005)

A small Nevada town is rocked by evidence of a gruesome slaying in their community. A house contains three pools of blood, but no bodies. Nick heads up the investigation and they find three family members shot and dumped in a nearby lake. While Nick is convinced that the young daughter may still be alive, Sara thinks he's becoming too emotionally involved because of his own recent kidnapping.

6-6. SECRETS AND FLIES (Nov 3, 2005)

Catherine gets an odd case: a young woman who apparently shot herself to death in her home. However, the autopsy reveals that she recently gave birth, even though she was a virgin. Meanwhile, Ecklie wants Grissom in court to refute the testimony of an entomologist so that a killer won't go free.

6-7. A BULLET RUNS THROUGH IT, PART 1 (Nov 10, 2005)

Part 1 of 2. This two-part episode focuses on Brass. Grissom's team has the unenviable task of investigating one of their own. When a high-speed chase results in the shooting death of a rookie police officer, evidence soon comes to light that he may not have been shot by fleeing gang members, but by friendly fire.

6-8. A BULLET RUNS THROUGH IT, PART 2 (Nov 17, 2005)

Part 2 of 2. As the investigation widens, the only suspect the police has is shot as he's being taken into custody. Grissom still pursues the unpleasant theory that friendly fire from a fellow cop caused the rookie's death.

6-9. DOG EAT DOG (Nov 24, 2005)

The world of competitive eating comes into the spotlight when an obese man is found dead in a dumpster outside a restaurant on Thanksgiving day. A golden retriever is a suspect in the death of a husband and wife who were on the verge of divorce. However, Nick and Sara aren't so sure they've got the right suspect.

6-10. STILL LIFE (Dec 8, 2005)

A distraught mother calls the police because her six-year-old boy has vanished from the park where he was playing on a swing set. She's convinced that her late husband's father has abducted her son. Nick receives a visit from Kelly Gordon, daughter of the man who kidnapped him and buried him alive.

6-11. WEREWOLVES (Jan 5, 2006)

The police receive an anonymous tip of a shooting death. When they arrive, they find a man with werewolf syndrome, a medical condition that causes excessive hair growth, dead in his home. The autopsy reveals a silver bullet in the man's chest. The CSIs believe that his death was more mundane than someone killing what they thought was a "werewolf": he was recently threatened by the owner of a gambling site for an unpaid debt, and he was engaged to be married.

6-12. DADDY'S LITTLE GIRL (Jan 19, 2006)

A motocross racer is slain while working in the garage of the house he shared with two women. Evidence comes to light that he'd planned to leave town with one of the women. Meanwhile, Nick discovers a disturbing link to his own past when he investigates the case of a woman who was fatally run over in a parking garage. It turns out she was the accountant for Kelly Gordon's father, the man who kidnapped him.

6-13. KISS-KISS, BYE-BYE (Jan 26, 2006)

An aging showgirl, who is well-connected and has possible mob ties, throws a lavish party that no one will ever forget—probably because there's a murder. While Grissom's team investigates a veritable who's who of suspects, Catherine discovers that her father, Sam Braun, is a prime suspect in the death.

6-14. KILLER (Feb 2, 2006)

A young woman accidentally runs her car into another vehicle, which results in her untimely death. It turns out the other driver strangled her to death and then fled the scene. Was it road rage, or is it linked to a dead man found murdered in an apartment building just a few blocks away from the accident scene?

6-15. PIRATES OF THE THIRD REICH (Feb 9, 2006)

The team tackles a case that becomes stranger with each new link of evidence that is discovered. A young woman's emaciated and abused body is found in the desert, and one of her eyeballs isn't even her own—it belongs to someone else. When the CSIs discover that the girl is the estranged daughter of Lady Heather ("Lady Heather's Box"), Grissom confronts her with the tragic news.

6-16. UP IN SMOKE (Mar 2, 2006)

Years ago, a sixteen-year-old vanished. Her corpse was never found and the CSIs never had enough evidence to gain a warrant to search the house of their prime suspect. They get a new chance when a man's charred body is found stuck in a chimney in the same house.

6-17. I LIKE TO WATCH (Mar 9, 2006)

Much to their dislike, the CSIs are ordered to let a reality show film crew follow them around on the job. Their latest investigation involves a fireman who apparently attacked and raped a woman. Evidence soon shows it was an imposter with a foot fetish who was responsible for the crime, and the woman may not have been his first victim. Meanwhile, Warrick's relationship with his new wife begins to show signs of stress.

6-18. THE UNUSUAL SUSPECT (Mar 30, 2006)

The case against a teenager charged in the slaying of two other students, whose nude bodies were found wrapped in a shower curtain and buried near a football field, seems airtight, until the suspect's twelve-year-old sister abruptly confesses to the crime on the witness stand. The prosecution is given seventy-two hours to re-examine the evidence before a verdict is delivered.

6-19. SPELLBOUND (Apr 6, 2006)

While doing a "reading" for some clients, a psychic predicts her own murder. Unfortunately, she's later found dead in her occult shop. While Grissom is certain that a rational scientific reason is behind the woman's demise, Greg isn't so sure, and reveals to Grissom that some "occult" expertise runs in his family.

6-20. POPPIN' TAGS (Apr 13, 2006)

When three teenagers are killed while helping to promote a rapper's new album, the CSI team delves into the world of musicians who will stop at nothing to promote themselves and eliminate the competition. Suspicion soon falls on those closest to the rapper, as they have their own motives as well.

6-21. RASHOMAMA (Apr 27, 2006)

A wedding goes very well until the newlyweds depart, only to find the murdered body of the groom's mother tied to the bumper of their car. The evidence is collected but trouble ensues when Nick's truck, parked at a nearby diner while he eats lunch, is stolen—with the evidence from the scene inside. This episode takes a unique visual look at how the CSI team operates.

6-22. TIME OF YOUR DEATH (May 4, 2006)

A high-stakes gambler and ladies man is living it up one minute in a luxury hotel, and the next, he's found dead outside on the asphalt. Clues lead the CSIs to uncover evidence that the man may have been an unknowing participant in living out his own fantasy of the weekend of his dreams.

6-23. BANG-BANG (May 11, 2006)

Part 1 of 2. A man accused of killing his wife and co-workers barricades himself and a hostage inside a casino's hotel room. While the CSIs search through evidence to determine if he had an accomplice in the killings, one of their own acts as hostage negotiator in a deadly, tense situation.

6-24. WAY TO GO (May 18, 2006)

Part 2 of 2. Grissom faces a tough decision when a teammate lies critically wounded in the hospital. Meanwhile, the team investigates the bizarre death of a man who was decapitated by a train. The death looks like a cover-up for murder, when they discover that his odd lifestyle of wearing corsets may have earned him some enemies.

CSI: Miami

SEASON ONE

1-1. GOLDEN PARACHUTE (Sep 23, 2002)

The team tackles the case of a corporate jet that crashes in the water, leaving only one survivor as well as a confusing mystery. One of the bodies is found miles away from the crash site.

1-2. LOSING FACE (Sep 30, 2002)

The team takes a personal interest in solving a case in which a bomb attached to a man goes off—claiming the life of one of Horatio's friends in the process. And the bomber isn't done with his chores, either....

1-3. WET FOOT/DRY FOOT (Oct 7, 2002)

Something fishy is afoot when a snagged shark yields part of a body. Soon the team's investigation leads to the smuggling of Cuban refugees—and the high price they pay for seeking freedom in the USA.

1-4. JUST ONE KISS (Oct 14, 2002)

When a young man's savagely abused body is found on a beach, and his female companion is raped and left for dead, suspicion falls on the sons of a wealthy businessman whom seem untouchable by the law.

1-5. ASHES TO ASHES (Oct 21, 2002)

The team tackles the shooting death of a much beloved priest who apparently had at least one enemy. A woman's death in a fiery car crash looks more like murder than an accident.

1-6. BROKEN (Oct 28, 2002)

A young girl is abducted from an indoor amusement park, then abused and murdered. The team will leave no stone unturned to find the man who committed the heinous crime.

1-7. BREATHLESS (Nov 4, 2002)

The body of a male exotic dancer is found in a garden, leading the team to a club that caters to wealthy, libidinous females who fulfill their fantasies in private. Meanwhile, another young man meets his maker—he "drops dead" on a sailboat after being stabbed and hit on the head.

1-8. SLAUGHTERHOUSE (Nov 11, 2002)

The team faces a horrible murder scene: nearly an entire family is brutally shot to death. Did the mother slaughter her family after experiencing post-partum depression, as the father suggests? The only true witness is a blood-soaked toddler found wandering the streets, and he's not talking.

1-9. KILL ZONE (Nov 18, 2002)

A sniper plagues Miami, racking up victims while the team rushes to stop him. Their main obstacle? The press, who are eager to gain ratings from the deaths.

1-10. A HORRIBLE MIND (Nov 25, 2002)

A professor studying torture through the ages ends up dead, hanging from a tree not far from his house. Did his research—which included killing animals—lead to his demise? Also, it looks like insurance fraud when a car is found underwater, but the CSIs quickly change their minds when they pop the trunk and find a nastily decomposing corpse.

1-11. CAMP FEAR (Dec 16, 2002)

The body of a young teenager is found alongside a rural highway. The team traces her to a juvenile detention camp that deals in problem youths. A man's burned body is found inside his house, and nobody seems to be crying over his death—especially not his ex-wife.

1-12. ENTRANCE WOUND (Jan 6, 2003)

A married man and his co-worker, looking for a little extracurricular romp, lose their ardor when they find a dead prostitute in their bungalow. Evidence soon leads to a family man who's been hiding a shady past. A German tourist is shot and killed during a carjacking, but the team suspects something is amiss, as the wife was left unharmed.

1-13. BUNK (Jan 27, 2003)

A man dies of poisoning when he enters a neighbor's house while looking for his dog. Meanwhile, an elderly lady is viciously killed at a retirement home.

1-14. FORCED ENTRY (Feb 3, 2003)

The team tackles two cases: When a crematorium owner is violently murdered, the CSI discover a lot of bodies that should have been cremated but weren't. Elsewhere, the nude corpse of a man is found tied to a bed. Evidence points toward sexual assault, but who did it, and why?

1-15. DEAD WOMAN WALKING (Feb 10, 2003)

When a mugger whose neck was broken is autopsied, it's found he was exposed to radiation. The team rushes to track the killer before an environmental lawyer who was exposed to a lethal dose dies of radiation poisoning.

1-16. EVIDENCE OF THINGS UNSEEN (Feb 17, 2003)

When a Russian immigrant is stabbed to death while enjoying himself at a peep-show booth, the only person who can identify the killer is the stripper who was entertaining him at the time.

1-17. SIMPLE MAN (Feb 24, 2003)

Horatio finds himself in a difficult position: he's ready to testify in a high-profile murder case until a second killing occurs that matches the profile of the first one. His team must determine if an innocent man is on trial while a serial killer is stalking Miami.

1-18. DISPO DAY (Mar 10, 2003)

An unmarked police convoy carrying confiscated drugs marked for incineration is hijacked and Speedle is shot, which brings back unhappy memories for Horatio of his brother's death. However, Internal Affairs thinks that the robbery was an inside job.

1-19. DOUBLE CAP (Apr 7, 2003)

A young woman in a bikini is shot dead execution-style, and Horatio's investigation is restricted when the feds show up and the murder weapon is linked to a case once investigated by Horatio's sister-in-law. Meanwhile, Calleigh brings her personal problems into the lab when her father's drinking problems escalate.

1-20. GRAVE YOUNG MEN (Apr 14, 2003)

When an ex-con's son goes missing, he goes to Horatio for help, but the evidence against him appears damning. Illegal drugs and spent ammo are found in the backyard where the boy spent his time, and clues lead the team to the body of another young boy. Meanwhile, Speedle's investigation of a man who died by asphyxiation is hampered by the deceased's girlfriend.

1-21. SPRING BREAK (Apr 28, 2003)

Two college students won't be graduating: The first is a young woman who is found with her neck broken and with human bite marks on her legs. The second case involves a young man who, although he was found at the bottom of a swimming pool, did not drown.

1-22. TINDER BOX (May 5, 2003)

Two cases keep the CSIs occupied: First, a prostitute is found dead in a judge's home. Second, both Delko and Speedle are enjoying some time off at a nightclub that catches fire. Over a dozen patrons are killed and evidence soon indicates that the arson may have been used to cover up a murder.

1-23. FREAKS AND TWEAKS (May 12, 2003)

A dead man bound in duct tape and a barn rigged with explosives are just the beginning of Horatio's problems: he learns that the victim knew his late brother. Meanwhile, a body shows up at the morgue that's alarmingly familiar to Alexx: it's the husband of her best friend.

1-24. BODY COUNT (May 19, 2003)

In this ninety-minute episode, an inmate is stabbed to death in prison, and when a medical helicopter arrives, it's actually manned by criminals breaking out three of their friends. Worse, two of the escapees were in jail for murder and have picked out their next targets.

SEASON TWO

2-1. BLOOD BROTHERS (Sep 22, 2003)

Horatio investigates the murder of a model intentionally run down outside of a Miami hotel by a driver who fled the scene. The situation goes from bad to worse when they find the killer and discover they can't arrest him due to his diplomatic immunity.

2-2. DEAD ZONE (Sep 29, 2003)

A man who recovers sunken treasure is found dead, pinned like a bug by a speargun spear to the wall of his multi-million-dollar yacht. Horatio learns that the man recently discovered a sunken Spanish galleon, and lots of folks wanted a piece of that pie. However, there's also the small matter of drug smuggling.

2-3. HARD TIME (Oct 6, 2003)

The team hunts for the individual responsible for luring a woman to a vacant condo and beating her with a piece of lumber before leaving her for dead. Horatio believes the attack was planned by a felon currently in prison for raping her.

2-4. DEATH GRIP (Oct 13, 2003)

When a teenage tennis phenom is abducted from her bedroom, the investigation leads to the waterways when a girl's arm is recovered in the stomach of an American crocodile. Alligator expert Jeff Corwin is called in to assist, but the forensic results turn up a surprising twist.

2-5. THE BEST DEFENSE (Oct 20, 2003)

A mysterious masked gunman is fingered when two young men are gunned down after hours in a bar. Calleigh's father wants her assistance with his new job—he's now a public defender whose first case involves the stabbing death of a woman.

2-6. HURRICANE ANTHONY (Nov 3, 2003)

When a couple tries to flee an oncoming hurricane, they're stopped when a man's body lands on their car. After the hurricane clears, the neighborhood exposes more deaths: another man is found impaled on a fence, and a woman whose house was recently robbed is found shot to death.

2-7. GRAND PRIX (Nov 10, 2003)

The qualifying race at the Miami Grand Prix Americas is shattered when a pit crew fuel man is mysteriously engulfed in invisible flames and perishes. When Horatio's team comes on the scene to investigate, they determine that it wasn't an accident, but murder.

2-8. BIG BROTHER (Nov 17, 2003)

Horatio learns a lot about the life and death of his brother when a woman shows up with a child she claims was fathered by Horatio's brother during his time as an undercover cop. And a stockbroker's death just might be linked to a voyeuristic Internet site.

2-9. BAIT (Nov 24, 2003)

Ouch. A woman found munched on by a shark turns out to have been shot first—and worked as bait for a private investigator hired by wives to catch their unfaithful husbands. The case becomes even more difficult for the CSIs when one of their co-workers becomes a leading suspect.

2-10. EXTREME (Dec 15, 2003)

The death of a young woman thrown off a parking garage at first looks like a kidnapping gone awry, until the CSI team turn up evidence that she was a thrill seeker involved with the wrong people. Delko inadvertently interferes with an investigation of a car-theft ring.

2-11. COMPLICATIONS (Jan 5, 2004)

When a prominent anesthesiologist from a plastic surgery clinic is found dead at his condo, the initial ruling of suicide soon turns to homicide when it turns out the husband of a patient who died while under the knife went to visit the physician the victim had assisted.

2-12. WITNESS TO MURDER (Jan 12, 2004)

When a diamond broker carrying millions in merchandise confronts a driver who hits his car, the driver kills him. The only person who can help out the CSI is the sole witness: a developmentally challenged man. Also, a body vanishes while on the way to the medical examiner's lab.

2-13. BLOOD MOON (Feb 2, 2004)

When a cigar maker is found hideously tortured in his store, the investigation leads Horatio to suspect the motive was revenge involving a group that helps Cuban refugees. Meanwhile, a young man is gunned down withdrawing cash from an ATM, but the attacker leaves the cash behind.

2-14. SLOW BURN (Feb 9, 2004)

A hunter is found shot to death near a controlled burn in the Everglades, and Alexx and Delko nearly die while investigating when the fire rages out of control. However, this latest fire discloses a second body, that of a young woman who was brutally beaten to death. At first it looks like her boyfriend is the likely killer, but Horatio suspects a sex offender.

2-15. STALKERAZZI (Feb 16, 2004)

When a celebrity photographer is found dead in his car following an accident, the evidence points Horatio's team toward an A-list movie star who may have been trying to hide compromising photos.

2-16. INVASION (Feb 23, 2004)

A former surfing champion's wife and son are tied up and beaten, and he vanishes, leaving behind a pool of blood. The plot thickens when drugs are found in the son's room, and the wife turns out to have been pregnant—and the child can't be the husband's. It appears that someone at the surfboard factory might have been supplying the son with drugs, but could also have a more intimate reason for murder.

2-17. MONEY FOR NOTHING (Mar 1, 2004)

A daring daytime robbery of over $3 million from an armored truck is interrupted when Horatio shows up. He shoots one of the thieves, but not before the truck's driver is killed. Although the accomplice escapes with the money, it turns out to be counterfeit, leading the CSI team back to the bank. Meanwhile, Yelina sees Horatio with his niece and makes an erroneous assumption.

2-18. WANNABE (Mar 22, 2004)

Speedle processes the scene of a man who was stabbed to death, and his investigation is compromised when forensics enthusiast Wally Shmagin makes off with a crucial piece of evidence. Speedle is able to find the young man but when it turns out his testimony could be crucial to the case, there could be problems. Across town, Delko and Calleigh probe the murder of a waitress who just may have had a winning lotto ticket.

2-19. DEADLINE (Mar 29, 2004)

A hotshot reporter's tale that a drug dealer killed a city councilman's aide during a visit to a seedy part of town begins to ring false when Horatio digs into the evidence.

2-20. THE OATH (Apr 19, 2004)

After a police officer pulls over a car and dies, evidence indicates that he wasn't shot at the scene. Horatio suspects that the shooting wasn't random when Internal Affairs gets involved in the case. Complicating the situation, Yelina begins to date the IAD officer in charge. Calleigh also aids a woman who was possibly being abused by one of the suspects.

2-21. NOT LANDING (May 3, 2004)

When a small plane crashes on a Miami beach and kills the pilot, evidence of illegal drug chemicals are found at the scene, prompting Horatio to suspect that the man's business partner might have sabotaged the craft. But when evidence indicates the pilot was dead before the crash, it seems that many of his well-to-do neighbors could have had a hand in his demise.

2-22. RAP SHEET (May 10, 2004)

A famous rap star refuses to talk to the police after one of his security guards is shot dead at a concert, yet evidence soon turns up that the security guard—not the rapper—might have been the intended target. Meanwhile, Alexx gets a shock when a dead body brought in from a car accident wakes up.

2-23. MIA/NYC - NONSTOP (May 17, 2004)

Pilot for the spin-off series *CSI: NY*. A teenage girl returns home from a party at an underage nightclub, only to find her parents brutally murdered. Horatio's team soon tracks the killer to New York City, where Horatio hooks up with Detective Mac Taylor, who is investigating the death of a police officer that may be related.

2-24. INNOCENT (May 24, 2004)

It looks like the CEO of a company that distributes adult films is responsible for the death of Ashley Anders, an adult actress whose strangled body is found in a park. An answering machine tape could provide crucial evidence to convict the man, but a lab accident erases it. IAD's Rick Stetler is put on the case when it appears that Delko was the last person to handle the tape.

SEASON THREE

3-1. LOST SON (Sep 20, 2004)

When a homicide victim's body is discovered on board a large yacht that crashes into a major bridge, his widow tells the police that just hours before, her husband had gone to pay a massive ransom to free their kidnapped son. When the trail leads to a jewelry store, one of Horatio's team is gunned down.

3-2. PRO PER (Sep 27, 2004)

The festivities at an exclusive party are interrupted when a cigarette boat speeds past, spraying bullets at the partygoers and killing a woman. Evidence points toward an ex-con who is summarily arrested, but he may go free when the star witness to the crime—the woman's son—refuses to testify against his mother's killer.

3-3. UNDER THE INFLUENCE (Oct 4, 2004)

A woman dies after being hit by a bus and her death just may be murder: Alexx finds a hand imprint on the decedent's back. Horatio assigns new CSI Ryan Wolfe to the case, which soon links to that of a man whose body is found down an elevator shaft in a nearby building. Meanwhile, Calleigh's father fears he may have killed someone while driving drunk.

3-4. MURDER IN A FLASH (Oct 11, 2004)

A "flash mob" is enticed to show up at a country club's golf course and lob golf balls into a sand trap, which contains the body of a high school student. Evidence ties the murder to a missing persons case involving a young woman, as well as student-teacher relationships that went well past the schoolroom.

3-5. LEGAL (Oct 18, 2004)

A teenage girl is found stabbed to death in the bathroom of a popular nightclub. An East European man is later found dead in the trunk of a car that crashes nearby. Horatio's team follows the evidence to a body spa that is not what it seems. Meanwhile, Calleigh and Ryan find disturbing evidence on the dead girl.

3-6. HELL NIGHT (Oct 25, 2004)

When jurors are brought to a crime scene, the last thing they expect to see is the defendant—a baseball player on trial for murdering his wife—dead in the kitchen with a meat cleaver through his skull. Meanwhile, Horatio must deal with a crime closer to home: Ray Jr. may have been involved in a prank that cost the life of a homeless man.

3-7. CRIME WAVE (Nov 8, 2004)

In this special ninety-minute episode, bank robbers take advantage of a tsunami that's headed toward Miami to commit their crime—

but the discovery of two bodies in a parking lot clue the police in. Meanwhile, after the water recedes, some dead bodies have been disinterred. One of them was never embalmed and was apparently the victim of a homicide. Horatio suspects that Yelina's boyfriend is physically abusing her.

3-8. **SPEED KILLS** (Nov 15, 2004)
After a night of speed dating, a man goes out to his car and is bludgeoned to death. Suspicion falls on two women, one of whom admits to vandalizing his car after he dumped her. When new evidence turns up, it seems that the dead man witnessed something at a Miami Heat basketball game that he shouldn't have seen.

3-9. **PIRATED** (Nov 22, 2004)
When several bodies from a ship's crew are found roped together and submerged in the ocean, their ship nowhere to be seen, modern-day pirates become the prime suspects in the multiple homicide investigation. Evidence leads the police to the rest of the crew, who escaped on a life raft, but their story of what happened doesn't match up to the evidence.

3-10. **AFTER THE FALL** (Nov 29, 2004)
A man on a sidewalk dies when another man falls off a building and lands on him. The CSIs investigate as a homicide when it turns out the victim possessed a sordid DVD involving a woman and a prominent Miami criminal judge. The team must delve further into the personal lives of the judge and others when the woman in the DVD is found dead.

3-11. **ADDICTION** (Dec 13, 2004)
A wealthy young couple leaves a restaurant, only to be attacked by a carjacker who fatally shoots the wife. The husband becomes a prime suspect in her death when evidence comes to light that he had a gambling addiction that could have bankrupted the company owned by him and his two brothers. Meanwhile, after Alexx shows convicted drunk drivers the potential results of their behavior, a mangled corpse, she hires one of them—a man who is soon accused of robbing the lab's dead.

3-12. **SHOOTOUT** (Jan 3, 2005)
When two gang members bring their fight to the emergency room, one of them is left dead after the gunplay. However, Horatio's team

discovers that a hospital employee may have alerted one of them to the other's whereabouts in the hospital, thus setting the tragedy into motion. Meanwhile, when Ryan checks out other patients present at the shooting, he suspects a mother may be abusing her baby.

3-13. COP KILLER (Jan 17, 2005)

A routine traffic stop results in a police officer shot to death and his ride-along—a seventeen-year-old boy—abducted by the killer. Evidence leads the team to another teenager who was present during the shooting. Meanwhile, the personal relationship between Horatio and Rebecca may dissolve when they don't see eye to eye on a case.

3-14. ONE NIGHT STAND (Feb 7, 2005)

One of Miami's hottest hotels may lose its five-star rating. A bellboy is shot dead, and the luggage he'd been handling leads the team to a counterfeiting ring. Meanwhile, a barely clad woman's body is found in a service elevator. Calleigh soon discovers that the woman and her husband had been attending a "friction" party that apparently may have gotten out of hand.

3-15. IDENTITY (Feb 14, 2005)

When a woman's slime-covered corpse is discovered in a poolside cabana, the killer turns out to be close by: it's a huge boa snake that the team soon links to a drug-smuggling operation. Horatio discovers that his nemesis Clavo Cruz may be behind the smuggling, yet diplomatic immunity may protect the criminal. Meanwhile, Ryan must contend with two women who both claim the same identity.

3-16. NOTHING TO LOSE (Feb 21, 2005)

In this ninety-minute episode, one crime begets another one. When local prisoners are brought in to control a wild fire in the Everglades, one of them, a convicted murderer, flees the scene. They also discover that the fire may have been set to hide the shooting death of a local college student. Horatio faces grim news at home: his niece has been diagnosed with cancer.

3-17. MONEY PLANE (Mar 7, 2005)

A corporate jet carrying over a billion dollars in checks crashes in a luxury neighborhood, and forensics determines that a body found inside the wreckage was dead before the crash occurred. The team learns that the victim, a socialite, might have discovered someone embezzling funds from a charity she headed. Meanwhile, Calleigh's job collides with her personal relationship with her ex-boyfriend, Detective Hagen.

3-18. GAME OVER (Mar 21, 2005)

High technology used for videogames provides the CSIs with a crucial piece of evidence when an extreme skateboarder and videogame tester appears to have died in an auto accident. Meanwhile, a person from Speedle's past returns to ask for Horatio's help: a former porn star once involved in one of Speedle's cases fears her new boyfriend will learn about her past if a stolen videotape she made with a past boyfriend is made public.

3-19. SEX & TAXES (Apr 11, 2005)

Two IRS agents are shot to death on the same day: one is found dead in his car, the other is killed while trying to repossess a yacht. Are the murders just coincidence, or is someone out to get IRS agents? Meanwhile, the professional relationship between Delko and Ryan takes a hit when Ryan takes credit for some of Delko's work.

3-20. KILLER DATE (Apr 18, 2005)

It's a busy day for the CSI team when a woman who runs a dating service (that does more than just offer dates) is smothered with a pillow. When Delko arrives at the scene, he discovers he's lost his police badge, and lands in hot water with Internal Affairs when the missing badge ends up used in a murder. Horatio learns shocking news about his late brother.

3-21. RECOIL (May 2, 2005)

Family disputes are often the most dangerous cases for police to investigate, and a custody battle at a courthouse turns out no differently when someone tries to kill a woman. It turns out the father of the daughter caught in the battle may not even be her biological father. At the lab, Calleigh's own father requires her expertise.

3-22. VENGEANCE (May 9, 2005)

This high school reunion will be one to remember: the former football star, who seems to have plenty of enemies, is murdered by someone who has apparently held a grudge for a decade. However, when Horatio's team arrives, they find that the crime scene has mysteriously already been processed, leading Horatio to disturbing information about his dead brother.

3-23. WHACKED (May 16, 2005)

When it appears that DNA evidence in a case is tainted, a condemned axe murder is given an eleventh-hour reprieve. Horatio's team must determine from other physical evidence if the man is truly guilty, for another double murder occurs that is suspiciously similar to the one they're re-investigating.

3-24. 10-7 (May 23, 2005)

Horatio's world is turned upside down when he finds a recent fingerprint of his supposedly dead brother while investigating a murder. When Ray Jr. is kidnapped, Horatio's brother comes out of his deep undercover assignment and the two men must work together to save the boy. Calleigh faces a professional crisis when an unknown assailant puts a gun to her head at a crime scene, and then later in the lab, the gunman's identity is revealed.

SEASON FOUR

4-1. FROM THE GRAVE (Sep 19, 2005)

Horatio is in the confessional of a church, talking to a priest about a killing in New York City that still haunts him, when shots ring out. Outside, he finds a correctional officer dying and the man's prisoner dead. Evidence soon leads to Miami's new "Mafia," the Mala Noche, whose leader is determined to see Horatio dead.

4-2. BLOOD IN THE WATER (Sep 26, 2004)

When a yacht catches fire, two young family members jump ship but instead of surviving, are attacked and killed by sharks. The CSIs discover that accelerant may have been used to start the fire. When a body is recovered, the parents say it's not their son, and even more puzzling, the partially eaten body has a bullet in it.

4-3. PREY (Oct 3, 2005)

When a visiting high school student on a class trip vanishes after a wild night of partying, her disappearance points to foul play; her rental car is found the next day with blood inside it. Even more suspicious is the hidden video camera inside, and evidence that the girl had sex in the back seat. Meanwhile, Stetler confronts Horatio about an old unsolved case from the detective's New York days.

4-4. 48 HOURS TO LIFE (Oct 10, 2005)

Horatio tries to prove an imprisoned young man innocent of the murder of a woman on a boat, despite the man's insistence on his own guilt. The CSIs discover that the woman was going through a rough divorce and was in the process of selling the boat. Before Horatio can prove the young man innocent, he stabs another inmate to death in a cell.

4-5. **THREE-WAY** (Oct 17, 2005)
When a pool boy at a five-star hotel is found dead on the hotel's lawn, suspicion falls on three wealthy housewives who were staying at the hotel. The man died shortly after visiting their penthouse suite. Meanwhile, an autopsy shows that a woman died due to a doctor's negligence, and Horatio discovers that someone is out to bring his team down.

4-6. **UNDER SUSPICION** (Oct 24, 2005)
The CSI team rushes into action when the last person to see a murdered woman alive turns out to be Horatio Caine, who insists he is being framed for the murder. And he may be right. When the team begins digging, it seems that a serial killer Horatio pursued ten years before just might be involved. Meanwhile, Alexx has concerns about Delko's finances and how he's handling them.

4-7. **FELONY FLIGHT** (Nov 7, 2005)
Part 1 of 2. Concludes with *CSI: NY*'s "Manhattan Manhunt." When an airplane crashes after being sabotaged, a serial killer who was being transferred from New York to Miami escapes and goes on a killing spree, abducting a college student. Detective Mac Taylor, who originally arrested the killer in New York, shows up to help Horatio capture the killer.

4-8. **NAILED** (Nov 14, 2005)
A recently separated woman dies a nasty death: her corpse is found with several nails shot through her torso and neck. When Delko is running late, Ryan shows up on the crime scene first and runs afoul of an intruder, who shoots him in the eye with the nail gun. Meanwhile, Stetler talks to Horatio about the man who murdered Horatio's mother over twenty years ago in New York.

4-9. **URBAN HELLRAISERS** (Nov 21, 2005)
After Delko loses his ATM card to the bank machine, he goes inside the bank. Shortly thereafter, three armed robbers burst in. The robbery goes awry when one of them tries to rape a woman and a shootout ensues, taking several lives. Evidence leads the team to a group of college students who are re-enacting a violent video game, and the CSIs must stop them before they escalate to even worse crimes.

4-10. SHATTERED (Nov 28, 2005)

Delko finds his life crumbling even further when a drug lord is gunned down in his palatial mansion, and a suspect who is arrested at the scene accuses Delko of selling him drugs. It doesn't take long for Internal Affairs to get involved. Evidence soon indicates there were two gunmen on the scene. Meanwhile, Calleigh makes a life-altering decision about her job in ballistics.

4-11. PAYBACK (Dec 19, 2005)

DNA testing technology sets a convicted rapist free after six years in prison. The CSIs re-examine the evidence and go after a suspect, but he is murdered before they can arrest him. Meanwhile, Alexx determines that a woman who supposedly died in a car accident instead died from a surgical error.

4-12. THE SCORE (Jan 9, 2006)

A man is found brutally murdered in a bedroom suite, stabbed multiple times with an ice pick, with the letter "L" written on his chest. He was attending a party at a private downtown club, and it seems someone may have spurned his advances. Meanwhile, Delko's sister, Marisol, is arrested for possession of marijuana but her motives are not what people think. Horatio tries to keep it in quiet, but the mole leaks the news.

4-13. SILENCER (Jan 23, 2006)

A day in the park turns deadly when a man and a woman watching dancers at a beach pavilion are gunned down. Horatio suspects that the Mala Noche gang is responsible for the shooting, but what is the connection between the dead female executive and a dangerous criminal gang? Meanwhile, personal relationships develop as Horatio sees Marisol, and Delko and Natalia's off-duty relationship continues to grow.

4-14. FADE OUT (Jan 30, 2006)

A man is gruesomely murdered, his body discovered hanging from a drawbridge with his eyes shot out. Although the crime reeks of a mob hit, Horatio's team soon discovers it mirrors a script written by some film students. But who is reenacting the crimes in their fictional story? Also, Ryan's eyesight begins to deteriorate, which could threaten his career.

4-15. SKELETONS (Feb 6, 2006)

When an alleged serial killer who eluded Horatio over a decade ago in New York shows up in Miami, the detective is horrified to discover that the killer, Walter Resden, is dating the daughter of one of his victims. Meanwhile, tensions run high at the lab when Natalia thinks she may be pregnant with a co-worker's baby.

4-16. DEVIANT (Feb 27, 2006)

When a registered sex offender living in Alexx's neighbor is beaten to death in a park, suspicion falls on Alexx. Days before the beating, Alexx put up signs in the neighborhood warning parents of the sex offender's presence. While Alexx may not be held criminally responsible, Horatio fears she could face civil penalties.

4-17. COLLISION (Mar 6, 2006)

A traffic accident claims a woman's life when her car smashes into a barrier, but soon another body turns up in the trunk of her car. That evidence leads Horatio to a crime where a $4 million necklace was stolen. Meanwhile, in order to solve the case, Natalia finds that she must confess a secret that could cost her more than her job.

4-18. DOUBLE JEOPARDY (Mar 13, 2006)

After a man is acquitted of his wife's murder, her stabbed corpse floats to the top of a pond. Knowing that the man can't be tried twice for the same crime, Horatio's team pores through unsolved cases, looking for other victims who may have been stabbed with the same weapon: a knife with a broken-off tip.

4-19. DRIVEN (Mar 20, 2006)

Marisol is present at a Coconut Grove day spa when three masked men rob a group of wealthy women, one of whom is shot when she fights back with pepper spray. It's not just a simple robbery, as the police discover that the shooter is now breaking into the women's homes. Ryan must face the repercussions of freezing at a shootout.

4-20. FREE FALL (Apr 10, 2006)

When a young couple are released from jail, they become "media darlings," but someone doesn't believe they're worthy of the acclaim, as attempts are made on their lives. Meanwhile, Calleigh has to work with an ex-boyfriend, who works for the U.S. Treasury, in order to help solve the case.

4-21. DEAD AIR (Apr 24, 2006)

A wrong number leads the police to a woman who has been kidnapped and made a frantic cell-phone from the trunk of a car. The kidnappers are demanding $5 million in ransom or they'll kill the woman. At the lab, Delko discovers that Natalia didn't invite him to a party she organized. Meanwhile, Horatio helps Marisol with a difficult decision.

4-22. OPEN WATER (May 1, 2006)

A millionaire on a honeymoon cruise is pushed overboard and eaten by sharks. The suspect list is large, until a large sum of cash is discovered missing from his room's safe and the team learns his new bride has a teenage daughter. Meanwhile, Horatio and Marisol's relationship moves to the next level.

4-23. SHOCK (May 8, 2006)

A local celebrity is found dead in her bathtub, and her rival, personal assistant, and boyfriend are all prime suspects in her demise. Because the murder took place at an A-list party, the CSI team has their work cut out for them as they determine which guests had motive to kill the woman. Meanwhile, Horatio discloses to Delko that he plans to marry Marisol.

4-24. RAMPAGE (May 15, 2006)

Horatio and Marisol's new life as husband and wife has barely begun when the Mala Noche gang trial is disrupted. A defendant shoots his way out of the courtroom when a witness helps him escape. The crime gang puts out a hit on Horatio, but someone else is shot instead. Meanwhile, Delko is being plagued by an ex-girlfriend who is harassing anyone she thinks is competition.

4-25. ONE OF OUR OWN (May 22, 2006)

The season finishes with Horatio mourning his loss while the team begins a manhunt to find the killer. Meanwhile, the CSI team is shocked when federal agents take over the lab in the search for stolen money from another case. Calleigh soon realizes she know who stole the money, and the mole's identity is revealed.

CSI: NY

SEASON ONE

1-1. BLINK (Sep 22, 2004)

A missing woman turns up dead, and soon evidence points Mac toward a serial killer who imprisons and tortures his victims. The police soon discover that one of his victims survived, but she can only communicate by blinking.

1-2. CREATURES OF THE NIGHT (Sep 29, 2004)

A young woman late for an event cuts through Central Park at night, but she is brutally assaulted and left with no memory of the attack. Despite a lack of evidence, Stella is determined to find her attacker. Meanwhile, Mac and Aiden must find a rat in order to solve the shooting death of a drug dealer.

1-3. AMERICAN DREAMERS (Oct 6, 2004)

When a skeleton dressed in clothing is found on a tour bus, the team's first thought is that it could be somebody's idea of a bad prank, until Dr. Hawkes determines that the bones belong to those of a youth missing for more than a decade.

1-4. GRAND MASTER (Oct 27, 2004)

The elation of an up-and-coming hip-hop deejay who wins a championship for spinners is short-lived when he's murdered. Meanwhile, Stella suspects foul play when a famous fashion designer is found dead in her penthouse swimming pool.

1-5. A MAN, A MILE (Nov 3, 2004)

Mac and Danny investigate the world of Sandhogs—men who work the tunnels underneath the city—when an explosion claims one of their members. Evidence indicates that the man was dead before the explosion. Meanwhile, the body of a teenage girl found near the East River turns out to be that of a middle-class girl trying to fit in at a fancy school.

1-6. OUTSIDE MAN (Nov 10, 2004)

Body parts abound when Mac and Stella try to find the owners of a human leg found near a loading dock and a human finger found in a freezer. Danny and Aiden deal with a mass murder at a Brooklyn diner where all the victims were shot and had bags placed over their heads.

1-7. RAIN (Nov 17, 2004)

A bank robbery in Chinatown goes horribly awry, leaving behind charred bodies and evidence that suggests it was an inside job. When the team questions the bank manager, they discover that her infant daughter is being held in order to force her cooperation in the crime.

1-8. THREE GENERATIONS ARE ENOUGH (Nov 24, 2004)

A trading floor is cleared when an abandoned briefcase is found, only the contents turn out to be not a bomb, but blood evidence of its missing owner, who is soon implicated in illegal trading. Meanwhile, a woman is found dead on the grounds of a church, leaving Stella to determine if the death was suicide or murder.

1-9. OFFICER BLUE (Dec 1, 2004)

A mounted officer investigating a fight in Central Park is shot and killed by a sniper. His horse is also wounded, but the bullet is lodged in the spine and its removal may prove fatal to the animal. Across town, Aiden probes the death of a young man who was found face down in an alley with burn marks on his face.

1-10. NIGHT MOTHER (Dec 15, 2004)

The case seems open and shut but Mac thinks otherwise when a woman is found dead, a wooden stake driven through her heart. It becomes clear that her blood-spattered assailant was sleepwalking and has no memory of the crime. Meanwhile, Danny and Aiden probe an apparent beating death of a pickpocket.

1-11. TRI-BOROUGH (Jan 5, 2005)

A man is found electrocuted on some subway tracks in Brooklyn, apparently the victim of an unfortunate accident—or was he? Meanwhile, Danny investigates the death of a Manhattan art dealer who was found shot to death in his gallery. In Queens, Aiden and Flack investigate the death of a construction worker.

1-12. RECYCLING (Jan 12, 2005)

A bicycle messenger was stabbed as he rode his route, but as Stella discovers, the man covered a lot of ground before he died. Meanwhile, Mac is thrust into the world of national kennel shows when a dog handler is found dead with a knitting needle speared through her. The investigations for both crimes have a common link: nobody particularly liked either of the victims.

1-13. TANGLEWOOD (Jan 26, 2005)

A young man is beaten with a baseball bat and left to die in a park. Clues link his death to that of another man who died in a robbery earlier that evening. An old tattoo links them both to the Tanglewood Boys gang, with which Danny has history. Meanwhile, Danny and Aiden discover a hit-and-run just may have been premeditated, and a store clerk is shot.

1-14. BLOOD, SWEAT, AND TEARS (Feb 9, 2005)

A box washes ashore on Coney Island and its contents—the body of a teenage boy—lead both Mac and Stella to the circus. The deceased was a member of a traveling circus which he yearned to leave. A second case involves a large pool of blood in a studio apartment, but no sign of a body.

1-15. 'TIL DEATH WE DO PART (Feb 16, 2005)

When a bride literally drops dead before she was to marry her wealthy fiancé, Mac suspects foul play but is stymied when the woman's father refuses an autopsy. Meanwhile, a dismembered human hand is found next to a dead man in an abandoned Staten Island monastery that some people believe to be haunted.

1-16. HUSH (Feb 28, 2005)

A longshoreman meets a gruesome fate when half of his body is found squashed under a huge shipping container on a flatbed truck. Mac and Stella track down the other half of the body at the docks. Aiden and Danny go to Queens where they investigate the death of a nude woman found near an expressway, the apparent victim of a car that slammed into a nearby tree.

1-17. THE FALL (Mar 2, 2005)

Flack's former training officer is assigned to the murder of an upscale wine shop owner who was apparently murdered by gang members, but the officer may be guilty of tampering with evidence. Meanwhile, a famous but much disliked movie producer falls to his death from a Chelsea apartment terrace.

1-18. THE DOVE COMMISSION (Mar 23, 2005)

When a commissioner who co-wrote a report documenting corruption in the New York City police department is shot dead the day before the findings were to be released, Mac and Stella find themselves under the gun to find the killer. Meanwhile, a gypsy cabdriver is found dead in his cab, the apparent victim of a robbery.

1-19. CRIME AND MISDEMEANOR (Apr 13, 2005)

A young woman whose throat was brutally slit is found at an industrial laundry facility, leading Mac and Stella to an expensive hotel where UN diplomats stay. When a street performer is found dead, Danny is determined to find out what happened.

1-20. SUPPLY AND DEMAND (Apr 27, 2005)

A college student is beaten and shot to death in his West Village apartment, the apparent victim of drug dealers whom he'd crossed.

The team must now track down his missing roommate. Meanwhile, Stella gets in trouble with Internal Affairs after she roughly questions a teenage suspect during interrogation.

1-21. ON THE JOB (May 4, 2005)

Danny finds himself under the scrutiny of Internal Affairs when he chases down and shoots a man whom he believed was a suspect he'd encountered earlier—only the dead man is actually an undercover cop. Danny claims the victim fired on him first, and it's up to Mac to clear Danny of the charges. Meanwhile, a nanny is killed in a restroom in Central Park.

1-22. THE CLOSER (May 11, 2005)

When a scantily clad woman runs into traffic and is killed by a delivery truck, the team discovers she was fleeing from an unseen assailant. A Boston Red Sox fan is found dead in a parking lot from a ruptured spleen after his team loses against New York.

1-23. WHAT YOU SEE IS WHAT YOU SEE (May 18 2005)

When Mac stops off at his favorite local coffee shop for breakfast, a gunman opens fire. Mac chooses to save a critically injured victim while the killer flees, but is stunned when evidence exonerates the killer, prompting him to conduct his own investigation.

SEASON TWO

2-1. SUMMER IN THE CITY (Sep 28, 2005)

Dr. Hawkes gets out into the field in season two and finds himself working with Mac to solve the case of an experienced climber who plummeted to his death off the Empire State Building. A clue may lie in a very tiny piece of evidence. Across town, Stella and Danny probe the murder of a fashion designer who is found dead wearing a diamond-studded bra worth millions. Aiden collects evidence against a rapist who attacked the same victim twice.

2-2. GRAND MURDER AT CENTRAL STATION (Oct 3, 2005)

The morning rush hour at Grand Central Station can be murder, as it is in the case of a plastic surgeon who dies after someone throws lye in his face and on his hands. Mac discovers that several patients had lodged malpractice suits against him, so there's no shortage of suspects. Stella finds herself investigating the world of "cuddle parties" after a blind woman is found dead on a Manhattan rooftop. Meanwhile, Aiden is determined to send a serial rapist to prison.

2-3. ZOO YORK (Oct 12, 2005)

Stella and Dr. Hawkes tackle the sensitive case of a debutante who was found dead on a carousel. The owner of a meat packing plant is mauled and devoured by a tiger at a New York animal conservatory, but it seems that his employees may have had something to do with his demise.

2-4. CORPORATE WARRIORS (Oct 19, 2005)

The team must tackle three cases. Mac investigates the grisly death of a businessman who was decapitated while sitting on a Central Park bench. Stella probes the death of a man who apparently beaten to death at a festival after allegedly trying to steal money. And arson seems to be the cause when a child dies in an apartment fire.

2-5. DANCING WITH THE FISHES (Oct 26, 2005)

A dancer who had a rival ends up plummeting from the Queensborough Bridge and crashing through a car windshield below. Meanwhile, a Roosevelt Island tram operator just days away from retirement is found dead inside the tram. A man meets a fishy death: he's murdered with a swordfish at a South Bronx fish market.

2-6. YOUNGBLOOD (Nov 2, 2005)

A wealthy businessman and a young woman are engaged in some amorous activity in an elevator when the doors open and someone blasts them with a shotgun. He dies, but she is left unharmed and flees the scene. Meanwhile, a lake in Central Park yields the weighed-down corpse of a murder victim.

2-7. MANHATTAN MANHUNT (Nov 9, 2005)

Conclusion of *CSI: Miami*'s "Felony Flight," which began with serial killer Henry Darius escaping from custody. The man flees Miami with Horatio Caine hot on his tail, and arrives in Manhattan. Before long he murders a group of teenagers in a luxury apartment where millions of dollars vanish from a high-security vault.

2-8. BAD BEAT (Nov 16, 2005)

A man who was caught cheating is tossed from a poker game, but allegedly returns later with a shotgun and kills a man by blasting a hole through the door. A female weather reporter is found drowned in Central Park, even though she was nowhere near any water. Evidence soon turns up that an affair with her boss may have been motivation enough for someone to kill her.

2-9. CITY OF THE DOLLS (Nov 23, 2005)

A doll clutched in the hand of a dead man may be the only clue to why someone killed the owner of a doll hospital. Across town, a terminally ill woman with only a few months to live is found dead in her bed. Is it suicide, or something more sinister?

2-10. JAMALOT (Nov 30, 2005)

Women's roller derby is a rough game, but it becomes lethal when the newest star of one team is attacked by members of another. A struggling author who could barely make ends meet is found dead, rolled up in an expensive Persian rug and tossed into a dumpster. His killer may be quite literate: passages from a book were scrawled over the corpse.

2-11. TRAPPED (Dec 14, 2005)

All the money in the world wasn't enough to protect a reclusive billionaire found with his throat slit in his bedroom. When Danny investigates further into the man's dwelling, he becomes trapped in the panic room. Across town, a stripper's body is found atop a scorching-hot klieg light. Evidence found on the body soon indicates that an irate customer may have been her murderer.

2-12. WASTED (Jan 18, 2006)

A young Russian model drops dead on the fashion runway, leading Mac and Danny to a second victim. Stella and Lindsay, acting on the confession of a man who walks into headquarters, find the body of his doctor in an alleyway. What's odd is that the doctor has leeches covering her body.

2-13. RISK (Jan 25, 2006)

When a commodities trader has a really bad day, he apparently takes his own life and is found hanging outside the window of his fortieth floor office, leaving behind angry clients who have lost millions. Danny literally comes across his next case when he stops a subway train from running over the body of a college student, the apparent victim of "subway surfing." However, murder is suspected when they find fish in the man's stomach and a shark tooth stuck in his hand.

2-14. STUCK ON YOU (Feb 1, 2006)

The entertainment industry has a rough night. In Greenwich Village, a young music promoter is found shot to death. Stella is viewing a photographer's premiering works at a swanky loft in Tribeca when the billionaire host of the party is shot from behind with an arrow. The shooter misses the host, but the man's date is pinned to the wall and dies.

2-15. FARE GAME (Mar 1, 2006)

Two crimes occupy the team: A woman who was known for suing restaurant critics is found dead in her bed, blindfolded and bound with a man's tie. Meanwhile, a member of law enforcement is found shot to death in a cemetery, the victim of a strange assassination game that may have gone too far.

2-16. COOL HUNTER (Mar 8, 2006)

A doorwoman is found floating in the rooftop water tower of an apartment building where, over the past decade, a number of people have mysteriously died. Across town, a man is found strangled on a swing set.

2-17. NECROPHILIA AMERICANA (Mar 22, 2006)

A museum diorama proves to be too life-like when an actual corpse is found on display. Although much of the victim's flesh was devoured by beetles, the team is able to determine that she was the curator and relative of a wealthy museum patron. Perhaps the only clue to solving the case lies with a six-year-old boy who may have witnessed the crime, but who refuses to talk. A second case is equally as odd: a man is found dead with foam insulation blocking his throat.

2-18. LIVE OR LET DIE (Mar 29, 2006)

When a medical helicopter is hijacked and an organ meant for donation is stolen, Mac and his team must recover the stolen organ before the transplant patient dies as well as find out who murdered a hospital intern during the crime. Stella and Lindsay discover that a restaurant hostess found dead in an alleyway was supplementing her income by engaging in phone sex.

2-19. SUPER MEN (Apr 12, 2006)

When a do-gooder tries to stop a mugging at an ATM, he's killed. The unusual part is that the man was dressed in a superhero cape and tights. Evidence soon indicates that the killer was involved in selling prescription medication to junkies. Lindsay and Danny investigate the death of a college football superstar found dead in his hotel room. The list of suspects is large, as the man had just been chosen as a first-round pick in the NFL draft and others wanted the spot.

2-20. **RUN SILENT, RUN DEEP** (Apr 19, 2006)

Mac is led to an end zone of Giants Stadium when he receives a phone call from a construction worker who confesses helping bury a body in that location. Unfortunately, the worker commits suicide before Mac can get more details, but the body the team unearths leads to disturbing information—that someone from the lab was present during the original crime. Meanwhile, Stella investigates the stabbing death of a bank executive.

2-21. **ALL ACCESS** (Apr 26, 2006)

Singer Kid Rock plays himself and becomes a murder suspect in this episode, in which his limousine driver is found shot to death. The team gets another difficult case: Stella's boyfriend has been shot to death, she's found covered in his blood, and she can't recall why she shot him.

2-22. **STEALING HOME** (May 3, 2006)

When a man is shot dead on the sidewalk, two women claim to be his wife. Mac, Stella, and Dr. Hawkes soon discover that the trio were involved in a trinogamous relationship that might not have been as happy as the widows claim. Meanwhile, a dead mermaid is found in the water off a ferry dock, and Lindsay takes the case more personally when it's discovered the victim is from her home state.

2-23. **HEROES** (May 10, 2006)

During Fleet Week, an annual NYC tradition that honors the military, a decorated Marine corporal is found stabbed to death in Central Park. A second case casts a dark pall over the team: the charred victim of a car fire turns out to be one of their own, Aiden Burn, who left the department after tampering with evidence. Stella soon discovers that Aiden was gathering crucial evidence to catch a serial rapist.

2-24. **CHARGE OF THIS POST** (May 17, 2006)

A mysterious bomber is setting off C-4 bombs across the city by utilizing random cell phones as detonators. When one of the team is critically injured in an explosion, it's a race against time to stop the bomber before he can strike again. For Mac, the bombings bring back memories of when a fellow Marine died during the Beirut barracks bombing.

Elyse Dickenson is the editor of Elyse's Comprehensive CSI Site, located at http://members.aol.com/JRD203/csi.htm.